FRANCHISING IN ASIA 2015

Legal and Business Considerations

KENDAL H. TYRE, JR., EXECUTIVE EDITOR
DIANA VILMENAY-HAMMOND, MANAGING EDITOR
PIERCE HAESUNG HAN, ASSISTANT EDITOR

LEXNOIR FOUNDATION

LexNoir Foundation is the charitable, educational arm of LexNoir, an international network of lawyers connecting the African Diaspora.

This book, *Franchising in Asia 2015: Legal and Business Considerations*, is published by LexNoir Foundation and reflects the points of view of the authors and editors as of the date of publication and does not necessarily represent the opinions, interpretations, or positions of the law firms or organizations with which they are affiliated, nor the opinions, interpretations, or positions of LexNoir Foundation or LexNoir.

www.lexnoir.org

Table of Contents

International Franchising in the Asian Context

Kendal H. Tyre, Jr., Diana Vilmenay-Hammond and Pierce Haesung Han
NIXON PEABODY LLP

Table of Contents (continued)

Page

Table of Contents (continued)

Franchising in Bangladesh

Dr. Mariam Khatoon and Nasir Doulah
DOULAH & DOULAH

Table of Contents (continued)

Franchising in Hong Kong

David Allison
BIRD & BIRD

Franchising in India

Preeti Mehta
KANGA & CO.

Franchising in Indonesia

Nurdin Adiwibowo, Freddy Karyadi, and Gustaaf Reerink
ABNR LAW

Table of Contents (continued)

Franchising in Japan

Kakuji Mitani
MOMO-O, MATSUO & NAMBA

Page

Franchising in Kazakhstan

Saule Akhmetova
GRATA LAW FIRM

Franchising in Malaysia

Wong Sai Fong and Michelle C.Y. Loi
SHEARN DELAMORE & CO.

Table of Contents (continued)

Table of Contents (continued)

Franchising in the Philippines

Maria Teresa D. Mercado-Ferrer
SYCIP SALAZAR HERNANDEZ & GATMAITAN

Table of Contents (continued)

Franchising in Taiwan

Patricia Ginsberg
PAMIR LAW GROUP

Franchising in Tajikistan

Rustam M. Nazrisho and Sherzod S. Sodatkadamov
NAZRISHO & MIRZOEV, LLC

Table of Contents (continued)

Page

Franchising in Thailand

Sriwan Puapondh and Alan Adcock
TILLEKE & GIBBINS

Franchising in Vietnam

Mai Thi Minh Hang and Ngo Viet Hoa
RUSSIN & VECCHI

Table of Contents (continued)

Appendices

Introduction

About the Editors

Kendal H. Tyre, Jr.—Kendal is a partner in the Washington, D.C., office of Nixon Peabody LLP. He handles domestic and cross-border transactions, including mergers and acquisitions, joint ventures, strategic alliances, licensing, and franchise matters. In his franchise and licensing practice, Kendal counsels domestic and international franchisors, franchisees, licensors, licensees, and distributors regarding U.S. state and federal franchise laws as well as foreign franchise legislation in a variety of jurisdictions. Kendal drafts and provides advice with regard to franchise and license agreements, disclosure documents, and area development agreements and has extensive experience drafting and negotiating a variety of other commercial agreements. His client base spans the United States and foreign countries, including South Africa, Kenya, and the United Kingdom.

Kendal is a frequent contributor to franchise publications and a frequent speaker at franchise programs held by the American Bar Association's Forum on Franchising and the International Franchise Association. Kendal is also the executive director of LexNoir Foundation.

E-mail address: ktyre@nixonpeabody.com

~

Diana Vilmenay-Hammond—Diana is an attorney in the Washington, D.C., office of Nixon Peabody LLP. She is a member of the firm's Franchise & Distribution team. In her franchise practice, Diana works with domestic and international franchisors on transactional and litigation matters. Specifically, she counsels franchisor clients regarding state and federal franchise laws, disclosure, and registration obligations. Diana drafts and negotiates various commercial agreements, including international franchise and development agreements. Diana has co-authored numerous articles on franchising and frequently co-hosted the Nixon Peabody franchise law webinar series. Topics have included:

- "Franchise Case Law Round-Up: Implications for Your Franchise";
- "Social Media Part II: Best Practices in Protecting Your Brand in the New Media"; and
- "The Awuah Case: Bellwether or Outlier."

Diana received her J.D. from Howard University School of Law and her B.A. from Georgetown University. She is a member of the American Bar Association (Forum on Franchising).

E-mail address: dvilmenay@nixonpeabody.com

~

Pierce Haesung Han—Pierce Haesung Han is an associate in Nixon Peabody's Business & Transactions group, where he works with clients on a broad range of matters including mergers and acquisitions, international commercial transactions, and federal securities law matters. Pierce focuses his practice on three main areas, assisting clients with a variety of complex business transactions.

- Mergers & Acquisitions: Providing assistance to both public and private clients with various mergers and acquisitions, performing due diligence, drafting and negotiating transaction documents, and facilitating closing and post-closing mechanics.
- International Commercial Transactions: Drafting and negotiating a variety of commercial agreements, including international franchise and development

agreements, license agreements, and purchase and sale agreements.

- Federal Securities Law Matters: Assisting public and private clients regarding federal securities laws and stock exchange rules relating to corporate governance and disclosure.

Pierce serves as the Secretary of the Asian Pacific Bar Association Educational Fund (an affiliate of the Asian Pacific American Bar Association of the Greater Washington, D.C., Area). Pierce received his J.D. from Georgetown University Law Center and his B.A. from Case Western Reserve University. He is admitted to practice in the State of New York and the District of Columbia.

E-mail address: phan@nixonpeabody.com

~

Introduction

Dedication

Kendal H. Tyre, Jr.: To Delores Marie, Dorothy Jacqueline, and Rose Marie

Diana Vilmenay-Hammond: To my family with lots of love

Pierce Haesung Han: To my parents, Dr. Peter and Ruth Han

Acknowledgment

This book could not have been written without the hard work and dedication of each of the contributing authors from various parts of the globe who are listed in *About the Authors*. Thank you.

We would like to acknowledge and extend our heartfelt gratitude to Maria Stallings, and Keri McWilliams of the Washington, D.C., office of Nixon Peabody LLP for their invaluable assistance in revising, proofing, and editing all the various editions of the manuscript.

To our family, friends, and others throughout the LexNoir community, words alone cannot express what we owe them for their encouragement that enabled us to complete this book—a special thanks to Liz for always going the extra mile with the kind of feedback that puts flesh on the bones and to Tim for being there since the beginning and always being ready to assist (and, more often than not, critique).

Introduction

About the Authors

Alan Adcock—Alan is based in Bangkok, Thailand, and is a partner and deputy director of the Tilleke & Gibbins intellectual property and regulatory affairs groups. Since 2005, Alan has received recognition by Asialaw Leading Lawyers Survey as one of Asia's leading business lawyers in the area of intellectual property, and he was named a top IP lawyer in Thailand by *Chambers Asia-Pacific 2013* and *WTR 1000 2013*. He is also recognized as one of the world's leading life sciences practitioners by *IAM Life Sciences 250* and *PLC Which Lawyer*. Alan has extensive experience in IP acquisitions, strategic structuring, technology transfer, and IP licensing and securitization agreements. He has handled various IP infringements and regulatory infractions involving labeling, advertising, clinical trials, product handling/warehousing, product registration, taxation, and import/export violations. Alan is also involved in the firm's leading patent and trade secret litigation practice, focusing mainly on the pharmaceutical, agrochemical, and material science sectors. He handles local pre-litigation strategy and litigation management for infringement and invalidation matters. Alan is a Co-Chair of the American Chamber of Commerce in Thailand's Food & AgriBusiness Committee and serves as the Thailand representative on the INTA Legislation & Regulation Committee, East Asia and Pacific Subcommittee. Alan speaks both Mandarin and English.

E-mail address: alan.a@tilleke.com

~

Nurdin Adiwibowo—Nurdin is a partner at ABNR Law in Jakarta, Indonesia. Nurdin joined ABNR as an associate in November 2000 and became a partner on January 1, 2012. He is a law graduate of University of Indonesia majoring in Business

Law. In 2000, he earned his LL.M. degree in The Netherlands, majoring in International Business Law. Prior to joining ABNR, he worked for a number of years for other prominent law firms in Jakarta. He is a registered capital market lawyer and has been involved in financing, corporate, and investment projects at ABNR, and has extensive regulatory knowledge in these areas. Nurdin speaks Indonesian and English.

E-mail address: nadiwibowo@abnrlaw.com

~

Saule Akhmetova—Saule is a partner and Director of the Almaty office of GRATA Kazakhstan. She graduated from the Al-Farabi Kazakh National University of Law with distinction in 1998. She then undertook extensive legal training with an oil company in Essen. Following this training, she returned to the Al-Farabi University for an LLM, which she obtained with distinction. Saule has extensive experience in corporate, oil and gas, contract, tax, and employment law, having been involved in transactions for a broad range of clients from a variety of sectors. Saule's practice is focused on oil producing companies and oil industry service companies, as well as different trade and industrial companies. She acts as a regular corporate adviser to a number of high profile international and Kazakh clients. Saule speaks Kazakh, Russian, and English.

E-mail address: sakhmetova@gratanet.com

~

David Allison—David is counsel within Bird & Bird's China IP team based in Hong Kong. With extensive experience in all major areas of intellectual property, including copyright, trademarks, patents, and registered designs, David has managed disputes dealing with infringement of trademarks and copyright as well as the misuse of confidential information and trade secrets. His particular areas of interest include contentious intellectual property disputes, the enforcement of intellectual property rights in both Hong Kong and mainland China, and the prosecution of trademark portfolios in Hong Kong and the greater China region. He also advises clients on non-contentious matters, particularly relating to personal data privacy. In addition to his litigation experience, David also has significant experience in the field of alternative dispute resolution. He is an accredited mediator and is a member of the Chartered Institute of Arbitrators. He also sits as a panelist for the Asian Domain Name Dispute Resolution Centre in Hong Kong. Prior to joining Bird & Bird, David worked for both multi-national and specialist law firms in Hong Kong and Australia in both IP and commercial litigation roles. He also acted as the Asia Pacific Regional IP Counsel for a major U.S. MNC based in Shanghai. David is qualified to practice law in the Supreme Court of Western Australia, the High Court of Australia, and the High Court of Hong Kong.

E-mail address: david.allison@twobirds.com

~

Brendon Carr—Brendon serves as senior foreign counsel at Yulchon in Seoul, South Korea. His practice focuses on corporate transactional work, including inbound foreign direct investment, corporate restructurings and privatizations of government-invested corporations, mergers and acquisitions, and joint ventures, as well as advising private and public companies and financial institutions on all related corporate, corporate governance, commercial, licensing, and securities law matters. He has primarily dealt with transactions in industries including alternative energy (clean technology), computers and software, automotive, hospitality, luxury and fashion, retailers, life sciences, cosmetics, financial services, advertising, and public utilities. In addition to his corporate transactional experience, Brendon also has significant experience in representing clients in employment and human resources matters and labor disputes in South Korea.

E-mail address: bcarr@yulchon.com

~

Nasir Doulah—Nasir is a partner at Doulah & Doulah in Dhaka, Bangladesh. His practice areas include corporate law, capital markets, M&A, banking and finance, and telecommunications. Nasir is one of the few legal experts on capital markets in Bangladesh. He is experienced in dealing with a variety of corporate matters, especially in corporate financing, corporate restructure and mergers and acquisitions. With his knowledge in banking and finance issues, he is serving a number of corporate offices and banks on all corporate issues. Nasir's recent deals include a custodian agreement finalization of ABN Amro and Morgan Stanley; providing assistance in regulatory matters for Bank of New York; negotiating for Al Aqeeq, UK in US$ 30 million equity investment; and finalizing lease financing on behalf of the General Electric Company. Nasir also serves as a consultant to investment companies such as Citibank, Etrade, etc. In M&A, he has facilitated transactions for three power plants in El-Paso and the sale of two oil companies. Lastly, he is involved in the restructuring of Khulna Power Company Ltd. He received honors in Law from the University of London and post-graduation in corporate finance. He is also a member of the Thomas Jefferson School of Law Tax and AML research teams. Nasir speaks Bangla and English.

E-mail address: ndoulah@doulah.com

Introduction

Wong Sai Fong—Mr. Wong is a partner at Shearn Delamore & Co. in Kuala Lumpur, Malaysia. Over the years, Mr. Wong has represented many multinationals in litigation and intellectual property enforcement matters. He also frequently appears as Senior Counsel in the High Court, Court of Appeal, and Federal Court on behalf of solicitors, and is often asked by intellectual property protection and enforcement coalitions to propose amendments to existing intellectual property laws or new laws to provide for better efficiency in the enforcement of intellectual property rights, and sits as a member on ad hoc government committees set up to review existing intellectual property laws or to propose amendments to existing laws. His non-litigation work includes advising on information technology, e-commerce telecommunications, franchising, entertainment, media, sponsorship, and merchandising matters and related agreements. He has been involved in unfair trade practice cases, the mediation or settlement of intellectual property related disputes, and representation of clients in dispute resolution matters.

E-mail address: saifong@shearndelamore.com

Shirshak Ghimire—Shirshak is an associate at Pradhan & Associates in Kathmandu, Nepal. Shirshak works in the areas of aviation, banking and finance, trade and commerce, corporate finance, M&A, technology, projects, telecommunication, etc. Shirshak received his B.A. and LL.B. from the National Law School of India University in Bangalore, India in 2011.

E-mail address: sghimire@pradhanlaw.com

Introduction

Patricia Ginsberg—Patricia is a partner based in Pamir Law Group's Taipei office. With an international law and business foundation and multi-lingual proficiencies, Patricia has focused her practice on international corporate and commercial transactions for multinational and local companies. She has represented and counseled clients investing from U.S. and Europe into Asia and also in the reverse direction. In addition, she has assisted Asian companies in projects within the Asian region. Her experiences include assisting clients in joint ventures, mergers and acquisitions, employments matters, structured management buyouts, technology licensing for technology-based clients, alternative dispute resolution, and assisting both lenders and borrowers in aircraft leasing and ship financings. While living in North America, Asia, and also Europe, Patricia gained valuable insights into issues faced by global businesses today. Her background provides her with keen awareness of Eastern and Western customs, often positioning her to bridge cultural and business gaps during legal/business negotiations and planning. Patricia received her B.A. from Wellesley College in 1995. She earned both her J.D. and M.A. from Washington University in St. Louis in 1998, where she was the recipient of the National Order of Barristers. She also received her M.B.A. from McGill University in 2004.

E-mail address: pginsberg@pamirlaw.com

Pierce Haesung Han—Pierce Haesung Han is an associate in Nixon Peabody's Business & Transactions group, where he works with clients on a broad range of matters including mergers and acquisitions, international commercial transactions, and federal securities law matters. Pierce focuses his practice on three main areas, assisting clients with a variety of complex business transactions.

- Mergers & Acquisitions: Providing assistance to both public and private clients with various mergers and acquisitions, performing due diligence, drafting and negotiating transaction documents, and facilitating closing and post-closing mechanics.
- International Commercial Transactions: Drafting and negotiating a variety of commercial agreements, including international franchise and development agreements, license agreements, and purchase and sale agreements.
- Federal Securities Law Matters: Assisting public and private clients regarding federal securities laws and stock exchange rules relating to corporate governance and disclosure.

Pierce serves as the Secretary of the Asian Pacific Bar Association Educational Fund (an affiliate of the Asian Pacific American Bar Association of the Greater Washington, D.C. Area). Pierce received his J.D. from Georgetown University Law Center and his B.A. from Case Western Reserve University. He is admitted to practice in the State of New York and the District of Columbia.

E-mail address: phan@nixonpeabody.com

~

Mai Thi Minh Hang—Hang is a partner at Russin & Vecchi in Hanoi, Vietnam. Hang's practice areas include banking, finance, telecommunications and mining, capital markets, and foreign investment. She has advised offshore clients who want to franchise their businesses in Vietnam. She assists a wide variety of clients on all aspects of business operation in Vietnam, including distribution in the form of direct selling. She assisted the Ministry of Industry and Trade in drafting regulations to implement the Commercial Code, which included government decrees on franchising and direct selling. She has published several articles on franchising and direct selling. Hang is commented by sources through legal directories, such as *Chambers* and *IFLR*, to be an excellent and diligent professional. Hang received a B.A. in Economics from Hanoi Foreign Trade University in 1997 and a LL.B. from Hanoi University of Law in 2001. Hang then attended Washington State University to receive an M.B.A. in 2003. Hang speaks Vietnamese and English.

E-mail address: mtmhang@russinvecchi.com.vn

~

Ngo Viet Hoa—Hoa is an Associate at Russin & Vecchi in Hanoi, Vietnam. Hoa's practice areas include corporate, commercial, and foreign investment. He has assisted clients on franchising, export, import, and distribution. Before joining Russin & Vecchi, Hoa worked for the Ministry of Industry and Trade in Vietnam ("MOIT"), as the director of Commercial Law Division. Hoa participated in drafting the Commercial Law 2005 and other legal documents which includes, among others, governmental decrees and ministerial circulars on franchising and distribution. He also took part as a legal advisor in negotiation of free trade agreements between Vietnam and its partners. Currently, although working with Russin & Vecchi, Hoa continues to provide inputs and comments on the draft laws and regulations at the request of the MOIT and the Vietnam Chamber of Commerce and Industry. Hoa received an LL.B. from Hanoi University of Law in 2002 and an LL.M. from the University of Melbourne Law School in 2009. Hoa speaks Vietnamese and English.

E-mail address: nvhoa@russinvecchi.com.vn

Introduction

Freddy Karyadi—Freddy is a partner at ABNR Law in Jakarta, Indonesia. Freddy joined ABNR as senior associate in July 2007 and became a partner on January 1, 2012. He studied law at University of Indonesia (1998) and Leiden University, majoring in International Tax Law (2002). He also graduated *cum laude* in 1997 from the Faculty of Economics of Trisakti University in Jakarta. He has participated in various trainings and seminars in Indonesia and abroad. Prior to joining ABNR, he worked for a number of years in other prominent law firms in Jakarta. In 2010, he was seconded to Loyens & Loeffs, Amsterdam Office, a prominent Dutch law firm. His special practice areas are capital markets, M&A, taxation, banking and corporate finance matters. He has represented numerous financial institutions, banks, private equity and funds, and multinational companies. He is a member of the editorial board of *Derivatives & Financial Instruments Journal*, International Bureau of Fiscal Documentation, the Netherlands, and is the regional correspondence for the Indonesia jurisdiction for *Tax Notes International* of Virginia, United States. He also contributes articles to *International Financial Law Review* and a number of national tax magazines, teaches in several universities and is a regular speaker in seminars and trainings. In addition to being an advocate and tax attorney, he is also a registered accountant (Ak) and a licensed tax consultant (brevet C). Freddy speaks Indonesian and English.

E-mail address: fkaryadi@abnrlaw.com

Dr. Mariam Khatoon—Dr. Khatoon is a partner at Doulah & Doulah in Dhaka, Bangladesh. Dr. Khatoon's practice areas include corporate law, commercial law, employment law, and intellectual property. She is highly experienced in the areas of corporate law and intellectual property matters. She has also finalized a number of key commercial deals and assisted in several foreign investments of Bangladesh by way of appropriate structurizations. Her clients include Intellisoft Yiecheng Logistics, Hewlett Packard, and Etihad Airways. Additionally, she is actively advising these companies in their day to day business, employment issues, and regulatory issues. Dr. Khatoon is a member of the Bangladesh Bar Council, Society for Research on Business Intellectual Inventions, Bangladesh Intellectual Property Organization, and the Association of European Lawyers. She received her B.A. and L.L.B. from Dhaka University, as well as her Doctorate in Philosophy, Intellectual Property Law. Dr. Khatoon speaks Bangla and English.

E-mail address: m.khatoon@doulah.com

Michelle C.Y. Loi—Michelle is a partner at Shearn Delamore & Co. in Kuala Lumpur, Malaysia. Michelle's area of practice is primarily contentious in nature. She has acted in court proceedings involving patent, trademark, copyright and design infringement, breaches of confidential information, and passing off. Her IP litigation experience transcends across a broad range of industries that include medical devices, food, movie, fashion, glove manufacture, oil palm, ink jet cartridges, digital transmission system, and pharmaceutical patents. She also represents clients in the Malaysian Intellectual Property Offices' opposition procedures as well as trade mark prosecution proceedings, and advises on domain name disputes. With respect to non-contentious areas, Michelle advises on Personal Data Protection Act, Food Act and Regulations, gaming regulations, franchising, as well as the IP and IT aspects of commercial transactions, which include licensing and technology transfers, software, and computer agreements.

E-mail address: michelle.loi@shearndelamore.com

Introduction

~

Keri McWilliams—Keri is a senior associate on the Franchise & Distribution team of Nixon Peabody LLP in Washington, D.C. Keri McWilliams works with franchisors to prepare and update franchise agreements and franchise disclosure documents in compliance with state, federal, and international franchise laws. She regularly counsels franchisors on sales compliance, franchisor/franchisee relationships, and international expansion. . Keri is also an experienced general commercial litigator, who has handled a wide range of cases including copyright, trademark, and other intellectual property disputes, breach of contract cases, non-competition disputes, collection cases, and shareholder disputes. Keri is an active member of the American Bar Association's Forum on Franchising, and an editor of The Franchise Lawyer. Keri received her J.D. from the Georgetown University Law Center and her B.F.A. from Washington University. She is admitted to practice in the District of Columbia and Minnesota.

E-mail address: kmcwilliams@nixonpeabody.com

~

Preeti Mehta—Preeti is a partner of Kanga & Co. in Mumbai, India. Preeti's practice is focused on foreign investment and joint ventures, mergers and acquisitions, private equity investment, corporate law, capital markets, franchising, and banking law. She has been recognized as one of the Leading Lawyers by the *International Who's Who of Merger & Acquisition Lawyers* and by *Chambers & Partners for Corporate and M&A*. Preeti is also internationally recognized for her franchise expertise and has been recognized as one of the Leading Lawyers by the *International Who's Who of Franchise Lawyers* for the last several years. She chairs the legal committee of the Executive

Council of the Franchise Association of India. Additionally, she serves on the Editorial Advisory Board of the *International Journal of Franchising Law* and has contributed to the India chapter of the *International Encyclopedia of Franchising*. Preeti received her B.A. and LLB from Bombay University in 1981 and 1984, respectively. She also completed specialized franchise coursework at the Middlesex University, U.K. in 2000. Preeti first became an Advocate of the High Court, Bombay and Member of the Bar Council of Maharashtra in 1984 before becoming a Solicitor in Bombay and England in 1987.

E-mail address: preet.mehta@kanagacompany.com

~

Maria Teresa D. Mercado-Ferrer—Tes is a partner at SyCip Law in Manila, Philippines. Her areas of practice cover banking, finance and securities; intellectual property, including licensing and franchising; mergers and acquisition; investments; and food and drugs. Some of the transactions she handled include the public offering of P75 billion series 2 preferred shares by San Miguel Corporation in 2012, the acquisition of Digital Telecommunications by Philippine Long Distance Company in 2011, and the acquisition of e-Telecare by Stream International in 2009. She is a member of Licensing Executives Society International, Licensing Executives Society-Philippines, and the UP Women Lawyers' Circle. She co-authored the Philippine chapter of *CCH Doing Business in Asia*.

E-mail address: mtmferrer@syciplaw.com

~

Kakuji Mitani—Kakuji is a partner at Momo-o, Matsuo & Namba in Tokyo, Japan. He passed the Japanese National Bar

Exam in 1999 and graduated from The University of Tokyo, Faculty of Law (LL.B.) in 2000. He then attended The Legal Training and Research Institute of the Supreme Court of Japan from 2001 to 2002 and was admitted to the Japanese Bar (The Dai-ichi Tokyo Bar Association in 2002). He began his career at Momo-o, Matsuo & Namba in 2002. In 2007, Kakuji graduated from Columbia University Law School with a Master of Laws degree and worked for Weil, Gotshal & Manges, New York City office, from 2007 to 2008. He was admitted to the New York Bar in 2008. Kakuji returned to Momo-o, Matsuo & Namba in 2008 and became partner in 2011. Kakuji speaks Japanese and English.

E-mail address: mitani@mmn-law.gr.jp

~

Rustam M. Nazrisho—Rustam is a senior partner at Nazrisho & Mirzoev, LLC in Dushanbe, Tajikistan. He obtained his Juris Doctor degree from New York Law School, and B.A. degree in international economics from Regents College, London and Long Island University, New York. Upon his graduation from law school, he joined the law firm of Bonfiglio & Asterita, LLC where he counseled a variety of clients in the finance sector, including banks, consumer credit companies, as well as private parties in purchases of residential and commercial properties. He later started his private practice and represented corporate clients in the United States in all aspects of commercial disputes. In 2011, he jointly, with a partner established the law firm of Nazrisho & Mirzoev, LLC. Since then Rustam has provided legal services to numerous national and international companies operating in Tajikistan. He assisted in providing legal support and maintenance of many various operations, including but not limited to advising international lenders in relation to loans to Tajikistani banks, issues surrounding participation in the Tajik securities market, guarantees, and collaterals. His practice encompasses corporate law, international finance law, litigation, real estate, and business transactions. Mr. Nazrisho is fluent in English, Russian and Spanish.

E-mail address: nazrisho@nmlaw.tj

Devendra Pradhan—Devendra is the founder and managing member of Pradhan & Associates in Kathmandu, Nepal. Before establishing Pradhan & Associates, Devendra worked with various law firms in Kathmandu for several years. He also worked with various law firms in New York and Washington, D.C. In addition to Nepal, Devendra is also admitted as an attorney at law in New York, District of Columbia, and various Federal Courts in the United States of America. Devendra focuses his practice on advising and representing foreign companies primarily in the area of aviation, telecommunications, technology, banking and finance, mergers and acquisitions, private equity, intellectual property, commercial arbitration, cross-border and international transactions, etc. He has been recognized as a leading lawyer in various areas of commercial law by *Who's Who Legal*, *Chambers Global* and *Chambers Asia*. *Who's Who Legal* has recognized him amongst the world's leading lawyers in the area of aviation, M&A, project finance and trademark for the last several years. Devendra regularly contributes scholarly articles on various topics of Nepalese commercial laws and on key issues of international laws in various national publications as well as in international law journals and international publications. Devendra received his bachelor's degree in law at Tribhuvan University in Kathmandu, Nepal in 1990. He later received his LL.M. in International Business Law in 2001 from American University, Washington College of Law in Washington, D.C.

E-mail address: dpradhan@pradhanlaw.com

Introduction

~

Sriwan Puapondh—Sriwan is an of counsel at Tilleke & Gibbins in Bangkok, Thailand, and, since 1999, has headed the firm's tax group. She is a highly regarded tax lawyer in Thailand with over 30 years of experience, including with Thailand's Revenue Department (10 years) and with such well-known firms such as General Motors (Thailand) Ltd., SGVN Legal & Tax Consultants Ltd., and Caltex Oil (Thailand) Ltd. She has extensive experience in international tax planning for cross-border transactions, expatriate tax planning, joint ventures, and mergers and acquisitions. She is also a frequent speaker at high-level conferences and top universities. Sriwan is widely regarded as a leading tax practitioner by her clients and independent legal publications, including the past ten editions of *The Legal 500 Asia Pacific*, *Chambers Asia-Pacific*, and *Practical Law Co*. The *Tax Directors Handbook 2011* named her as one of the top 250 tax lawyers in the world. Swiran speaks both Thai and English.

E-mail address: sriwan.p@tilleke.com

~

Gustaaf Reerink—Gustaaf is a foreign counsel at ABNR Law in Jakarta, Indonesia. Gustaaf graduated from Leiden University in the Netherlands, where he earned an LL.M in private law, an MA in Indonesian studies, and a PhD in law, governance, and development. In addition, he studied law at King's College London and the School of Oriental and African Studies in London and studied French at the University of Burgundy in Dijon. Prior to joining ABNR, he worked as an associate in the Amsterdam and Brussels offices of De Brauw Blackstone Westbroek. His practice encompasses foreign investment, corporate, mergers and acquisitions, energy and mineral resources, and related regulatory and compliance matters. He regularly publishes articles and gives presentations on Indonesian legal matters, and serves as a guest lecturer at several Indonesian universities. He is admitted to the Amsterdam Bar and is a registered foreign lawyer in Indonesia. Gustaaf speaks Dutch, English, French, and Indonesian.

E-mail address: greerink@abnrlaw.com

~

Sherzod S. Sodatkadamov—Sherzod is a senior associate at Nazrisho & Mirzoev, LLC in Dushanbe, Tajikistan. He graduated from the Tajik National University, Faculty of Law. He started his career working with the non-governmental organizations. Afterwards he served as lawyer in private companies where his practice was mostly focused on Civil Law. Since joining Nazrisho & Mirzoev, LLC, Sherzod expanded his practice. During his practice in the firm he became involved in several large investment projects in Tajikistan in such diverse areas as corporate issues, transactions, real estate, etc. He has advised nonprofit organizations on labor and employment related matters. He also has contributed to the annual report of the World Bank "*Doing Business.*" Sherzod knows Tajik, Russian and English.

E-mail address: ssherzod@nmlaw.tj

~

Kendal H. Tyre, Jr.—Kendal is a partner in the Washington, D.C., office of Nixon Peabody LLP. He handles domestic and cross-border transactions, including mergers and acquisitions, joint ventures, strategic alliances, licensing, and franchise matters. In his franchise and licensing practice, Kendal counsels domestic and international franchisors, franchisees, licensors, licensees, and distributors regarding U.S. state and federal franchise laws as well as foreign franchise legislation in a variety of jurisdictions. Kendal drafts and provides advice with regard to franchise and license agreements, disclosure documents, and area development agreements and has extensive experience drafting and negotiating a variety of other commercial agreements. His client base spans the United States and foreign countries, including South Africa, Kenya, and the United Kingdom.

Kendal is a frequent contributor to franchise publications and a frequent speaker at franchise programs held by the American Bar Association's Forum on Franchising and the International Franchise Association. Kendal is also the executive director of LexNoir Foundation.

E-mail address: ktyre@nixonpeabody.com

~

Diana Vilmenay-Hammond—Diana is an attorney in the Washington, D.C., office of Nixon Peabody LLP. She is a member of the firm's Franchise & Distribution Team. In her franchise practice, Diana works with domestic and international franchisors on transactional and litigation matters. Specifically, she counsels franchisor clients regarding state and federal franchise laws, disclosure, and registration obligations. Diana drafts and negotiates various commercial agreements, including international franchise and development agreements. Diana has co-authored numerous articles on franchising and frequently co-hosted the Nixon Peabody franchise law webinar series. Topics have included:

- "Franchise Case Law Round-Up: Implications for Your Franchise";
- "Social Media Part II: Best Practices in Protecting Your Brand in the New Media"; and

- "The Awuah Case: Bellwether or Outlier."

Diana received her J.D. from Howard University School of Law and her B.A. from Georgetown University. She is a member of the American Bar Association (Forum on Franchising).

Email address: dvilmenay@nixonpeabody.com

~

Kelly F. Xiang—Kelly serves as a Chinese Legal Consultant in the Shanghai, China office of Nixon Peabody LLP. She focuses her practice on cross-border matters involving China, including all forms of foreign direct investments in China, market entries, mergers and acquisitions, commercial franchising, labor and employment, immigration, taxes, licensing, regulatory issues, general corporate matters, and IP-related matters including trademark, branding and licensing.

E-mail address: kxiang@nixonpeabody.com

Introduction

About the Book

Franchising in Asia 2015: Legal and Business Considerations serves as a practical, succinct, easy-to-use reference tool for lawyers, business people, and academics to use in navigating the myriad laws and business issues impacting franchise arrangements in Asia.

It provides an overview of the franchise industry in Asia and addresses the typical legal issues confronted when expanding a franchise system overseas, and particularly in Asia. Finally, the book also covers those laws governing franchising in 15 Asian jurisdictions — Bangladesh, China, India, Indonesia, Japan, Kazakhstan, Malaysia, Nepal, Philippines, South Korea, Taiwan, Tajikistan, Thailand, and Vietnam as well as Hong Kong.

In each chapter devoted to a particular country, an author, who is a legal expert in the designated jurisdiction, addresses the basic questions that a franchise lawyer would need to know to competently represent a client in expanding their franchise system to that country.

Each country chapter organizes a discussion of each country's laws under various headings and in a uniform format. Topics were sent to each country's author in the form of a questionnaire attached as *Appendix A*, and each author drafted responses to the questions presented. A general overview relating to the political and economic history of the country at the beginning of each chapter provides an initial context for the regulatory framework.[1]

The authors for each chapter are listed at the beginning of a chapter and their biographical information is listed in the previous section, *About the Authors*.

---

[1] The source of information for these sections is the Central Intelligence Agency, https://www.cia.gov/library/publications/the-world-factbook/ (last visited June 7, 2015).

Introduction

Counsel should always consult with local counsel in the relevant jurisdiction instead of relying solely on the information contained in this book. The laws governing franchising in Asia are evolving and local counsel in the various jurisdictions are best positioned to provide timely, relevant advice applying the current law to the particular facts of a case.

International Franchising in the Asian Context

Kendal H. Tyre, Jr., Diana Vilmenay-Hammond and Pierce Haesung Han

NIXON PEABODY LLP

Washington, D.C. (U.S.)

I. Industry Overview

Asia is currently home to the world's second-, third-, and tenth-largest economies[2] measured by gross domestic product (GDP) and five of the twenty G20 Members.[3] The emerging Asia region, which includes Southeast Asia, China and India, is projected to grow by 6.9% per year from 2014 to 2018.[4]

Despite the global economic downturn, the economies of the Association of Southeast Asian Nations (ASEAN)[5], which includes Brunei, Cambodia, Indonesia, Laos, Malaysia, Myanmar (Burma), Philippines, Singapore, Thailand and

---

2 Andrew Bergman, *World's largest economies*, CNNMONEY, *available at* http://money.cnn.com/news/economy/world_economies_gdp/ (last visited June 7, 2015).

3 *G20 Members*, G20, *available at* https://www.g20.org/about_g20/g20_members (last visited June 7, 2015).

4 *Economic Outlook for Southeast Asia, China and India 2014*, OECD, *available at* http://www.oecd.org/site/seao/Pocket%20Edition%20SAEO2014.pdf (last visited June 7, 2015).

5 *ASEAN Member States*, ASEAN, *available at* http://www.asean.org/asean/asean-member-states (last visited June 7, 2015).

Vietnam, have continued to experience steady growth, supported by strong domestic consumption and investment. The Asia Pacific region as a whole was forecasted to experience 4.7% retail growth in 2014, up from 4.3% in 2013.[6] However, the International Monetary Fund has expressed concern over the region and the "middle-income trap" where rapidly growing economies become stagnate at middle-income levels and fail to graduate into the high-income levels of advanced economies.[7]

Recent Expansion into Asia. Against this backdrop, franchising in Asia has experienced consistent and exponential growth in recent years. The news headlines cite the growth taking place.

Starbucks recently opened its 625th store in South Korea, after first arriving in the country in 1999.[8] Additionally, the company expected to operate more than 1,000 stores in China by the end of 2014.[9] Berkshire Hathaway Inc., which owns Dairy Queen and operates more than 600 stores in China, is expanding into Taiwan and Vietnam.[10] Johnny Rockets opened its second location in Malaysia less than six months after opening its first

---

6 Raphael Moreau, *Year of the Horse: Outlook for Retailing in Asia Pacific in 2014 and Beyond*, EUROMONITOR INTERNATIONAL, *available at* http://blog.euromonitor.com/2014/02/year-of-the-horse-outlook-for-retailing-in-asia-pacific-in-2014-and-beyond.html (last visited June 7, 2015).

7 *I.M.F. Warns of 'Middle-Income Trap' in Asia*, THE NEW YORK TIMES, *available at* http://www.nytimes.com/2013/04/30/business/global/30iht-asiaecon30.html (last visited June 7, 2015).

8 Matt Viser, *Dunkin' Donuts jumps on Asia's coffee craze*, BOSTON GLOBE, Mar. 30, 2014, *available at* http://www.bostonglobe.com/news/world/2014/03/29/from-massachusetts-seoul-dunkin-donuts-finds-new-markets-coffee-craze-sweeps-asia/aykwWhGnFNjG85ahVxJIFL/story.html (last visited June 7, 2015).

9 *Id.*

10 Alexandria Baca, *Buffett's Dairy Queen Targets Asia With Red-Bean Flavor*, BLOOMBERG L.P., Jan. 21, 2014, *available at* http://www.bloomberg.com/news/2014-01-22/buffett-s-dairy-queen-targets-asia-with-red-bean-flavor.html (last visited June 7, 2015).

restaurant in the country on October 28, 2013.[11] The company has 11 total restaurants in Southeast Asia, with six outlets in the Philippines and three in Indonesia.[12] Johnny Rockets' expansion has continued into India, first opening its doors on January 28, 2014, with multiple other locations set to open over the next several months.[13] The world's largest food chain, Subway, has an ambitious target of 10,000 stores by 2020 in Asia.[14]

International franchisors expanding across the region are not limited to food and beverage franchises but range from clothing retail to luxury hotels.[15]

Franchise Specific Programs in Asia. Certain Asian countries have focused on the growth of the franchise industry to spur overall economic growth. Malaysia, for example, has set specific franchise industry goals to contribute 9.4 percent to the country's

---

11 *Johnny Rockets Continues To Sizzle In Malaysia*, PR NEWSWIRE, Mar. 28, 2014, *available at* http://www.prnewswire.com/news-releases/johnny-rockets-continues-to-sizzle-in-malaysia-252964471.html (last visited June 7, 2015).

12 *Id.*

13 *International Restaurant Chain, Johnny Rockets, Opens First Restaurant In India*, PR NEWSWIRE, Feb. 4, 2014, *available at* http://www.prnewswire.com/news-releases/international-restaurant-chain-johnny-rockets-opens-first-restaurant-in-india-243571211.html (last visited June 7, 2015).

14 Liz Lee, *Up close and personal with Fred DeLuca*, STAR PUBLICATIONS, Apr. 6, 2013, *available at* http://www.thestar.com.my/Business/Business-News/2013/04/06/Up-close-and-personal-with-Fred-DeLuca/ (last visited June 7, 2015).

15 Gap Inc. announced plans to open five franchise operated stores in the Philippines in 2014, with continued expansion in Japan and its first store in China. *Gap Inc: Old Navy's New Asian Expansion Story*, Mar. 31, 2014, *available at* http://www.forbes.com/sites/greatspeculations/2014/03/31/gap-inc-old-navys-new-asian-expansion-story/ (last visited June 7, 2015). Hyatt Hotels Corporation has aggressive overseas expansion, with Asia as its focus. Anjali Raval, *Hyatt opens up and bets on expansion*, THE FINANCIAL TIMES LTD, Mar. 18, 2014, *available at* http://www.ft.com/cms/s/0/99c6bdf4-ae45-11e3-974d-00144feab7de.html#axzz2xZqGIHek (last visited June 7, 2015).

GDP and to become a leading franchise hub in the Southeast Asia region by the year 2020.[16] In order to accomplish these goals, Malaysia has adopted the National Franchise Development Blueprint: 2012–2016 to provide clear goals and a strategic direction for the franchise industry in the country. The Malaysian Ministry of Domestic Trade, Co-Operatives and Consumerism has also pledged to double its efforts to meet these targets. It has established a specific unit within the ministry, the Perbadanan Nasional Bhd (PNS), to oversee and facilitate franchise development. The PNS provides training for franchisors, franchisees, franchise consultants, and the public on issues related to the operation and management of franchise businesses.

Several development programs have also been created to help spur franchise growth. For example, the Franchise Development Programme is a marketing program aimed at bringing together franchisors with prospective franchisees that operate small and medium enterprises in the commercial, service, and industrial sectors. Another program assists local entrepreneurs who have products that have the potential to be franchised but who do not possess the know-how or capabilities to franchise these products. Through the program, eligible local entrepreneurs are appointed a qualified franchise consultant to guide them through the process, such as work documentation and procedures, until the opening of a prototype outlet or store and the entering into a contractual arrangement with a prospective franchisee. The cost of the consultation is borne by the program.

Several financial schemes have also been created to help franchises find financing. The Franchise Development Assistance Fund encourages local entrepreneurs to turn their

---

[16] *See* Kendal H. Tyre, Jr. and Pierce Haesung Han, *Tapping Into Malaysia's Aggressive Franchising Goals*, LAW 360, http://www.law360.com/articles/491545/tapping-into-malaysia-s-aggressive-franchising-goals (last visited June 7, 2015); *see also* Kendal H. Tyre, Jr. and Pierce Haesung Han, *Malaysian Government Actively Promotes Growth in Franchise Sector*, NIXON PEABODY FRANCHISE LAW ALERT (October 2013).

conventional businesses into franchised businesses. Through the fund, businesses that have successfully been developed as franchises are eligible for reimbursements of up to 90 percent for the overall franchise system development costs incurred for a maximum amount of approximately US$ 31,118. To provide yet another option for financing, the PNS has also launched the Franchise Micro-Financing Scheme that allows prospective entrepreneurs to use microfinancing for franchises. This allows those with lower incomes the opportunity to start businesses and learn a trade with less business risk. In 2012, the PNS allocated approximately US$ 2.5 million, of which approximately US$ 1.9 million was disbursed as of early April 2013. The ministry has stated that it is not averse to pumping more funds into the scheme.

Legislative Reforms. The robust growth of franchising is likely to continue as legislative and economic reforms take hold on the Asian continent. Some Asian governments have enacted legislative reforms to address the ever changing business and legal landscape in the franchise industry. For example, in February 2014, South Korea amended the Fair Transactions in Franchise Business Act to better address franchise relationship issues and heighten disclosure requirements.[17] The Fair Transactions in Franchise Business Act first became effective on November 1, 2002 and was amended in 2008 and again in 2010.

This amendment added several new provisions to the Fair Transactions in Franchise Business Act. It requires franchisors to bear up to 40% of the remodeling costs of the franchised business and to restrict franchisors from requiring their franchisees to remodel only once every five to seven years and for justifiable reasons. These restrictions would not apply to situations where the franchisee voluntarily remodels or must remodel to improve conditions due to sanitary or other safety concerns.

---

[17] *See* Kendal H. Tyre, Jr. and Pierce Haesung Han, *South Korea Adopts Major Amendments to the Fair Transactions in Franchise Business Act*, NIXON PEABODY FRANCHISE LAW ALERT (January 2014).

The amendment further restricts franchisors from requiring franchisees to operate the franchised business during specific business hours under certain circumstances. For example, franchisees will be permitted to reduce their business hours if profits generated from operation of the franchised business during night hours do not cover or are not greater than losses for operating at night. In addition, a franchisee may also reduce business hours if there are unavoidable circumstances, such as illness or the treatment of an illness that prevents normal operation during business hours.

Additionally, the amendment requires franchisors to specifically define the business area or territory of the franchisee in each franchise agreement. During the term of such franchise agreement, the franchisor is restricted from directly or indirectly (through affiliates or other related entities) operating a similar business within the franchisee's territory without justifiable reasons.

The amendment requires franchisors over a certain size to provide additional information to prospective franchisees on projected sales revenue and the relevant calculation methods for these projections. A franchisor must maintain such information for five years from the date of execution of the franchise agreement.

The heightened disclosure obligations also include the requirement of franchisors to specify whether they have violated the Fair Transactions in Franchise Business Act's general terms and conditions, information regarding business support received by the franchisor from affiliates or third parties and details about the closest 10 franchised businesses.

The amendment permits franchisees of the same franchise system to form trade associations or organizations similar to a trade union to protect their rights. These franchisee organizations can collectively consult and negotiate with the franchisor to amend the terms and conditions of their franchise relationship. Franchisors are restricted from penalizing franchisees on the grounds of forming or becoming involved with such organizations and will be subject to corrective measures or fines, when and if they do so.

The amendment requires franchisors to refund franchise fees under certain circumstances. For example, franchisees are now entitled to request refunds of franchise fees within four months of execution of the franchise agreement if franchisors provide false, exaggerated, or misleading disclosures. The amendment now grants the chairman of the board of audit and inspection and the administrator of the small and medium business administration the right to file criminal complaints of violations of the Act with the Korea Fair Trade Commission, which previously was an exclusive right of the prosecutor general. These amendments to the Act represent a substantial shift to protect franchisees in South Korea.

Coupled with the aforementioned legislative reforms, South Korea has also increased fines and the power of regulatory entities. In October of 2014, the South Korea Fair Trade Commission, the country's antitrust agency, fined the largest coffee franchise in South Korea for violating the Fair Transactions in Franchise Business Act.[18] Caffe Bene, a company worth 176.2 billion won (approximately US$171 million), has more than 1,860 stores in 14 different countries worldwide, with 735 franchisees throughout South Korea.

The South Korea FTC fined Caffe Bene the maximum possible penalty of 1.9 billion won (approximately US$ 1.88 million) for passing costs on to its franchisees. The FTC found that Caffe Bene violated the Fair Transactions in Franchise Business Act and specific provisions of its franchise agreements with franchisees that provided that the costs of marketing and promotions would be shared equally.

---

[18] *See* Kendal H. Tyre, Jr. and Pierce Haesung Han, *South Korea's Fair Trade Commission Imposes Largest Possible Fine on Franchise for Unfair Practices*, NIXON PEABODY FRANCHISE LAW ALERT (October 2014).

Upon further investigation, the FTC also found that Caffe Bene required its franchisees to redesign their store locations, purchase "necessary equipment" from headquarters or a designated third-party, and purchase additional items that were actually listed as "optional" in the franchise agreements. Caffe Bene attained sales of 181.3 billion won (approximately US$ 176 million), nearly 56% of its total sales, during the period between November 2008 and April 2012, largely due to the interior remodeling and equipment sales to its franchisees. The fine imposed on Caffe Bene is the largest fine ever levied by the South Korea FTC and clearly shows the agency's intent to enforce the act and stop abusive franchisors from overpowering their franchisees.

II. Legal and Contractual Overview

A. Due Diligence

At the beginning of a transaction, franchisors should concentrate on certain due diligence topics including intellectual property and certain local laws and regulations of the target country (i.e., those relating to disclosure, registration and taxes) as well as issues related to supply chain and the background of the franchisee. Each of these due diligence items can present barriers to the franchise system from a time and expense perspective whether it relates to waiting periods associated with disclosure or government agency approval of registration, or repatriating funds out of the target country or importing products into the region.

1. Intellectual Property

The intellectual property analysis should be beyond whether to take the requisite steps to protect the franchisor's principal trademarks. The parties' focus should be on intellectual property issues that may impact their financial position over the course of the agreement and in the event of termination. A few examples are highlighted below:

a. Trademark registration

Trademark registration may often take many months (or years) to complete. During the negotiation, the parties must determine who bears the risk if a primary trademark needs to be changed because of a valid third-party claim. Franchise agreements typically provide that the franchisee bears all responsibility (including related costs) for changes or modifications to the marks. This risk is more difficult to impose on a franchisee if the trademarks are not yet registered. In international deals, when significant funds are expended by the franchise at the onset (area fee, lease commitments, etc.), an alternative approach is to consider a cost sharing mechanism. One example is having the franchisor cover a portion or all of the franchisee's costs to replace signage and/or provide indemnification.

b. Registered user or similar agreements

Often franchisees are required to show governmental authorities evidence of their ability to use the franchisor's trademarks in the target country. The franchisor should confirm whether registration of a user agreement (or similar agreement) is necessary or just advisable and determine. It should also determine what type of document should be filed, if any. Often, preparing and registering a short form trademark agreement after execution of the full franchise agreement is preferable because it keeps the principal deal terms confidential. Further, the franchisor should analyze whether registration of this document could trigger agency or dealer protection, which may significantly change the monetary considerations associated with termination or non-renewal.[19]

---

[19] *See infra* at 31-33.

c. Injunctive relief

The franchisor's timetable and procedure to obtain injunction relief against a franchisee for trademark infringement or failure to de-identify after termination are not topics typically covered by the parties during the negotiation; however, it is important for the franchisor to know as part of its overall risk assessment. This particular issue in the assessment may not prevent a deal from closing, but it may be a tipping point, particularly if a franchisor is prioritizing a list of target countries for its international expansion.

d. Ownership of innovations

If the franchisee contends that the target country does not allow for the franchisor to have ownership of innovations, the franchisor should be prepared to offer an alternative. One potential way to remedy this situation is to immediately transfer innovations rights to the franchisor. This gives ultimate ownership to the franchisor and addresses the public policy issue.

2. Local Laws and Regulations

Franchisors need to determine at the outset what local laws impact the sales process, the drafting of the contracts, and the process for effectuating the documents. Set out below are some initial considerations for local counsel:

a. Laws regulating franchising

Counsel must be aware of laws regulating franchising to avoid unnecessary surprises. Disclosure and/or registration laws, for example, can significantly impact the timing and expense related to a transaction, and may dictate behavior in the sales process and negotiation phase.

b. Laws impacting franchising

Certain laws governing other businesses or industries generally may impact how a franchisor conducts business in the country, gathers information from the prospect, and drafts agreements.

c. Local ownership restrictions

A franchisor should confirm whether local ownership restrictions exist so that it can require the franchisee to identify a local partner. If the existing franchisee is unable to find a partner suitable to the franchisee and franchisor, any time spent on negotiation may have been unnecessary.

3. Tax

Tax planning issues should be assessed by a franchisor when determining of how it wants to structure the franchisor entity. Other initial tax considerations include the following:

a. Withholding taxes

A franchisor must understand the foreign withholding tax rates that may impact the fees remitted by the franchisee. It must assess whether it can take a tax credit, as well as how and if a different characterization of fees may be more tax efficient and how such fees should be addressed in the franchise agreement.[20]

b. Gross-up clauses

A franchisor should determine at the outset whether it wants to include a gross-up clause. Such a clause requires that the franchisee pay the withholding tax, provide evidence of the payment to the franchisor, and pay the full royalty amount as stated in the franchise agreement. Because these clauses can be extremely contentious, a franchisor should determine at the

---

20 *See infra* at 42-44.

beginning of a negotiation whether it is a critical element to the deal.[21]

c. Transfer pricing

When the parties are located in different jurisdictions, counsel should take into account the imposition of transfer pricing rule as it structures the inter-company relationships between a franchisor and its affiliates and subsidiaries. Transfer pricing restrictions require prices paid for goods and services between related parties be similar to those prices that are charged between unrelated parties. The commercial terms of any inter-company agreements should be assessed from this perspective.

4. Supply Chain

Counsel and the appropriate business person should conduct due diligence on the potential supply chain of the target country and determine whether alternative products are a viable option. Various restrictions on certain food items are common. Therefore, counsel should advise clients at any early stage if such limitations will cause problems with the importation of these goods to the target country.[22] The costs associated with

---

21 *Id.*

22 For example, many sub-Saharan Africa countries are still in the early stages of supply chain development. African franchisees are required to maintain adequate supplies of the products that fuel their businesses and those products must also meet the franchisor's particular quality standards. For instance, KFC and other fast food brands require adequate supplies of chicken that meet their standards. This may be difficult in certain African countries where the supply of chickens from local chicken farmers fail to meet the franchisor's criteria for not only food safety and security but also quality and quantity. South African KFC's sell almost 10% of the nation's commercially grown chickens. In these instances, local franchisees are required to purchase their supply from outside the country from franchisor-approved suppliers. To ensure adequate supply needs are met and to cut costs, some franchisors are working with their franchisees to secure local suppliers. See *International Franchising in the African Context*, FRANCHISING IN AFRICA 2014: LEGAL AND BUSINESS CONSIDERATIONS, 9

(Footnote continued on next page)

taxes and tariffs on these goods can undermine the pricing model and make the business unviable, if due diligence in this area is not thorough.

5. Franchisee Information

Often, an important element to a successful franchise relationship is finding the right partner. Once the right franchisee is found, the legal aspects of franchisee due diligence, are critical.

In United States, anti-terrorism laws prohibit a franchisor from conducting business with certain individuals or entities. As part of its due diligence, U.S. franchisors must confirm that its potential franchisee is not deemed a "specially designated national and blocked person" ("SDN"). A list of these individuals and entities is maintained by the U.S. Department of Treasury's Office of Foreign Assets Control ("OFAC").

Some information on the background of potential franchisees can also be obtained from third parties or other resources. For example, franchisors based in the U.S. should check if the prospective franchisee is listed on certain lists maintained by the Bureau of Industry and Security ("BIS") of the U.S. Department of Commerce. BIS maintains the Denied Persons List. This list identifies those individuals who have been denied export privileges. BIS Entity List designates those organizations that BIS has determined present a high level of proliferation concerns. Finally, the Unverified Parties List is a list maintained by BIS of parties to transactions for which BIS could not perform a pre-license check or a post-license verification.

(Footnote continued from previous page)

(Kendal H. Tyre, Jr., Diana Vilmenay-Hammond, and Courtney L. Lindsay II, eds. LexNoir Foundation 2014).

Further, third parties can provide more in-depth background checks, including items such as media hits, credit and financial history, litigation reviews, and financial information.

To ensure that the background check of the franchisee is complete, franchisors should confirm who its shareholders are, whether that it has authority to enter into the agreement, and whether the person signing on behalf of the franchisee is authorized to do so.

U.S. franchisors are subject to the Foreign Corrupt Practices Act ("FCPA"). As a result, the franchisor should determine if the prospective franchisee or any of the principals of the franchisee is an official of a foreign political party, a foreign official, a foreign political candidate, or an officer of a public international organization.

Finally, the franchisor should obtain directly from the franchisee information relating to any personal guarantees or obligations currently imposed on the franchisee entity and each principal, résumés for each principal and key employees, financial statements and past years' tax returns for the company and each principal, and any banking and accounting information.

B. Letter of Intent

International franchise transactions may be complex. Negotiations may be lengthy, depending on the parties, the country, applicable laws. Often, letters of intent are used prior to executing binding, definitive agreements. They contain some of the key business and legal terms, but are not as comprehensive as the franchise agreement.

1. Assessing the Business Rationale

Letters of intent may not be appropriate for every franchise transaction. Often, the goal of a letter of intent is to make a complex deal more efficient and cost effective. To accomplish this goal, the parties must understand at the outset that it is not to be heavily negotiated.

Requiring a deposit as part of the letter of intent is one way to vet candidates and to off-set the franchisor's own expenses. Franchisors should consider determine whether the deposit will be refundable to the candidate, whether it will be deducted from any other fees paid by that such candidate and whether franchise laws are triggered upon taking any deposit.[23]

2. Application of Franchise Laws

Compliance with registration and/or disclosure laws becomes more complicated with franchisors that enter into letters of intent, because the applicability of the franchise laws in many jurisdictions is unclear, and local counsel may be reluctant to give a firm answer on whether such laws apply to a letter of intent, given the ambiguity.[24]

3. Advantages of a Letter of Intent

The advantages of a letter of intent can be significant. Entering into a letter of intent demonstrates the seriousness of the parties. A letter of intent may identify difficult issues prior to the negotiation of the franchise agreement, resulting in the saving of time and money. Finally, a letter of intent where confidentiality covenants can be used provides comfort to the parties that their disclosures will be kept confidential.

4. Disadvantages of a Letter of Intent

Entering into a letter of intent also has some significant risks. The negotiation of the letter of intent can easily expand into a negotiation of all terms and conditions. However, it should be

---

[23] *See infra* notes 27 through 50 and accompanying text.

[24] S. Goldman, G. Knack, G. Mondragon, and A. Loewinger, *Using Letters of Intent, Term Sheets and Other Interim Deal Documents in International Franchising* (Paper Presented at IBA/IFA 26th Annual Joint Conference, May 2010) at 5. In IBA/IFA 26th Annual Joint Conference – Managing Risks in International Franchising, May 18-19, 2010, Washington, DC.

limited to the key business terms—royalties, area development fees, marketing fees, territory, and development schedule.

One significant risk of entering into a letter of intent is not drafting the document carefully. In *Texaco, Inc. v. Pennzoil Co.*, a U.S. court found that the "memorandum of agreement" had the essential elements of a contract, despite having open terms and referencing a future definitive agreement.[25] The court concluded that the memorandum, in connection with the press releases issued by the parties demonstrated an intent to be bound. This resulted in an award to Pennzoil of over US$ 10 billion.

If the letter of intent is intended to be non-binding, drafters should use words such as "would," "possible" and "proposed." The parties should use binding words such as "shall" and "must" only if meant. Moreover, the franchisor's post-signing conduct should be consistent with the non-binding nature of the document.

C. Standard Structures

When structuring the contractual arrangement for international franchise expansion, typical formats include single-unit franchise agreements, master franchise agreements, area development agreements, joint venture agreements, or area representative agreements. Often, international franchise agreements do not follow a standard form. In fact, they may be negotiated documents that take the form of a hybrid of these typical arrangements.

There are disadvantages and advantages for each form of international franchise agreement.

1. Unit Franchise Agreements

Franchise systems expanding into target countries with geographic proximity, or with similar languages, laws, customs,

---

[25] 729 S.W.2d 768 (Tex. App 1987).

and cultural considerations will often offer new franchises to single-unit operators. They will simply amend the form of unit franchise agreement to conform to domestic standards in the target country. Under a single-unit franchise arrangement, the franchisee will acquire the right to open and operate only one unit for a specific location in a country.

Expansion through traditional single-unit agreements with different franchisees slows growth. It also results in increased cost to the franchisor in recruiting different prospective franchisees and providing operational support and training to each franchise arrangement. However, one or two single-unit agreements may be useful to test a concept in a new market, or to evaluate potential partners for area development or master franchise arrangements. In some instances, a single-unit franchisee may ask the franchisor to approve them for a second unit, then a third, and so on, after proving they are capable operators. This is often called "sequential franchising."

2. Area Development Agreements

When the franchisee is well-financed, the parties may enter into an area development agreement. It is also common when the franchisee has corporate operational experience, and when expanding into target markets where language, laws, customs, and cultural considerations vary dramatically from those in the domestic market. Under this form of agreement, the franchisee—commonly known as the area developer—develops all franchise units in the target country by itself, or through affiliated corporations. For example, a franchisee could be granted the right to open five store locations between 2015 and 2020. The development agreement governs the overall relationship. Typically, it specifies the territory, the time frame, and the specific number of franchise units that the franchisee is authorized to open. A specified form of unit franchise agreement will be entered into with the area developer for each unit developed.

An area development arrangement enhances growth, eliminates the need to recruit perspective franchisees, and concentrates operational support to one franchisee, the area developer. However, the success of a franchise system using area development as an expansion strategy depends heavily on the expertise, business skill, and motivation of the area developers.

3. Master Franchise Agreements

Many franchisors expand internationally through master franchise arrangements. The master franchise agreement is entered into with the master franchisee, who is known as the sub-franchisor, and contemplates that the master franchisee will enter into subfranchise agreements with individual unit franchisees in the target market. The franchisor is typically not a party to the individual subfranchise agreements between the master franchisee and the subfranchisees. If the target country has applicable franchise registration or disclosure laws, the master franchise arrangement may result in two levels of registration and disclosure—one for the franchisor and master franchisee relationship and another for the master franchisee and subfranchisee relationship.

The master franchise arrangement typically results in rapid target market penetration and accelerated franchise system growth. It also attracts investors with the necessary financial resources and business experience. In less developed target markets, master franchise arrangements facilitate entry into the target market. Risk is allocated between the parties because much of the development and operational expansion risk is with the master franchisee. Under the master franchise arrangement, the strain on the franchisor's financial and management resources is less than what would be the case in direct unit franchising. If the master franchisee is successful, the return on invested capital to a franchisor is significant.

The disadvantage of a master franchise relationship to the franchisor is that the franchisor loses control of the sales process and operations in the target market. In addition, it may also need to comply with registration and disclosure laws in the target country. The franchisor shares fees from the subfranchisees with the master franchisee and so its profits are diluted. If the relationship fails and the master franchise agreement is terminated, the franchisor risks incurring the expense required to salvage the franchise system in the target market.

4. Area Representative Agreements

An area representative arrangement is another means to expand internationally. In this arrangement, the franchisor enters into an agreement with a local developer who is charged with expanding the franchise system in the target market, although the franchise agreements with individual franchisees are entered into directly between the franchisor and the franchisees.

The franchise agreements acknowledge the role of the area representative in servicing the franchisees. The area representative solicits and screens prospective franchisees and assumes post-sale operational responsibilities including recruitment, site selection assistance, training, advertising, inspections, operational assistance, and product and service sourcing. Typical fees payable to the area representative include a portion of the initial franchise fees, royalty fees, and perhaps other payments made by franchisees to the franchisor. Typically, the area representative receives 40 to 60 percent of the initial franchise fee and the ongoing royalties.

The advantage of an area representative structure is that the franchisor retains less contractual control over the franchise system but maintains a local presence in the market at a lower operational cost. Often, this means a more direct and efficient response to franchisees' needs.

There are some disadvantages of the area representative arrangement. The franchisor may be subject to vicarious liability claims based on the acts of the area representative. Moreover, it may be difficult to replace an area representative that does not adequately perform. Finally, profits are diluted to the franchisor since they must be shared with the area representative.

In some jurisdictions, the arrangement may result in complex franchise registration or disclosure compliance issues. Normally, there is no need for a separate registration and disclosure relating to the area representative arrangements. However, the area representative will often be registered as a broker where broker registration is required. Disclosure of the area representative arrangement in the franchisor's disclosure document, including the scope of the responsibilities of the area representative, is typically included.

5. Joint Ventures

International franchise arrangements may take the form of a joint venture agreement. Typically, a joint venture entity is established in the target market. The entity is often jointly owned by the franchisor and a local joint venture partner. The joint venture may take the form of a corporation, limited liability company, partnership, limited partnership, or another legal entity organized under the laws of the target country. The franchisor and the joint venture entity will often enter into a master franchise agreement. The joint venture entity will subsequently enter into subfranchise agreements with franchisees in the target market.

The franchisor and joint venture partner each contribute to the joint venture entity. The franchisor will typically contribute licensed rights to the use of trademarks and other intellectual property. It may also provide ongoing operational support. The domestic joint venture partner will often contribute investment capital, human resources, management, operational responsibilities, and certain services to franchisees.

A joint venture arrangement provides several advantages. Such arrangement:

- allows for rapid development and expansion of the franchise system in the target market,
- permits shared risk between the franchisor and the joint venture partner because costs are allocated between the parties,

- brings local market expertise and experience of the joint venture partner to enhance development,
- results in more control by the franchisor than a master franchise or area development arrangement because of the franchisor's equity ownership in the joint venture entity, and
- provides more potential for profit to the franchisor since it holds a direct ownership interest in the joint venture entity whose value may appreciate with the future success of the franchise system in the international market. In addition, the profit sharing in a joint venture arrangement may not be restricted to royalties, but could include dividends or other forms of corporate reinvestment.

The disadvantage of a joint venture arrangement is that the agreements are often complex and subject to extensive negotiation.

D. Using Local Counsel

1. Retaining Local Counsel – Franchisor vs. Outside Counsel

Diligent vetting of local counsel in the target country is necessary. A franchisor can retain local counsel to provide legal services directly the franchisor. Alternatively, a franchisor can work through its existing domestic counsel to identify local counsel.

2. Finding the Right Local Counsel

Various sources may be used to identify competent local counsel. Referrals tend to be a reliable source of information on local counsel with the requisite skills. To find local counsel in a particular jurisdiction, one could also consult databases or listings of lawyers published by:

- American Bar Association Forum on Franchising;
- International Bar Association;
- *Chambers Global;*
- *International Who's Who of Franchise Lawyers*;
- Local franchise associations or other relevant trade organizations that operate in the jurisdiction in which local counsel is required.[26]

3. Working with Local Counsel

Local counsel should advise on the laws and policies of the target market. Without the advice of local counsel, a franchisor may expend resources on issues that may not be useful or applicable in the target country. Lawyers must recognize foreign legal issues and counseling clients on matters on which he or she has no ability to advise.

III. Typical Target Country Legal Issues

A franchisor expanding internationally must review and analyze the laws and regulations of the target country that impact the documents used for international expansion. Often, these laws and regulations dictate the modifications and changes to the franchise system that are necessary for its successful deployment in the target country.

A. Pre-Sale Disclosure

Many countries require disclosure of specific information to potential franchisees prior to the execution of an agreement or the payment of any money by the franchisee. The scope and types of information vary from country to country. The goal of most disclosure laws is to ensure that franchisees receive information necessary to make an informed decision. Compliance with some disclosure laws can be difficult due to the

[26] In Section XI (Other Significant Matters) of each country chapter of this book, there is a listing of what, if any, local franchise associations are active in the relevant Asian jurisdictions surveyed.

vague wording of the relevant legislation. In the case of newly enacted legislation, government regulators may not have had sufficient time to consider how the disclosure law should be interpreted and this may exacerbate the problem. Experienced local counsel should be retained if there are any questions regarding the interpretation of a country's disclosure requirements.

Many foreign laws specify that a certain number of days must pass between delivery of the disclosure document to the franchisee and the execution of an agreement or payment of money by the franchisee (e.g., Australia—14 calendar days; Brazil—10 calendar days; Indonesia[27]—14 calendar days; Mexico—30 business days). Some countries (e.g., Romania) have no specified waiting period after the disclosure document is delivered. Jurisdictions outside of Asia that require disclosure to potential franchisees include Australia,[28] Belgium,[29] Brazil,[30] Canada (Alberta, Ontario, Prince Edward Island, New Brunswick, and Manitoba),[31] France,[32] Germany,[33] Italy,[34]

---

27 *See* Nurdin Adiwibowo, Freddy Karyadi, and Gustaaf Reerink, *Franchising in Indonesia*, in FRANCHISING IN ASIA 2015: LEGAL AND BUSINESS CONSIDERATIONS 125 (Kendal H. Tyre, Jr., Diana Vilmenay-Hammond, and Pierce Haesung Han, eds. LexNoir Foundation 2015).

28 *Franchising Code of Conduct, Competition and Consumer (Industry Codes—Franchising) Regulation 2014.*

29 The *Law of 19 December 2005.*

30 *Brazilian Federal Law Number 8955/94* adopted on December 15, 1994, and effective as of February 14, 1995.

31 *Franchises Act, RSA 1980 cF-17* (Alberta); *Ontario Regulation 581/00, amendment to O. Reg. 199/05* (Ontario); *Franchises Act R.S.P.E.I. 1988, Cap. F14.1* (Prince Edward Island); *The Franchise Act, S.N.B. 2007, c. F-23.5, Mediation Regulation—Franchises Act, N.B. Reg. 2010-93* and *Disclosure Regulation—Franchises Act, N.B. Reg. 2010-92* (New Brunswick); *The Franchises Act, C.C.S.M. c. F156* and Man. Reg. 29/2012 (Manitoba).

32 *Articles L330-3 and R-330-1*of the Commercial Code of France.

Mexico,[35] Romania,[36] South Africa,[37] Spain,[38] Sweden,[39] Tunisia,[40] and United States.[41]

About half of the Asian countries surveyed[42] require franchisors to provide pre-sale disclosure to prospective franchisees. These countries include China,[43] Indonesia,[44] Japan,[45] Kazakhstan,[46] Malaysia,[47] South Korea,[48] Taiwan,[49] and Vietnam.[50]

(Footnote continued from previous page)

33 German pre-contractual disclosure requirements have been derived from German case law and from the German Franchise Association's code of ethics.

34 *Law Number 129/04*, effective as of May 25, 2004.

35 Article 142 of the *Mexican Industrial Property Law* and the *Regulations of the Industrial Property Law.*

36 *Government Ordinance number 52/1997*, as amended by *Law number 79/1998.*

37 *Consumer Protection Act 68 of 2008, and related regulations.*

38 Article 62 of *Spanish Act 7/1996 of January 15, 1996,* as amended by *Act 1/2010* and the *Royal Decree 201/2010 of February 26.*

39 *Act on franchisor's Obligations to Provide Information* (*lagen 2006:484 om franchisegivares informationsskyldighet*), effective as of October 1, 2006.

40 *Law n° 2009-69*, Article 15, dated August 12, 2009.

41 16 C.F.R. Part 436, *Disclosure Requirements and Prohibitions Concerning Franchising*, effective as of July 1, 2007, ("FTC Franchise Rule"). There are also 15 U.S. states that have adopted their own disclosure, registration, or notice laws.

42 Any reference in this book to "surveyed" Asian countries or jurisdictions refers to the countries reviewed in the latter portion of this work—namely, Bangladesh, China, Hong Kong, India, Indonesia, Japan, Kazakhstan, Malaysia, Nepal, Philippines, South Korea, Taiwan, Tajikistan, Thailand and Vietnam.

43 *See* Kelly F. Xiang, *Franchising in China*, in FRANCHISING IN ASIA 2015: LEGAL AND BUSINESS CONSIDERATIONS 92 (Kendal H. Tyre, Jr., Diana Vilmenay-Hammond, and Pierce Haesung Han, eds. LexNoir Foundation 2015).

B. Government Approvals, Registrations, Filing Requirements

An increasing number of countries have enacted regulations specifically affecting franchising. Some countries have self-regulatory or voluntary disclosure requirements issued through government agencies or promoted through franchise associations. Often, these laws include disclosure document requirements requiring the preparation and delivery of a disclosure document at a certain time before the execution of the definitive franchise documents. Certain countries have enacted franchise laws requiring registrations, approvals, and/or filings

---

(Footnote continued from previous page)

44 *See* Adiwibowo, Karyadi, and Reerink, *supra* note 27 at 125.

45 *See* Kakuji Mitani, *Franchising in Japan*, in FRANCHISING IN ASIA 2015: LEGAL AND BUSINESS CONSIDERATIONS 147 (Kendal H. Tyre, Jr., Diana Vilmenay-Hammond, and Pierce Haesung Han, eds. LexNoir Foundation 2015).

46 *See* Saule Akhmetova, *Franchising in Kazakhstan*, in FRANCHISING IN ASIA 2015: LEGAL AND BUSINESS CONSIDERATIONS 159 (Kendal H. Tyre, Jr., Diana Vilmenay-Hammond, and Pierce Haesung Han, eds. LexNoir Foundation 2015).

47 *See* Wong Sai Fong and Michelle C.Y. Loi, *Franchising in Malaysia*, in FRANCHISING IN ASIA 2015: LEGAL AND BUSINESS CONSIDERATIONS 172 (Kendal H. Tyre, Jr., Diana Vilmenay-Hammond, and Pierce Haesung Han, eds. LexNoir Foundation 2015).

48 *See* Brendon Carr, *Franchising in South Korea*, in FRANCHISING IN ASIA 2015: LEGAL AND BUSINESS CONSIDERATIONS 221 (Kendal H. Tyre, Jr., Diana Vilmenay-Hammond, and Pierce Haesung Han, eds. LexNoir Foundation 2015).

49 *See* Patricia Ginsberg, *Franchising in Taiwan*, in FRANCHISING IN ASIA 2015: LEGAL AND BUSINESS CONSIDERATIONS 232 (Kendal H. Tyre, Jr., Diana Vilmenay-Hammond, and Pierce Haesung Han, eds. LexNoir Foundation 2015).

50 *See* Mai Thi Minh Hang and Ngo Viet Hoa, *Franchising in Vietnam*, in FRANCHISING IN ASIA 2015: LEGAL AND BUSINESS CONSIDERATIONS 284 (Kendal H. Tyre, Jr., Diana Vilmenay-Hammond, and Pierce Haesung Han, eds. LexNoir Foundation 2015).

with local government authorities before the offer or sale of a franchise. Other typical requirements could include, for example, competition authority approvals, trademark license filings, and central bank approvals. Compliance with these laws is important to ensure the enforceability of the franchise agreement. A few examples of these regulatory requirements are explored below:

1. Franchisor Registration

Before expanding to the target country, franchise counsel must determine whether the franchisor needs to register with any governmental authorities prior to offering or selling franchises in that jurisdiction. For example, a franchisor planning to sell franchises in Malaysia,[51] Indonesia,[52] or Vietnam[53] must first complete a filing with the relevant governing authority. Some foreign registrations and filings must be updated annually and/or when an individual franchise is sold.[54] Compliance with registration requirements is critical. Franchisors may be prohibited from entering into or enforcing a franchise agreement before the approval of the franchisor's registration or filing. In some jurisdictions, the approval process may focus on one specific aspect of the franchise agreement. Registration is

---

51 Section 6(1) of the *Franchise Act 1998* as amended by the Franchise (Amendment) Act 2012; *see also* Wong and Loi, *supra* note 47, at 173-175.

52 *Regulation of the Minister of Trade No. 53/M-DAG/PER/8/2012*, dated August 24, 2012; *see also* Adiwibowo, Karyadi, and Reerink, *supra* note 27, at 126.

53 *Commercial Law*, adopted by the National Assembly on June 14, 2005; *Decree No. 35/2006/ND-CP* dated March 31, 2006, and *Circular No. 09/ 2006/TT-BTM of the Ministry of Industry and Trade*, dated May 25, 2006; *see also* Hang and Hoa, *supra* note 50, at 286-287.

54 *See Section 6(1) of the Franchise Act 1998* as amended by the Franchise (Amendment) Act 2012 (Malaysia) and *Regulation of the Minister of Trade No. 53/M-DAG/PER/8/2012*, dated August 24, 2012 (Indonesia); *Commercial Law*, adopted by the National Assembly on June 14, 2005; *Decree No. 35/2006/ND-CP* dated March 31, 2006, and *Circular No. 09/2006/TT-BTM of the Ministry of Industry and Trade*, dated May 25, 2006 (Vietnam).

required or recommended in many of the surveyed Asian countries.

2. Government Approvals

Many countries regulate the franchise relationship itself, as opposed to or in addition to regulating the offer and sale of the franchise opportunity. These countries require the franchisor to submit transactions for approval of their specific terms and conditions, including types and amounts of fees, choice of law provisions, termination rights, non-competition provisions, and/or remittance of payments abroad.

For example, with the exception of Hong Kong,[55] Tajikistan,[56] and Vietnam,[57] the Asian jurisdictions surveyed require central bank approval to remit payments abroad. Certain countries only require approvals for payments over a specific threshold.[58]

3. Trademark License Filings

Trademark offices in some countries require the filing of the franchise agreement or a short form license agreement that shows that the trademarks used in the franchise system have been licensed to the local franchisee for use in the target country. Generally, the documents must be translated into the local language before their submission.

---

55 *See* David Allison, *Franchising in Hong Kong*, in FRANCHISING IN ASIA 2015: LEGAL AND BUSINESS CONSIDERATIONS 103 (Kendal H. Tyre, Jr., Diana Vilmenay-Hammond, and Pierce Haesung Han, eds. LexNoir Foundation 2015).

56 *See* Rustam M. Nazrisho and Sherzod S. Sodatkadamov, *Franchising in Tajikistan*, in FRANCHISING IN ASIA 2015: LEGAL AND BUSINESS CONSIDERATIONS 249 (Kendal H. Tyre, Jr., Diana Vilmenay-Hammond, and Pierce Haesung Han, eds. LexNoir Foundation 2015).

57 *See* Hang and Hoa, *supra* note 50 at 286.

58 *See infra* at 29.

Although some trademark offices provide only a ministerial review of the terms and conditions of the licensing arrangement, failure to file with these authorities can have serious repercussions. In Mexico, for example, which is typical of many countries, the filing is not technically required but is highly recommended because the failure to file can result in an inability to pursue claims against third-party infringing parties.[59] In Russia, approval of a trademark license agreement by the trademark office must occur prior to the granting of a valid trademark license. A failure to register will invalidate the trademark license portions of the franchise agreement.[60]

In those Asian countries surveyed, most require (or the authors recommend) the filing of a registered user agreement or a short trademark license agreement with the trademark authorities. In many cases, such a filing would enable parties to pursue claims against third-party infringers.

C. Relationship Laws

Some jurisdictions have enacted relationship legislation in addition to or as an alternative to the more common disclosure and registration laws described above. While disclosure laws strive to provide protection to the franchisee prior to executing a franchise agreement, relationship laws aim to protect the on-going business arrangement of the parties after signing a franchise agreement. These relationship laws restrict franchisors' power over franchisees in certain areas of the franchise arrangement.

A practitioner should review whether a jurisdiction's relationship laws apply when considering the following issues:[61]

---

59 *Industrial Property Law* (as last amended April 2012).

60 *Part IV of the Russian Civil Code,* which came into effect on January 1, 2008.

61 With the few exceptions of "disclosure only" jurisdictions, the majority of franchise regulations around the world contain both pre-contractual

(Footnote continued on next page)

- good faith and fair dealing;
- general release or waivers of claims;
- franchise associations and the right to associate;
- dispute resolution rules, including applicable law and venue;
- governing law and venue issues;
- franchise transfers;
- renewals;
- termination;
- procurement; and
- encroachment on franchisee territories.

D. Currency Restrictions and Funds Repatriation

Some target countries require that any commercial transactions within their borders be conducted in the domestic currency of the country. Other countries restrict the amount of domestic currency that can be converted into foreign currency, restrict the amount of foreign currency that can be withdrawn from the country, or prohibit funds to be expatriated at all.

If appropriate funds cannot be withdrawn from the target country, it may be necessary to leave all profits earned in the target country for further expansion opportunities or as an offset against expenses incurred in the country. As an alternative, the

---

(Footnote continued from previous page)

disclosure and on-going relationship components; a small number of other countries have chosen to use "relationship only" regulations. Certain countries, such as Australia, Belarus, Canada, China, Lithuania, Macau, Malaysia, Romania, Russia, South Africa, South Korea, Ukraine, the United States, and Vietnam, have enacted either franchise specific or consumer protection legislation which features explicit relationship regulations. In contrast, other countries, such as Albania, Angola, Estonia, France, Georgia, Indonesia, Italy, Japan, Kyrgyzstan, Mexico, Moldova, Mongolia, the Province of Quebec in Canada, Saudi Arabia, Tunisia, and Venezuela, have more minimalist regulatory regimes with respect to franchise relationship laws that arise out of their respective Civil Codes.

franchisor may acquire products available in the target country with domestic currency, and thereafter sell such products in the free market to obtain freely tradable currency.

E. Anti-trust, Competition, and Trade Practice Laws

Most developed countries have anti-trust, competition, or trade practice laws that are applicable to franchise operations. For example, laws impacting suggested pricing, misleading advertising, price discrimination, co-operative advertising allowances, telemarketing, tying, exclusive dealing, and market restriction must be analyzed and incorporated as necessary into the franchisor's documents and into the franchise system.

Anti-trust or competition laws typically address two types of activity: collusion among parties that limits consumers' choices in selecting products or services, and abuse of franchisor's superior bargaining position to the detriment of the other party to an agreement.

Most franchisors use in-term and post-term covenants not to compete to protect their systems. Typically, non-compete covenants are enforceable if they include reasonable limitations as to the time, geographic area, and the scope of activity restricted. Some countries, however, have additional restrictions on non-compete provisions. For example, in certain circumstances, European Union countries may restrict in-term covenants not to compete to five years (and post-term covenants to one year).[62]

In those Asian countries surveyed, with a few exceptions, covenants not-to-compete are generally enforceable, so long as the restraint is reasonable, limited in scope and geography, and

[62] Frank Zaid and Kendal Tyre, International Franchising Basic Track Workshop: *A World Tour of The Basics of International Franchising*, (Paper Presented at the International Franchise Association's 38th Annual Legal Symposium, May 2005) at 7.

necessary to protect the interests of the individual or entity who seeks to enforce the restraint.

F. Governing Law and Venue

Each party to the franchise agreement typically desires the governing law of the agreement to be the law of its home country. Depending on the jurisdiction of the transaction, the contractual arrangement may be required to be governed by local law. It may also be required to have a venue within such jurisdictions. Agreements that provide otherwise may be unenforceable.

Often parties will seek remedies before courts in the target country even if only to enforce arbitral or decisions granted in the home jurisdiction. In most countries, such will generally uphold the parties choice of law, unless it conflicts with domestic public policy.

In those Asian jurisdictions surveyed, Indonesia,[63] Malaysia[64] and the Philippines[65] specifically require that local law must govern the franchise agreement.

G. Agency Laws

The relationship between franchisor and franchisee is not typically considered an agency relationship in most countries. In certain countries, however, franchisees are deemed agents of the franchisor and are subject to commercial agent or sales representative laws. These laws protect sales agents who market and distribute the products or services of a principal. They often

---

63 *See* Adiwibowo, Karyadi, and Reerink, *supra* note 27 at 134.

64 *See* Wong and Loi, *supra* note 47 at 182.

65 *See* Maria Teresa D. Mercado-Ferrer, *Franchising in the Philippines*, in FRANCHISING IN ASIA 2015: LEGAL AND BUSINESS CONSIDERATIONS 212 (Kendal H. Tyre, Jr., Diana Vilmenay-Hammond, and Pierce Haesung Han, eds. LexNoir Foundation 2015).

entitle the franchisee to reasonable compensation or indemnification, which is triggered upon a termination of the relationship without "good cause." Compensation in some instances may be triggered regardless of the reason upon any termination or expiration of the franchise agreement. Other agency laws in some countries define "good cause" narrowly such that a franchisee will almost certainly be entitled to compensation upon any expiration or termination of the agreement.

For example, in several Middle Eastern countries, the amount of compensation that may be owed to the franchisee under an agency law varies from country to country. However, it is often left to the discretion of local courts. They typically consider the circumstances as a whole. This would include the franchisee's actual investment and a reasonable prediction of future profits. A standard award would be the equivalent of one year's total profits (averaged over four to five years) of the franchisee. Compensation for the goodwill of the business and any unused inventory could also be awarded.[66] The amount of compensation may be higher if the parties have a long-term relationship and the franchisee shows extensive investment in the franchise.

If agency laws are deemed applicable in certain target countries, local courts may assume jurisdictions notwithstanding a contrary jurisdiction and/or venue clauses in the parties' agreement. Moreover, there are even special agency law courts that are made up of agents who hear the cases.[67]

One method for avoiding registration is to ensure that the franchisee itself is at least partially owned by foreign nationals of the target country, and thus ineligible to serve as a commercial agent. Alternatively, franchisors include features in the agreement that would make the overall relationship more

---

[66] Zaid and Tyre, *supra* note 62, at 8.

[67] Joyce Mazero and J. Perry Maisonneuve, *Franchising in the Middle East and North Africa*, (Paper Presented at the American Bar Association 32nd Annual Forum on Franchising, October 14–16, 2009) at 10.

difficult to register, refrain from execution formalities required in the registration process, and seek protection against the exposure arising out of registration under the commercial agencies law.

H. Arbitration

Many international franchisors turn to arbitration as a means of dispute resolution due to the uncertainty and lack of development of judicial systems in a number of foreign countries. A franchisor expanding internationally should review the local laws of the target country with respect to the ability to enforce arbitral decisions. International treaties or target country laws relating to the enforcement of an international arbitration award must also be analyzed. Over 148 countries have adopted the *Convention on the Recognition and Enforcement of Foreign Arbitral Awards* (the "New York Convention"). Under the New York Convention, arbitration awards are recognized and enforced with little interference from foreign courts in the signatory countries.

Arbitration is popular because of the perception that it will be conducted in a neutral setting, and because the parties can tailor the procedural rules to be used in their arbitration. Some of the disadvantages of arbitration include the potential high costs, the potential for unpredictable results stemming from the arbitrators not being bound by legal precedent, and the concern that arbitration awards are not generally appealable.

Of those Asian countries surveyed, all but Taiwan[68] are signatories to the New York Convention. Taiwan is not a party to the convention because it is not a member of the United Nations, however, foreign arbitral awards are nevertheless recognized and enforced in Taiwan.[69]

---

[68] *See* Ginsberg, *supra* note 49 at 241.

[69] *See infra* at 62-63.

I. Transfer Restrictions

A franchisor may freely establish conditions for the transfer of any interests in the franchisee, the franchise agreement, or the assets of the franchised business in most jurisdictions. In addition, a franchisor may wish to impose such restrictions in the franchisee's charter documents to ensure that the franchisee cannot assign its interests to a third-party without the franchisor's consent. However, local laws must be reviewed to determine whether there are limitations impacting such restrictions. Injunctive relief to prevent an improper transfer may not be available in all jurisdictions. Some countries may limit relief to the termination of the franchise agreement or damages. A franchisor, unless restricted by statute to act reasonably, may seek to reserve the right to act unreasonably and arbitrarily when refusing transfer requests.

J. Import and Customs Laws

A franchisor must carefully review local laws regarding customs and duties in the target country. A franchisor's ability to export personnel, products and materials to the target country is vital to the success of the system. In some cases, domestic goods or services produced in a home market are critical to the supply chain in preparing retail products in the foreign market. Any restrictions that are imposed on such distribution can have a substantial impact on the franchise business.

Counsel to a franchisor should discuss with local counsel:

- whether government approvals are necessary to import products, equipment, and services for the franchise system;
- which party assumes the expense for visas or work permits; and
- whether the target country has specified duties for the items to be imported.

K. Guarantees and Other Security

Guarantees can be used to reduce risk. The personal or corporate assets of the guarantor provide additional collateral or security to the franchisor. When seeking additional security, the franchisor should request:

- □ bank guarantees;
- □ letters of credit;
- □ a personal guarantee from the individual shareholders or a corporate guarantee from the parents of the corporate franchisee;
- □ an indemnity from the guarantors in favor of the franchisor; and/or
- □ a security interest in its assets of the franchisee or its affiliates.

Of those Asian countries surveyed, India[70] has particular requirements regarding guarantees. Typically, corporate or personal guarantees by a resident of India in favor of a non-resident franchisor will require prior approval of the Reserve Bank of India; such approval can take two to three months for approval.

L. Termination and Renewal Issues

The term of an international franchise agreement is typically expressed for a certain number of years and extension or renewal rights are usually included. Conditions of renewal will be similar to those provided for in the franchisor's home country unit franchise agreement.

Post-term rights and obligations of the parties must be provided for in the agreement, if the document expires or terminates. By

---

[70] *See* Preeti Mehta, *Franchising in India*, in FRANCHISING IN ASIA 2015: LEGAL AND BUSINESS CONSIDERATIONS 113 (Kendal H. Tyre, Jr., Diana Vilmenay-Hammond, and Pierce Haesung Han, eds. LexNoir Foundation 2015).

way of example, the franchisee may be allowed to continue as a subfranchisor on a non-exclusive basis and to operate its existing owned or operated outlets. However, further development rights for additional units will normally terminate. Alternatively, if the franchisee is precluded from continued operation of the franchise system, de-identification obligations of the franchisee and its subfranchisees must be stipulated. In some instances, the franchisor may include a right to purchase or otherwise take assignment of the franchisee's and the subfranchisees' outlets on expiration.

Of those Asian countries surveyed, China,[71] Malaysia,[72] South Korea,[73] and Vietnam[74] have specific laws relating to the termination of a franchise agreement. For example, in China, the franchisee has the right to unilaterally terminate the franchise agreement within a certain amount of time after the agreement is signed. Malaysia requires that franchise agreements can only be terminated for "good cause." In South Korea, franchisors are required to notify the franchisee of its decision not to renew a franchise agreement at least six (6) months prior to scheduled expiration. Failure to do so will provide the franchisee the right to demand renewal on the then-current terms of the franchise agreement. In Vietnam, a party to a commercial contract may unilaterally terminate the agreement for breach. In addition, both the franchisor and franchisee have special rights to unilaterally terminate a franchise agreement under certain circumstances such as the franchisor's failure to provide background and guiding documents to a franchisee or the franchisee's failure to maintain its business registration certificate.

Finally, many target countries have general agency laws requiring that the franchisor have "good cause" to terminate or fail to renew a franchise agreement, provide the franchisee prior

---

71 Xiang, *supra* note 43 at 96-97.

72 Wong and Loi, *supra* note 47 at 177-179.

73 Carr, *supra* note 48 at 225.

74 Hang and Hoa, *supra* note 50 at 291.

notice of a termination or non-renewal, and give the franchisee an opportunity to cure a breach.[75] In most target countries "good cause" for termination includes franchisee's failure to comply with material provisions of the agreement, including a failure to make payments under the agreement, and a felony, abandonment, fraud, bankruptcy, or insolvency of the franchisee.

M. Privacy/IT

Specific privacy laws control the manner in which information is obtained, stored and used. Often these laws are of critical importance when such information is transferred across international borders. As a result, the practices of the franchisor should be modified to account for local laws in the target country, after consultation with local counsel.

Franchisors should also require the franchisees to adopt adequate security safeguards for their computer systems and abide by the franchisor's privacy policies regarding the collection, protection and destruction of customer information. Franchisor should ensure that these policies comply with the data protection and privacy laws of the target country and home country.

The franchise agreement should provide that the protection of customer information and privacy are a continuing obligation of the franchisee surviving the termination or expiration of the agreement. The franchisee should also require prompt notification to the franchisor of any material security breaches.

N. Execution Formalities

Each country has its own execution formalities, including witness requirements, spousal acknowledgements, notarization requirements, legalization requirements, or payment of stamp duties. Franchise agreements may also need to be authenticated

---

[75] *See* European Franchise Federation website, http://www.eff-franchise.com/spip.php?rubrique21 (last visited June 7, 2015). *See also* Zaid and Tyre, *supra* note 62, at 29.

before they are deemed enforceable by the courts of a particular jurisdiction. In some countries, the execution procedures differ depending on the location of the party when it executes the agreement. Others require that any documents required for government approval must be translated into the local language and that the translated form of the agreement must be signed. If possible, franchisors should specify in their franchise agreements that regardless of whether the agreement is translated into another language, the English language version of the document must be executed by the parties and will govern any dispute between the parties.

Most of the Asian jurisdictions surveyed had no requirement that a franchise agreement be translated into the local language to be enforceable. English is generally acceptable. However, where an agreement is required to be filed or registered with a government authority or enforced by a local court, local laws often require that the agreement must be translated into the local language.

IV. Drafting International Franchise Agreements — Typical Legal Terms

There is no such document as a "standard" franchise agreement, but rather a checklist of "standard" issues that must be considered before drafting a franchise agreement. Drafting an agreement before an issues list has been canvassed will only prove to be problematic.

Preparing a "standard" form of international franchise agreement complicates the issue further. The typical drafting issues must be considered in addition to legal, socio-economic, cultural, linguistic, and commercial factors of two or more countries. A number of these issues are explained below[76]:

---

[76] Portions of this section were adapted from Zaid and Tyre, International Franchising Basic Track Workshop: *A World Tour of The Basics of International Franchising*, *supra* note 62.

Franchising in the Asian Context

A. Territorial Rights and Limitations

The franchisor must define the scope of the franchise system for which exclusivity is being granted. Most franchisees will seek a franchise agreement that provides them the exclusive geographical right, license, and privilege to use the franchise system in a local segment of the market or the entire jurisdiction. Exclusivity issues are not, however, limited to geographical considerations.

It is not uncommon for a franchisor to grant third parties exclusive or reserved rights to sell the franchisor's products or services within the exclusive territory. If this is the case, these rights must be specifically carved out in any documents being drafted or under consideration.

Notwithstanding the exclusive rights granted to a franchisee, most international franchisors reserve to themselves certain rights, such as the right to acquire a competitor or be acquired by a competitor, to sell the same or similar products or services associated with the franchise system or the right to sell such products or services through other channels of trade, including the Internet, or to specific customers, and national or international accounts. These reserved rights often place the franchisor in competition with the franchisee or its subfranchisees, so the franchisor may be required to disclose those reservations depending on the laws of the relevant jurisdictions.

Because an international franchisor imparts know-how, trade secrets, and confidential information relating to the operation of the franchised business, the franchisee should covenant to deal exclusively with the franchisor and the franchise system, and not to compete (at least during the term of the franchise agreement). Any such covenants require a number of drafting considerations, including the geographical scope of the restriction, to whom the covenant will apply, and exceptions for potential existing businesses of the franchisee.

Exclusivity in terms of the territorial restrictions applicable to the franchisee should be clearly defined. A map or description of the boundaries as they exist at the time of executing the franchise agreement could be included in the agreement.

Finally, if international franchisees wish to expand the franchise system beyond the boundaries of the target country to adjoining countries, rights of first refusal or options to develop additional countries may be provided for in an international franchise agreement. These rights are often granted when the adjoining countries have similar cultural, language, and/or commercial characteristics. These rights may also require that certain quotas or target sales figures be reached before the rights may be exercised or may have time restrictions on the exercise of the options following which the options will be forfeited.

B. Fees

The initial fee for international franchise rights is typically calculated in one of two ways. It is either a fixed fee or a fee based on quota or performance. International franchisors may frequently underestimate the costs involved in expanding their franchise systems internationally, particularly in less developed or emerging target countries, accordingly some franchisors control their cost by requiring the reimbursement of their expenses in developing products and services for the franchise system for target markets.

Examples of reimbursed costs may include expenses incurred in connection with governmental reviews, registrations, and approvals; and expenses incurred by the franchisor for training the franchisee and its staff, communications expenses, translation and other development costs for the operations manual and other materials, and legal and other professional costs incurred related to the development of the franchise system documents.

As for "development" fees incurred by the franchisor for the opening of individual franchisee locations, the agreement may provide for payment to the franchisor for fees for a specific number of initial or additional outlets. Fees may be incurred on a fixed-amount basis, a per unit basis, or in accordance with some formula basis. Agreements typically express continuing fees as a royalty percentage of gross sales or revenues of the franchisee. Continuing fees may also be expressed on a fixed-fee basis for each unit developed. Fees may be expressed on a constant or variable percentage. Alternatively, the agreement may provide for minimum periodic fees, usually on a quarterly or annual basis.

Definitions of gross or net sales typically provide for certain exclusions, including refunds, discounts, taxes, and other similar nonprofit items to the franchisee. In some instances, the fees will be subject to an inflation factor or adjustment based on a cost of living or other index. This type of adjustment is especially important in jurisdictions with historically high inflation records.

The agreement must describe the mechanics for payment, including the frequency of payment, any interest on late payments, and the methods of payment. For example, the agreement could provide for payment to a designated bank account of a franchisor. If withholding taxes are exigible on fees paid to the international franchisor from the target country, the agreement may be written to break up specific components of the fees into certain services that may not be subject to withholding tax. These components may include technical assistance services, training, rights to know-how, trademark license fees, site selection, inspection, and consultation fees.

1. Currency

The franchise agreement may provide for a particular conversion method to the franchisor's home country currency that results in a specific payment in that currency on a particular date. A franchise agreement should allow the franchisor to select a different currency, designate the source from which the exchange rate quotations are to be obtained, and specify the conversion date on which the franchisee must purchase the required currency. Typically, the currency conversion date is the date on which periodic payments are due under the agreement. For reimbursements and other irregular payments, the currency conversion date should be the date the franchisor incurs the expense or the date it issues an invoice. For late payments, the conversion date should be, at the franchisor's option, either the date payment was due or the date of actual payment. If currency conversion is not possible because of governmental regulations or other factors, alternatives for the franchisor should be stipulated, including the possibility of payment in tangible or intangible property. If currency conversion continues, the agreement may provide for a suspension or termination of the franchise agreement after a specified period.

If subfranchising is involved, the franchisor may require payment by subfranchisees directly to the franchisor to avoid the risk of non-payment by the franchisee.

2. Withholding Taxes

Withholding taxes will normally be charged on royalty, interest, and similar payments from a franchisee to a franchisor residing outside of the target country. The franchisee will generally be required to calculate, withhold, and remit such taxes to the target country tax authorities. The franchisee will also be required to provide the franchisor tax receipts for the payments made so that the franchisor can claim foreign tax credits in its home country.

Some international franchisors require a gross up of all fees including a component for any taxes withheld in the target country. The "tax gross-up" method shifts the burden of target country withholding taxes to the franchisee. The franchisee pays both the withholding tax and the royalties (or other applicable fees) at the full contract rate agreed to by the parties. If the franchisor reimburses the franchisee for its withholding tax payments to the extent that the franchisor receives foreign tax credits for withholding taxes paid by the franchisee, the franchisor can mitigate the negative financial impact on the franchisee. This mitigation method is complicated by the complexities of calculating allowable foreign tax credits. It may not work where the target country government objects to any provision that benefits the franchisor at the franchisee's expense.

Sophisticated franchisee parties will often resist a gross-up requirement as a result of the additional financial burden it represents. A franchisor that is expecting such a response may choose to increase the fees it would have otherwise expected to receive before engaging in negotiations on the gross up so that if the gross-up provision is lost in negotiation (such that taxes are withheld) the franchisor will be less impacted by the reduced income.

The "unbundling" method is another technique for avoiding foreign withholding tax issues. "Passive" income, such as royalties, is taxed in some target countries at higher rates than "active" income earned for the provision of services. Such services would include field supervision, training, and business counseling. The "unbundling" method separates the fees assessed for trademark and business system usage—the passive income—and the fees that compensate the franchisor for training, consultation, and other benefits or services provided by franchisor—the active income. Each set of unbundled fees are subsequently taxed at the applicable rate. This may result in tax savings for the franchisor.

As in most countries across the globe, including those Asian nations surveyed here, the applicable taxes can be reduced if the entity receiving the payment is incorporated in a country with which the taxing jurisdiction has a double taxation agreement.

Of those Asian countries surveyed, Kazakhstan[77] raises another issue to consider when analyzing the tax and corporate structure of a deal. Kazakhstan, not unlike many other countries in Asia and elsewhere, maintains a tax blacklist[78] of 60 jurisdictions that

---

77 *See* Akhmetova, *supra* note 46 at 162.

78 Kate Habershon and Bakhytzhan O. Kadyrov, *Luxembourg Has Been Removed from the Kazakhstan Tax Blacklist*, MORGAN LEWIS & BOCKIUS LLP, Feb. 9, 2015, *available at*

(Footnote continued on next page)

it considers countries with privileged tax regimes that are perceived to be non-cooperative in Kazakhstan's efforts to drive transparency in tax affairs and effective exchange of information to combat such things as money laundering, tax fraud and terrorist financing. Any commercial arrangement between Kazakhstan entities and those from a blacklisted jurisdiction triggers various disadvantages including higher withholding taxes on payment made to those jurisdictions and increased transfer pricing scrutiny/adjustments.

C. Development of Territory

International franchise agreements often specify development rights and obligations of the franchisee defined in terms of a specific number of outlets that are required to be owned and operated by the franchisee or by sub-franchisees. These rights will often be defined in a development schedule. The schedule will typically specify a minimum number of outlets to be opened and operated within a certain period.

The international franchise agreement will specify the aggregate number of outlets that must be opened and in operation at the end of each development period. The relevant provision must also cover any closed or terminated outlets and the ability of the franchisee to carry forward outlets developed beyond the schedule requirements.

Some drafters of international franchise agreements extend development obligations in certain countries to political subdivisions or geographic territories rather than expressing them on a broader target country or other geographic basis.

In most agreements, the franchisee is required to own and operate at least one and perhaps more franchise outlets. The

---

(Footnote continued from previous page)

http://www.morganlewis.com/pubs/luxembourg-has-been-removed-from-the-kazakhstan-tax-blacklist (last visited June 7, 2015).

agreement may provide that the franchisee must open and operate a certain number of outlets itself or own and operate outlets for a certain period before being allowed to subfranchise. The franchisee may also be required to own and operate a specified number of outlets during the term of the agreement to be allowed to continue subfranchising.

For outlets to be developed by subfranchisees, the franchisor may require certain information before approving such outlets or subfranchisees. The franchisor may stipulate site selection criteria and franchisee selection criteria rather than approving each outlet and subfranchisee individually. As an alternative, the franchisor may require the right to approve each site either during an initial period or during the entire term of the franchise agreement.

As for development obligations, the franchisor must establish clear growth targets with the franchisee. Often, development targets in international franchise agreements are not met.[79] To counter this, international franchisors should consider growth incentives and providing rewards for good performance. For example, if a franchisee opens more than "x" complying units in a particular city or region within "y" period, it may be granted the right of first refusal over additional territory.

If the franchisee fails to comply with its development obligations, a number of alternatives may be triggered. The most severe would be the termination of the franchise agreement. Alternatively, the franchisee's development rights may be

---

[79] Arturs Kalnins, *Biting Off More Than They Can Chew: Unfulfilled Development Commitments in International Master Franchising Ventures*, 5.12 *CHR REPORTS* 1, 8 (2005). Specifically, research revealed that in a sample of 142 ventures of 53 U.S.-based franchisors in 37 countries: (1) only 55 (39 percent) of the ventures survived to the end of the development term which was typically five years; (2) the median number of units that were intended to be open was 34; (3) of the 55 ventures that survived to the end of the development term, the median number of units opened was 3; and (4) only six (11 percent) of the ventures satisfied their development obligations.

terminated. Under this scenario, the franchisee would continue to service existing subfranchisees. The franchisee may also trigger the right to continue limited development on a right of first refusal basis, or its exclusivity may be terminated. This would allow the franchisee to continue developing but in competition with the franchisor or some other newly appointed franchisee.

Surrendering of a portion of the territory for which exclusive rights were granted could be another consequence of failing to comply with the development schedule. This would permit the franchisor to further develop the territory or to enter into a franchise or other agreement with a new franchisee or developer.

Yet another alternative when drafting development obligations is to require the parties to renegotiate a reduced development schedule. This may be a viable option particularly when the franchisee may be able to demonstrate that the original development schedule was unrealistic because of economic or market changes.

D. Term and Post-Term Rights and Obligations

The term of an international franchise agreement is typically expressed for a certain number of years and extension or renewal rights are usually included. Conditions of renewal will be similar to those provided for in the franchisor's home country unit franchise agreement.

Post-term rights and obligations of the parties must be provided for in the agreement, if the document expires or terminates. The franchisee may be allowed to continue as a subfranchisor on a non-exclusive basis and to operate its existing owned or operated outlets. However, further development rights for additional units will normally terminate. Alternatively, if the franchisee is precluded from continued operation of the franchise system, de-identification obligations of the franchisee and its subfranchisees must be stipulated. In some instances, the franchisor may include a right to purchase the franchisee's and the subfranchisees' outlets on expiration.

Upon expiration or termination of the international franchise agreement, typical post-term covenants include return of the franchisor's proprietary materials, including operations manuals, agreements, advertising and promotional materials, products and supplies, and trademarked products on a pre-determined formula or third-party determination basis.

As indicated above, the post-term non-compete covenant of the franchisee requires an understanding and application of applicable laws in the target country, as well as the definition of prohibited activities, the geographical scope of application, and the time period for the covenant. A drafter will also need to determine the persons to whom the covenant applies, such as the franchisee, principals of the franchisee, family members, and designated shareholders.

E. System Adaptation and Modification

Often franchisors must modify their franchise systems so that they will be accepted in the target country. The franchisor's trademarks are one of the essential elements of the franchise system that may be subject to modification. The franchisor must determine whether its trademarks can be used in the target country or whether they must be modified. The franchisor must also ensure that it complies with all appropriate legal requirements to maintain continuing ownership of its principal trademarks and any modified or translated versions.

Other typical franchise system modifications in the target country include site and franchisee selection procedures, specifications for system facility, equipment, fixtures, furnishings, decor, signage, and location standards.

Some international franchisors maintain approval rights over each and every such change and modification, but this approach is often impractical. The franchisor approves certain critical matters relating to the franchise system and retains a right to approve, at its option, less critical changes in the system. The franchisee will typically be required to modify or change the operations manual to comply with local standards, but in any event the franchise agreement should specifically state that all modified versions of the operations manual will be owned by the franchisor including specifically all copyrights in and to the modified versions.

The form of subfranchise agreement used by the franchisee for subfranchisees is often attached as an exhibit to the international franchise agreement and requires approval by the franchisor. An international franchisor will often require approval of any modifications, or may allow for some non-material changes to comply with local requirements. If the franchisee develops the form of subfranchise agreement, the franchisor should prescribe certain mandatory provisions and an absolute right to approve the form of subfranchise agreement. Finally, there should be a separate form of subfranchise agreement for each such unit owned and operated by the franchisee or its affiliate.

F. Governmental Approvals

In a number of jurisdictions, governmental authorities must approve the proposed franchise agreement prior to the parties entering into the agreement or enforcing its terms and conditions. Often these governmental approvals will be a condition precedent to the effectiveness of the franchise agreement in the jurisdiction. The franchise agreement should stipulate which party is responsible for obtaining such approvals. Other pre-conditions in the franchise agreement that may be stipulated include foreign investment notifications or approvals, completion of trademark registrations and obtaining visas or work permits for certain specified personnel.

G. Proprietary Marks

One of the earliest considerations that an international franchisor should undertake in respect of international franchising is the protection of its trademark around the world. The franchisor must determine the availability of its trademarks in the target country. If the trademarks have not been registered, applications should be applied for as soon as possible after the relevant searches are undertaken to identify the existence of the same or confusingly similar trademarks. Once the registration process is underway, the franchisor's principal trademarks should be registered for additional classes of products and services, if possible, to allow for future expansion. If modified, translated, substitute, or additional trademarks are necessary, the franchisor should protect and register those trademarks as well.

Subject to the trademark laws of the target country, the franchise agreement should impose upon the franchisee and all subfranchisees proper provisions for use of the franchisor's trademarks. Often these provisions are similar to those that would typically be provided for in the home country unit franchise agreement. The agreement must further stipulate:

- □ compliance with any registered user or licensing registrations in the target country;
- □ marking and public notification of ownership; and
- □ legal proceedings to protect the trademarks against infringing uses.

The franchise agreement should also provide that translated versions of its trademarks, and new trademarks in the future, regardless of whether they are introduced by the franchisee, subfranchisees, or otherwise, will be owned by the franchisor. It will also provide for the right of the franchisor to substitute new, different, or modified trademarks for use in the target country, with a provision concerning the financial or other obligations of the franchisor if it exercises such right.[80]

---

[80] *See supra* at 27-28.

H. Franchisor's Obligations

The franchisor will often provide certain services to and fulfill certain obligations to international franchisees on a periodic and continuing basis. For example, a franchisor will typically conduct an initial training session for the franchisee. Topics typically covered during such training include site selection, operating systems, systems standards, and marketing. If the international franchise agreement provides for subfranchising, training may also include the recruitment and training of subfranchisees, the servicing of subfranchisees, and the sourcing of equipment and products for subfranchisees.

Following the initial training, the franchisor may mandate periodic additional training related to the introduction of new products and services, the modifications to existing facilities and/or system standards. Subsequent training sessions may take the form of conferences, seminars, or workshops. Attendees may include representatives of the franchisor and/or the relevant suppliers.

The international franchise agreement must specify where the training session will be conducted, the costs of who will cover the costs related to such training and what, if any, support franchises may provide with respect to obtaining any travel visa to attend such training sessions.

If the training will be conducted in a particular language, such as English, the franchisor should specify this in the franchise agreement and, if appropriate, stipulate that training program attendees must be fluent in the designated language and/or provide that the franchisee will be responsible for the expense of any interpreter required for the program attendees.

The franchise agreement should mandate that the franchisee and its designated personnel satisfactorily complete all initial training programs. If the franchisee and its personnel fail to satisfactorily complete the initial training, the consequences should be set forth in the agreement. For example, the franchisee could be required to attend additional training at the franchisee's expense or replace any personnel that did not successfully complete training or, at the discretion of the franchisor, terminate the agreement.

The franchise agreement may also specify certain ongoing assistance to be provided by the franchisor, such as:

- □ periodic inspections of outlets to ensure they comply with the system standards;
- □ support consultations with the franchisee with respect to operating problems and changes in system standards; and
- □ additional services and assistance requested by the franchisee that may incur a charge at designated per diem or other rates.

I. Franchisee's Reporting and Payment Obligations

An international franchisor will typically require certain reports submitted to it relating to the performance of the franchised units in the target country. The reports will cover units of the franchisee and, if applicable, any subfranchisee. The franchise agreement must therefore prescribe the type and frequency of reports required, including operational reports outlining the number of outlets opened or under development, the identification of subfranchisees, the locations of all outlets, the revenues from each outlet and other operating statistics submitted to the franchisor.

Financial statements will generally also be submitted to the franchisor. The financial reporting requirement in some target countries may differ from generally accepted accounting principles in the franchisor's home country. Consequently, conversion of financial statements and reports may be required.

The agreement may specify that reporting obligations may be satisfied by electronic means, including e-mail, and this may require special computer hardware and/or software as required by the franchisor.

Special payment terms may be required in certain target countries, especially where there are temporary or permanent restrictions on payment. For example, a franchisor may require payments to a designated bank or other financial institution or intermediary located in the target country. The franchisor could also require payment in the form of tangible property or drawdown payments against deposits lodged in the franchisor's home country.

Finally, a franchisor will typically require the right to: (i) inspect rights of the franchisee's and subfranchisees' outlets, (ii) audit statements submitted by the franchisee, and (iii) review the books and records of the franchisee and outlets operated by the franchisee and subfranchisees.

The franchisee may also be required to furnish franchisor copies of inspection reports performed by the franchisee and related to outlets operated by the franchisee and subfranchisees. The parties will typically negotiate whether the inspection and audit rights of the franchisor must be subject to prior notice.

J. Other Franchisee Obligations

A typical international franchise agreement will contain additional obligations pertaining to the franchisee. This may include site selection, acquisition, and development, training, system standard compliance, insurance policies and maintenance, target country law compliance, advertising and promotion, supplier arrangements and, if applicable, selection of subfranchisees and training and assistance to subfranchisees.

K. Training

The franchisor should require the franchisee and its key personnel to be competent in the English language and be trained as required in the franchisor's policies. Consider the following points:

- ☐ franchisee's personnel should be required to complete training;
- ☐ parameters of any initial training program and ongoing training should be specified, including wages, fees, travel expenses, visas and related costs;
- ☐ any agreement should specify who will bear the costs for initial training and/or ongoing training; and
- ☐ types of ongoing assistance the franchisor will provide and in what format.

L. Supply and Suppliers

Prior to entering into an international franchise agreement, the franchisor must investigate anti-trust and competition laws of the target country, particularly as they relate to supplier matters. Often, the parties will negotiate the franchisor's right to designate approved suppliers or sources of products and services. Often the supplier or a source of products or services will include the franchisor or the franchisor's affiliates. If the franchisor receives rebates, advertising allowances, concessions, or other payments from designated suppliers, subject to target country anti-trust of competition laws, the franchisor should disclose such payments in the franchise agreement.

The franchisor will typically provide standards and specifications for approval of suppliers to the franchisee. The franchisor may stipulate a right to limit the number of suppliers, to inspect and monitor the supplier's premises and facilities, to receive samples of the supplier or source of products to ensure such samples comply with the franchisor's standards for testing purposes, and to change or disapprove an approved supplier or source of supply upon notice to the franchisee.

If the franchisor will share with the franchisee and/or its subfranchisee any rebates or other payments from suppliers, the franchise agreements should disclose these payments.

For goods or supplies sold to or provided by approved suppliers to the franchisee for use in connection with the franchise in the target country, the franchise agreement should restrict, subject to the target country's anti-trust or competition laws, resales outside the target country, to prevent grey marketing or unauthorized parallel importation in other foreign countries, where another franchisee has already been appointed or may be appointed in the future.

M. Advertising and Marketing Fund

Franchisors may administer a national advertising fund in their home countries as part of their franchise system. Franchisees in these domestic systems often contribute a percentage of gross sales to the fund. Similarly, an international franchise agreement typically establishes and administers an advertising and marketing fund for the target country to which franchisees must contribute. In forming an advertising and marketing fund in the target country, the franchisor must consider what the franchisee will contribute and the benefits to be obtained. The franchisee should have access to any advertising promotions and marketing materials, and to use such materials in the target country, subject to any necessary translations and modifications based on the customs, culture, and local laws of the target country. The franchisee's contribution to the fund may be a percentage of aggregate revenues from the franchise system in the target country, or an individual percentage of royalties or fixed fees paid by the franchise units of a franchisee or subfranchisee.

The right of the franchisor to approve marketing programs in the target country must also be addressed in the franchise agreement. The agreement should provide the criteria for granting approval, the time limits for granting such approval, and the method by which approval must be obtained by the franchisee. Alternatively, the franchisor could require the franchisee to consult with the franchisor before initiating a marketing program of a material nature, if the franchisor does not retain rights to approve such programs.

N. Transfer and Assignment

The personal qualifications of controlling shareholders of its international franchisees are of vital importance to international franchisors. As a result, a franchisor will generally restrict the ability of an international franchisee from transferring its ownership interests, the franchise agreement, or all or substantially all of the franchisee's assets without the franchisor's prior approval. Also, it may strengthen the enforceability of a transfer restriction if the international franchise agreement contains an acknowledgment by the franchisee that the restrictions are reasonable and necessary for the proper management of the system.

In some instances, franchisors require franchisees to place transfer restrictions in their organizational documents to prohibit transfers to innocent third parties by putting them on notice of the restrictions. This technique is permissible in most jurisdictions. However, some target countries, such as Taiwan, for example, will not allow transfer restrictions in a company's articles.[81] The practice is also not customary in Australia.[82] Several countries permit the placement of transfer restrictions in organizational documents subject to certain restrictions. Panama permits certain transfer restrictions in an entity's charter documents except that an absolute prohibition of share transfers will be void, and Costa Rica requires shareholder approval and several other conditions before transfer restrictions can be added to a company's articles.[83]

---

81 Zaid and Tyre, *supra* note 62, at 26.

82 *Id.* Australia has, however, codified that right to impose reasonable transfer restrictions. *See Australia's Franchising Code of Conduct*, Clause 20.

83 Joyce Mazero, *Impact of Other Local Laws*, in FUNDAMENTALS OF INTERNATIONAL FRANCHISING, 240-41, ABA Forum of Franchising (Richard M. Asbill & Steven M. Goldman eds, 2001). *See also* Zaid and Tyre, *supra* note 62, at 26.

The franchise agreement should provide whether change in control of the franchisee is prohibited or subject to the approval of the franchisor.

A drafter of the franchise agreement may limit the right of the franchisee to transfer the franchise agreement, or to transfer a controlling interest in the franchisee, subject to the franchisor's right of first refusal. Typically, these transfers are subject to the franchisor's right of first refusal, unless the transfer involves a non-controlling interest below a specified ownership level, transfers among existing shareholders or owners, or a public offering of securities in the franchisee entity.

The franchisor may often restrict a public sale of equity interests in the franchisee entity or permit a public offering only after with the franchisor's prior approval. If the franchisor allows a public offering, it typically will require the original owners to retain a minimum threshold of ownership of the franchisee entity and require prior approval of the prospectus or any other registration document filed with a regulatory authority. The franchisor will want to confirm that references to the franchise agreement, the franchisor, and the franchise system are accurate. The franchisor will also usually require indemnities.

In those Asian countries surveyed, the authors were asked to advise whether there are any restrictions on a franchisor's ability to restrict transfers by a master franchise including any interest in or assets of the master franchisee. Transfers are generally permissible so long as the other party gives prior consent.

O. Liquidated Damages

Most target countries enforce liquidated damage provisions. As a result, franchisors often include them in international franchise agreements, because damages may be difficult to prove in foreign courts and other proceedings. They also deter the franchisee from engaging in activities that could cause irreparable harm to the franchisor, such as violations of transfer restrictions, non-competition, confidentiality, and trademark or other intellectual property protections. Foreign courts review liquidated damage amounts to ensure that the amount of damages stipulated is commensurate with the damages of the franchisor. As a result, the franchise agreement should only provide for that amount of liquidated damages based on a reasonable expectation of the damages that may occur. Foreign courts view excessive liquidated damage amounts as a penalty and reduce such amounts to an amount that approximates the actual damages resulting from the breach. Moreover, in certain target countries, the inclusion of liquidated damage amounts in an international franchise agreement may not be beneficial to the franchisor. In the Dominican Republic, for example, the courts may use the amounts specified as liquidated damages as a cap on damages, even if actual damages exceed such amount.[84]

P. Indemnification

Indemnification provisions allocate losses and expenses between the parties. In drafting these provisions, the parties should address (i) who is indemnified; (ii) who initiates, controls, and pays for an indemnitee's legal counsel; (iii) who has authority to settle disputes; (iv) whether the parties must mitigate damages; and (v) whether the indemnification provision survives termination of the agreement.

In international franchise agreements, the franchisees are usually required to indemnify franchisors for any losses or expenses involving (i) any lawsuit, dispute resolution proceeding, settlement, or investigation; (ii) a breach of the agreement; and (iii) any acts and omissions in the construction or operation of the franchisee's unit(s). Moreover, in some instances, franchisors indemnify franchisees for third-party actions related to the franchisee's authorized use of the franchisor's trademarks.

Most target countries will enforce indemnification provisions provided that parties are not indemnified for their own gross negligence or intentional acts. Italy and other countries,

---

[84] Mazero, *supra* note 83, at 280-81.

however, will generally require mitigation of damages.[85] Moreover, in other jurisdictions, drafters should be aware that overly broad indemnification provisions are vulnerable to challenge. In these target countries, indemnification is often restricted to what was reasonably foreseeable at the time of execution of the franchise agreement.

Q. Default and Termination

An international franchise agreement stipulates a variety of items constituting default of the agreement. Cure periods may be negotiated for certain events, but others will provide for the right of the franchisor to terminate the franchise agreement.

Standard defaults include a breach of representations or warranties by the franchisee. Other defaults may include franchisee's failure to comply with the development schedule; failure to meet target quotas or development obligations; and breach of any bankruptcy or insolvency provisions of the agreement.

In addition, there may be certain events, which if not met, result in termination. These events include failure to obtain any required government approvals, failure to register trademarks, and compliance with exchange controls that prevent payment of fees to the franchisor for some period of time.

Depending on the negotiation of the parties, cure periods will provide the franchisee a reasonable period of time to cure those defaults that can be cured.

A few examples of points to consider when working with local counsel to draft provisions related to renewal, expiration and termination:

With respect to renewals, the drafters need to consider the number and length of renewal terms. Also important is ensuring

---

[85] *Id.* at 266.

that there are conditions for renewals including execution of the then-current form of international unit franchise agreement conformed for use in accordance with the local territory; execution of a release; satisfactory operation of the franchised business; ensuring that there are no defaults or monetary obligations; confirming that the store or it complies with then-current requirements for the franchised business; renovations including all repairs, replacements or acquisitions of updated furniture, fixtures, equipment and computer hardware and software; and training.

In terms of expiration, the franchisee or the franchisor typically provides notice of its election not to renew within a certain time frame prior to the end of the then-current term. If the franchisor elects not to renew and the lease underlying the franchise agreement has not expired, the international franchise agreement provide the franchisor an option to operate the franchised business until the lease expires or buy back the franchised business at an established value. Conditions on expiration also include return of the franchisor's proprietary materials and payment of all fees due.

For terminations, the applicable events warranting termination of the franchise agreement include failure to pay fees when due and failure to comply with system standards or insolvency.

Upon expiration or termination of the international franchise agreement, typical post-term covenants include return of the franchisor's proprietary materials, including operations manuals, agreements, advertising and promotional materials, products and supplies, and trademarked products on a pre-determined formula or third-party determination basis.

As indicated above, the post-term non-compete covenant of the franchisee requires an understanding and application of applicable laws in the target country, as well as the definition of prohibited activities, the geographical scope of application, and the time period for the covenant. A drafter will also need to determine the persons to whom the covenant applies, such as the franchisee, principals of the franchisee, family members, and designated shareholders.

R. Dispute Resolution

Because parties to the franchise agreement typically want to avoid judicial proceedings, it is common for alternative dispute resolution methods and requirements to be specified in the agreement.

The first step in attempting to resolve any dispute in many international franchise agreements is the requirement that the senior executives of the parties meet in an attempt to resolve any disputed issues prior to the commencement of any further dispute resolution proceedings. The agreement should require the parties to meet in good faith to resolve the dispute. It should also specify who are the required participants, the location of any meeting, the minimum period of time for the meeting, and who incurs the costs of such meeting.

If the senior executive officers of the parties are unable to resolve the dispute, non-binding third-party mediation is typically the next step. The agreement should provide for who the mediator will be or how the mediator will be selected, the place of mediation, the procedures for mediation, and who incurs the costs of the mediation.

If mediation cannot resolve a dispute, the agreement may provide for formal arbitration. However, certain dispute items may fall out the purview of arbitration so that the parties may seek immediate relief. These items include equitable remedies, remedies with respect to use or misuse of the franchisor's trademarks, and remedies with respect to non-payment.

All details concerning the arbitration should be provided in the international franchise agreements, including whether the arbitration will be held in the home country, the target country, or in a neutral location. Arbitration rules should also be specified. Typical rules include the rules of the American Arbitration Association (Commercial Arbitration or International

Arbitration Rules), the International Chamber of Commerce, the United Nations Conference on International Trade Law (UNCITRL), and the London Court of International Arbitration.

The agreement should specify the number of arbitrators, how they will be selected, the language of the arbitral records, the jurisdiction for enforcement of the arbitral award, the governing law, and who has responsibility for expenses and fees of the arbitration as well as responsibility for payment of each party's own fees and expenses.

If any disputes are to be resolved by judicial determination, provisions must be included in the franchise agreement specifying a number of items. Each of the franchisor and the franchisee will typically want the governing law of the franchise agreement to be the law of its home country. Regardless of the choice of law, in many cases, parties to the franchise agreement will seek remedies before target country courts even if only to enforce arbitral or judicial awards or decisions granted in the home country.

The laws of the target country will also control intellectual property issues (e.g., trademark infringement claims), currency restrictions imposed by the target country, withholding taxes, disclosure requirements, and competition restrictions.

In providing for choice of forum, the franchisor may want to designate the forum for dispute resolution within the home country, while the franchisee may want to designate the forum within the target country. To resolve the issue, the agreement could provide that the courts of the domicile of the party that does not commence legal proceedings will serve as the choice of forum. Another alternative is to confer concurrent jurisdiction on the courts of the domicile of each party.

Because the judicial systems in some target countries do not recognize equitable remedies, the parties may need to specifically provide for preliminary relief in the form of interlocutory injunctions, temporary restraining orders, orders of specific performance, and other similar types of relief in the agreement.

It will also be necessary to specify who is responsible for fees and costs, although in some judicial systems it is within the discretion of the court to order costs. Nevertheless often the losing party pays all fees, expenses, and costs of the other party.

Other dispute-related issues to cover in an international franchise agreement include a period of time for asserting claims, severability of agreement provisions, waiver of jury trial, and waiver of exemplary or punitive damages.

In those Asian countries surveyed, the country authors were asked to confirm whether the choice of law of a foreign jurisdiction would likely be upheld under the law of his or her country. They were also asked to confirm whether a court in his or her country would honor an election of international arbitration dispute resolution. Most of the answers were consistent. It is preferred that the franchise agreement be governed by and interpreted under the laws of the Asian target country; however, in a number of cases, the courts will generally hold the parties to the laws of another jurisdiction so long as the parties have agreed to it and the choice of law does not conflict with domestic public policy. In short, courts in the countries surveyed would likely honor an election of international arbitration dispute resolution and enforce arbitral judgments. Moreover, Bangladesh,[86] China,[87] Hong Kong,[88] India,[89] Indonesia,[90] Japan,[91] Kazakhstan,[92] Malaysia,[93] Nepal,[94]

---

86 *See* Dr. Mariam Khatoon and Nasir Doulah, *Franchising in Bangladesh*, in FRANCHISING IN ASIA 2015: LEGAL AND BUSINESS CONSIDERATIONS 79 (Kendal H. Tyre, Jr., Diana Vilmenay-Hammond, and Pierce Haesung Han, eds. LexNoir Foundation 2015).

87 *See* Xiang, *supra* note 43 at 98.

88 *See* Allison, *supra* note 55 at 107.

89 *See* Mehta, *supra* note 70 at 118-119.

90 *See* Adiwibowo, Karyadi, and Reerink, *supra* note 27 at 134.

Philippines,[95] South Korea,[96] Tajikistan,[97] Thailand[98] and Vietnam[99] are all signatories to the New York Convention so an arbitral award under international rules will likely be enforced in these jurisdictions. Taiwan is not a signatory to the convention.

S. Consequences of Termination

The consequences of terminating an international franchise agreement can be complicated, especially if subfranchisees are involved. As a preliminary matter, it must be determined whether the agreement will provide that the franchisee has any continuing rights to operate the franchisee's own outlets and those of subfranchisees post-termination. If a franchisee will be prohibited from continuing operation, the agreement must, upon termination, automatically reassign subfranchise agreements to the franchisor. It may also provide for a right to purchase existing outlets on a pre-determined formula basis. The franchisor will need to review the laws affecting the preparation of conditional assignments in the target country to draft the

---

(Footnote continued from previous page)

91 *See* Mitani, *supra* note 45 at 154.

92 *See* Akhmetova, *supra* note 46 at 166.

93 *See* Wong and Loi, *supra* note 47 at 183.

94 *See* Devendra Pradhan, *Franchising in Nepal*, in FRANCHISING IN ASIA 2015: LEGAL AND BUSINESS CONSIDERATIONS 195 (Kendal H. Tyre, Jr., Diana Vilmenay-Hammond, and Pierce Haesung Han, eds. LexNoir Foundation 2015).

95 *See* Mercado-Ferrer, *supra* note 65 at 214.

96 *See* Carr, *supra* note 48 at 226.

97 *See* Nazrisho and Sodatkadamov, *supra* note 56 at 254.

98 See Sriwan Puapondh and Alan Adcock, Franchising in Thailand, in FRANCHISING IN ASIA 2015: LEGAL AND BUSINESS CONSIDERATIONS 276 (Kendal H. Tyre, Jr., Diana Vilmenay-Hammond, and Pierce Haesung Han, eds. LexNoir Foundation 2015).

99 *See* Hang and Hoa, *supra* note 50 at 293.

appropriate assignment provisions in both the franchise agreement and the individual unit subfranchise agreements.

If the franchisee is to be barred from further involvement in the franchise system, appropriate covenants should be included in the agreement relating to non-competition, non-solicitation, non-use of trade secrets and confidential information, and cessation of all use of trademarks and proprietary products.

The agreement may also provide for conditional rights of assignment of all leases and subleases entered into by the franchisee. As a precautionary measure, the franchisor should review the enforceability of such provisions under the target country laws as well as any formal requirements for drafting the appropriate assignment language.

Finally, the franchise agreement should provide the franchisor with an option to require a defaulting franchisee to sell the agreement and related rights and assign any subfranchise agreements to a qualified third-party purchaser designated by the franchisor. This allows the franchisor to locate a new franchisee and to assign to the new franchisee the system rights.

T. General Agreement Provisions

An international franchise agreement should include the general contract provisions that would typically be included in a contract, such as provisions relating to the entire agreement, the binding effect of the agreement, counterparts, governing language, effective headings, notices, and independent contractors.

Appropriate disclaimers should also be included and adapted for the laws of the target country. Relevant disclaimers may provide that:

- □ the franchise system is proprietary,
- □ the franchisee had an opportunity to obtain independent advice and counsel,

- □ the franchisee assumed the risks of entering into the international franchise agreement,
- □ the franchised business has adequate capitalization and working capital,
- □ the franchisee has provided adequate representations and warranties relating to financial statements submitted by to franchisor, as well as to the identity of and ownership interests of shareholders and principals of the franchisee entity, and
- □ the franchisee has acknowledged that it does not and will not operate any competitive business.

V. Conclusions

Asia is a rapidly changing region, and franchising is increasingly seen as a viable means to expand businesses, spur the development of SMEs, and increase foreign investment. Given these factors, counsel and business executives in the franchise industry should understand the impact and consequences of various franchise structures, the law of the target countries in which the franchise will operate, and the options in drafting key contractual provisions of the international franchise agreement. Moreover, a suitable international franchise arrangement for a particular franchise system in a specific target country, whether in Asia or elsewhere, must be determined on an individual basis. A franchisor's appetite for international growth, the ability to relinquish control, the desire for capital or debt reduction, and the willingness to share fees must be analyzed. In addition, some thought must be given to certain cultural and business considerations including availability of product, supplies and sites, the receptiveness and adaptability of the franchise concept in the target market, and the sophistication of potential investors. Throughout the expansion process, it is critical that the franchisor obtain experienced legal, accounting, banking, and other professional advice in the target country and that an appropriate selection be made of the franchisee in the target country to launch a successful franchise venture in Asia.

Franchising in Bangladesh

Dr. Mariam Khatoon and Nasir Doulah

DOULAH & DOULAH

Dhakah, Bangladesh

Bangladesh

I. Introduction

A. Historical Background of the Country

At the closure of World War II, it was clear that European colonialism had run its course and Indian independence was inevitable. The independence of India was attained from Britain in 1947 but the struggle was bitter and divisive, especially in Bengal, which was a part of India and where the fight for self-government was complicated by internal religious conflict. The British, realizing any agreement between the Muslims and Hindus was impossible, decided to partition the subcontinent into India and Pakistan with Bengal and Punjab, the two overwhelmingly Muslim regions, on opposite sides of India.

Inequalities between the two regions (i.e., East and West Pakistan) soon stirred up a sense of Bengali nationalism that had not been reckoned with during the push for Muslim independence. The drive to reinstate the Bangla language metamorphosed into a push for self-government and when the Awami League, a Bengali nationalistic party, won a majority in the 1971 national elections, the president of Pakistan, faced with this result, postponed opening the National Assembly. Riots and strikes broke out in East Pakistan, the independent state of Bangladesh was unilaterally announced, and Pakistan sent troops to quell the rebellion.

The ensuing war was one of the shortest and bloodiest of modern times followed by the emergence of Bangladesh. Sheikh Mujib, one of the founders of the Awami League, became the country's first prime minister in January 1972; he was assassinated in 1975 during a period of crisis.

The ruined and decimated new country experienced famine in 1973–74, followed by martial law, successive military coups and political assassinations. In 1979, Bangladesh began a short-lived experiment with democracy led by the overwhelmingly popular President Zia, who established good relationships with the West and the oil-rich Islamic countries. His assassination in 1981 ultimately returned the country to a military government until 1991.

From thereon Bangladesh has been under a democracy but political fighting between the BNP and the Awami League became too acrimonious to exploit the potential of the country to its fullest extent possible.

B. Economy of the Country

Bangladesh is a developing nation. However, the poverty rate has declined by 25% since 1990, and per-capita GDP has doubled from 1975 levels. Dhaka and Chittagong, the country's two largest cities, as well as other urban centers, have been the driving force behind much of the recent growth.

Bangladesh has seen a dramatic increase in foreign direct investment. In order to enhance economic growth, the government set up several export processing zones to attract foreign investment. These are managed by the Bangladesh Export Processing Zone Authority.

Lack of infrastructure is still being considered as a hurdle towards foreign direct investment and financing. The insufficient power supply constitutes an obstacle to growth.

One significant contributor to the development of the economy has been the widespread propagation of microcredit by Muhammad Yunus (awarded the Nobel Peace Prize in 2006) through the Grameen Bank.

The Bangladesh government is planning for construction of the largest deep sea port in South Asia at Sonadia Island. The 500 billion taka project will be completed in multiple phases and enable Bangladesh to service the whole region as a maritime transport and logistics hub.

Recently, the government of Bangladesh has launched high-speed modern DEMU trains and is also going to construct a metro rail system and a high-speed electric powered intercity bullet rail network. The government has yet to source funds for the first large scale PPP project under the PPP framework (i.e., the Elevated Expressway). A number of countries including Russia, Malaysia, and China have proposed necessary financing. A number of power projects are under implementation with significant financing from international donors, multilateral bodies, and development banks.

Bangladesh is one of world's largest producers of: rice (4th), potato (11th), mango (9th), pineapple (16th), tropical fruit (5th), onion (16th), banana (17th), jute (2nd), and tea (11th). More than three-quarters of Bangladesh's export earnings came from the garment industry in 2005. The industry began attracting foreign investors in the 1980s because of cheap labor and low conversion cost. In the 2011–12 fiscal year, the industry exported US$ 18 billion worth of products where in 2002 the exported amount was US$ 5 billion. Bangladesh has been ranked as the 4th largest clothing exporter by the WTO (The World Trade Organization). According to *The Economist*, Bangladesh is the world's third-largest clothes-export industry. The industry now employs more than 3 million workers, 90% of whom are women. There has also been a significant growth to Bangladesh's ship building industry in the last few years. The required ships and vessels in the country are being produced by local shipbuilders.

C. Franchise Overview

In recent times, the franchise market has been one of the fastest growing primarily due to the potential of franchising as a powerful tool to stimulate the growth of SMEs. This has led to increased employment, helped to ensure sustainable economic growth and, importantly, facilitated broader access to the economy.

No specific legislation exists to control the franchise industry in Bangladesh leaving the sector unregulated. As a result, the courts have grappled with the classification and treatment of the franchise relationship in terms of the common law of Bangladesh. Although courts have in the past equated the franchise relationship to that of a fiduciary relationship, the concept of a fiduciary relationship conflicts with the reciprocal nature of a franchise agreement.

Recently, a *Competition Act, 2012* (the "CA") and *Consumer Protection Act, 2009* (the "CPA") has been enacted in Bangladesh with the establishment of a Competition Commission and Consumer Rights Protection Committee still under implementation phase. These two regulatory authorities may address franchise issues thus enabling the market to benefit from the requirement of franchise specific rules and regulations.

II. Regulatory Requirements

A. Pre-Sale Disclosure

Please describe any pre-sale franchise disclosure or similar requirements that may apply to franchise transactions.

There is no pre-sale franchise disclosure or similar requirements applicable to franchise transactions in Bangladesh.

B. Governmental Approvals, Registrations, Filing Requirements

Please describe any necessary government approvals, registrations or filing requirements that may apply to franchise transactions.

While there are no government approvals or filing registration requirements specific to franchising in Bangladesh, existing exchange control rules apply to franchising. The current Bangladeshi exchange control measures are set out in the *Foreign Exchange Regulation Act, 1947* (the "FERA") and the *Guide to Foreign Exchange Transactions* (the "GFET") issued by the Central Bank of Bangladesh ("Bangladesh Bank").

Bangladesh

The Central Bank of Bangladesh ("Bangladesh Bank") has wide discretion with respect to exchange control measures and this discretion is exercised on a case-by-case basis. In terms of FERA (without approval granted by the Bangladesh Bank or a person authorized by the Bangladesh Bank, i.e., an "Authorized Dealer"), no person is permitted to make any payment to, or in favor, or on behalf of, a person resident outside Bangladesh, or place any sum to the credit of such person.

Typically, in a franchise agreement, the franchisee pays the franchisor a royalty for the use of the brand name and operating system required to operate the business. The payment of royalties under a franchise agreement by a Bangladeshi franchisee to a non-resident franchisor requires exchange control approval from the Bangladesh Bank. This means that a formal application requesting approval of the franchise agreement should be made to the Bangladesh Bank as per the GFET.

Where the terms of the franchise agreement includes the manufacturing of products within Bangladesh, the franchise first has to be registered with the Board of Investment (the "BoI"). Under such circumstances, the BoI examines the license agreement and approves payment of royalties. Where no local manufacturing is involved, BoI does not intervene in the proceedings and Bangladesh Bank itself applies its discretion in approving the franchise transaction.

However, all agreements that contain any clauses that stipulate down payments, minimum payments, and one-off payments will be considered for recommendation to the Bangladesh Bank by the BoI. The Bangladesh Bank applies a set of procedures that it has developed over time and that are set out in the GFET to be applied by the BoI when considering the recommendation of license agreements. However, the GFET is also applied by the BoI in approving agreements where no local manufacturing is involved. See also Section V (Trademarks) of this chapter relating to non-mandatory recordal of licenses under the *Trade Marks Act, 2000*.

Both of the approvals from the Bangladesh Bank and BoI take approximately one month to be approved. Along with a specific form (attached as Annex-1), an audited return from the last year has to be filed for such approval from the Bangladesh Bank. The required form for approval from BoI is attached as Annex-2 along with a list of required documents. However, in the event manufacturing is not involved, for royalties below 6%, prior permission from the Bangladesh Bank is not required.

C. Limits of Fees and Typical Term of Franchise Agreement

Please describe any limits upon the nature and extent of fees and the term of a typical franchise agreement.

Pursuant to the GFET of the Bangladesh Bank, generally the BoI and the Bangladesh Bank would approve payments of royalties of between 6% and 8% of the revenue generated in the closed year excluding any taxes such as value-added tax irrespective of the nature of goods and services. Down payments/up-front payments other than nominal amounts will be considered only if actual costs of transferring technology (tangible items) are involved.

The applications must clearly quantify and substantiate such costs. Payments for trademarks will be considered if such trademarks are linked to the furnishing of technology. Payment for the use of a trademark shall be considered in such a way that the total royalty payment (i.e., for the use of the trademark and the provision of technology) should not exceed the maximum percentages as stated above.

The GFET specifically provides that exchange control approval will normally be granted for the transaction as a whole. However, for each remittance an application has to be filed to the Bangladesh Bank along with historical data.

III. Currency

If all payments under a franchise agreement must be made in immediately available U.S. Dollars, please advise as to any restrictions, reporting requirements, or regulations concerning the exchange, repatriation or remittance of U.S. Dollars.

Any payments by a franchisee who is a resident of Bangladesh will be subject to exchange control requirements imposed by the Bangladesh Bank. A Bangladeshi franchisee will not be permitted to make payments under a franchise agreement offshore (whether these are structured as franchise fees, royalties, or any other type of payment) without prior approval from the Bangladesh Bank. The Bangladesh Bank will consider the terms of such payment and approval will normally be for a specified period of time. Approval will need to be renewed when appropriate.

If there is any substantive amendment of the terms of a franchise agreement in relation to such payment, the parties may need to seek approval from the Bangladesh Bank for the amended structure of the payments. The Bangladesh Bank may refuse to approve payments under a franchise agreement where it considers the amounts of such payment excessive in relation to the counter-consideration received by the franchisee. Additionally, the Bangladesh Bank may refuse to grant approval for such payments in longer term agreements.

As per the GFET, royalties may be based on any of the freely exchangeable international currencies such as USD, EUR, GBP, etc.

IV. Taxes, Tariffs, and Duties

Please do not provide any in-depth comments on tax structuring. However, please provide your general comments on the typical amount of withholding tax that would apply and whether a "gross-up" provision contained in a franchise agreement would be enforceable in your country.

Bangladesh

A. General taxation principles

In terms of the *Income Tax Ordinance, 1984* (the "Income Tax Act"), Bangladeshi tax residents are taxed on their worldwide income and non-residents are taxed on Bangladesh sourced and deemed sourced income, subject however to relief afforded by a double taxation agreement ("DTA") where applicable. On the assumption that the franchisor is not a resident of Bangladesh, the franchisor will be taxed in Bangladesh on Bangladesh sourced and deemed sourced income only, subject to DTA relief.

Bangladesh has double taxation agreements with thirty two countries, including Belgium, Canada, China, Denmark, France, Germany, India, Indonesia, Italy, Japan, Malaysia, Norway, Pakistan, Philippines, Poland, Republic of Korea, Romania, Singapore, Sri Lanka, Sweden, Switzerland, Thailand, The Netherlands, Turkey, United Kingdom, United States, and Vietnam.

In general, a company that is incorporated in Bangladesh will be treated as a resident for tax purposes. All other companies, including branches of foreign companies, are treated as non-resident companies. Dual resident status is not recognized in Bangladesh. A company is tax resident in Bangladesh for income tax purposes if:

- the company is incorporated in Bangladesh;
- the company has its head office in Bangladesh;
- the company has its center of management in Bangladesh; or
- the company's directors, in their capacity as directors, exercise control of the company in Bangladesh, even if the directors' decision-making also occurs outside Bangladesh.

If a company is resident in Bangladesh and also resident under the domestic laws of the country with which Bangladesh has a DTA, relevant provisions in that agreement will determine where the company is considered resident for the purposes of applying the DTA. The Income Tax Act defines income as "any income, profits or gains, from whatever source derived."

B. Bangladesh taxation treatment of royalty income received by a non-resident

For Bangladesh tax purposes, royalty income received by a non-resident is statutorily deemed to have accrued from a source within Bangladesh including:

- the use or right of use, or the grant of permission to use, in Bangladesh, of any patent, trademark, design or copyright or any model, plan, pattern, formula or process or any other property or right of a similar nature; and
- payments for the imparting of, or undertaking to impart, any scientific, technical, industrial, or commercial knowledge or information for use in Bangladesh, or the rendering of, or the undertaking to render, any assistance or service in connection with the application or utilization of such knowledge or information, wheresoever such knowledge or information has been obtained or imparted or assistance or services is rendered or to be rendered.

Such deemed Bangladesh sourced royalty income is taxed in the hands of the non-resident receiving it by a final withholding tax calculated at the rate of 10%.

C. Reduction of the withholding tax by a DTA

All of the thirty-two DTAs Bangladesh has entered into stipulate a withholding tax of 10% on the royalties received. As such, there is no additional reduction of the withholding tax by a DTA.

D. Enforceability of a "gross-up" provision contained in a franchise agreement

Provided that any gross-up provisions contained in a franchise agreement do not contravene the GFET, as discussed above, they are enforceable under Bangladesh law. However, gross-up conditions should include the maximum limit for remittance of royalties so that the income tax withheld is actually part of the total receivables of the franchisor.

V. Trademarks

Please advise us as to whether there are any special requirements for granting a valid trademark license, including the use of a registered user agreement or a short trademark license agreement and any required filing of such an agreement with the trademark authorities.

There are no specific requirements for a trademark license to be valid in Bangladesh. The *Trade Marks Act, 2000* provides for the recordal of licensees as registered users; however, such recordal is not mandatory. To grant a franchisee use of the brand, the brand must be applied for or registered with the Trademark Registration Authority of Bangladesh. The user/license agreement becomes effective from the date of registration if such application for recordation is lodged with respect to a trademark that is not registered.

VI. Restrictions on Transfer

Please advise as to whether there are any restrictions (1) on a franchisor to restrict transfers by a master franchisee, any interest in a master franchisee, or the assets of the master franchisee, or (2) the ability of a master franchisee to control and/or restrict transfers of a subfranchisee's rights under a master franchise agreement, interest in the subfranchisee, or the assets of the subfranchisee.

Under Bangladesh law, it is permissible for an agreement to stipulate certain restrictions on transfers as well as pre-emptive rights in favor of the franchisor, in instances where the master franchisee intends to dispose of the business, the assets of the franchising entity or its controlling interest in the franchise entity. A franchise agreement may also provide for so-called "step-in" rights in favor of the franchisor where there are concerns relating to the prudent management of the franchise entity and franchisee.

VII. Termination

Please advise us as to any laws relating to termination in your country, such as agency laws, required indemnity provisions, notice or "good cause" requirements, or other laws affecting termination of a franchise agreement. Please describe.

Under Bangladesh law, the parties to an agreement are free to stipulate the basis upon which either is entitled to terminate the agreement between them. This will include any ancillary agreements, such as licensing or agency agreements. Generally, agreements provide for termination on notice, upon breach of the agreement, default or insolvency.

VIII. Governing Law, Jurisdiction, and Dispute Resolution

A. Choice of Law of Foreign Jurisdiction

Please confirm whether the choice of law of a foreign jurisdiction would likely to be upheld under the law of the country, except for certain matters such as trademarks, bankruptcy, and competition matters, which we assume would be governed by the law in your country.

Pursuant to Bangladesh Bank recommendations, every effort should be made to ensure that agreements are construed and interpreted under the laws and jurisdiction of Bangladesh. However, where parties have elected for the laws of another jurisdiction to govern, the courts will generally uphold the parties' choice. Submission to the jurisdiction of the forum is recognized as a basis for the competence of a foreign court to enforce a foreign judgment.

However, according to the *Code of Civil Procedure of Bangladesh*, all foreign judgments are not enforceable in Bangladesh. Judgments from countries with which Bangladesh has a reciprocal arrangement are enforceable in Bangladesh. Bangladesh has such reciprocal arrangements with Australia, Fiji, India, New Zealand, Pakistan, Singapore, and the United Kingdom. Such foreign judgments are enforceable subject to the following requirements:

- the foreign judgment must be conclusive and given on the merits of the case;
- the judgment must have pronounced by a court of competent jurisdiction (i.e., the agreement between the parties refer to said court or the judgment debtor must have been carrying on business or have been ordinarily resident within the jurisdiction of the foreign court). Alternatively, the judgment debtor must have voluntarily appeared or otherwise submitted or agreed to submit to the jurisdiction of that court;
- the judgment must be capable of enforcement in the original court;
- the judgment debtor, if he was the defendant in the original proceedings, must have been duly served with the process of the original court;
- the judgment must not have been obtained by fraud or be in respect of a cause of action;
- the judgment is not contrary to Bangladesh public policy or a refusal to recognize the laws of Bangladesh where applicable;
- where it sustains a claim founded on a breach of any law in force in Bangladesh; and
- where there is no pending or possible intended appeal against the judgment of the original court.

B. International Arbitration Dispute Resolution

Please confirm that a court in your country would honor an election of international arbitration dispute resolution, and therefore refuse to hear any disputes arising under a franchise agreement.

As stated above, the Bangladesh courts will give effect to the parties' right to freedom of contract, and to the legal system under which they choose to contract. However, this will not necessarily be the case at all times. Where, for example, public policy considerations are at play or where gross irregularity has occurred in the conclusion of the agreement or an arbitral award, the courts may elect to apply the principles of Bangladesh law.

Bangladesh is a signatory to the *Convention on the Recognition and Enforcement of Foreign Arbitral Awards* (the "New York Convention"). Foreign arbitral awards including arbitration awards from any country that is a signatory to the New York Convention are enforceable in Bangladesh as per the *Arbitration Act, 2001*. ICC and UNCITRAL arbitration rules with Singapore as the venue are frequently used in local contracts and agreements.

Awards from international arbitration are referred to as foreign arbitral awards and have to be filed with the District Court for enforcement. No appeal lies against an enforcement verdict from the local courts. However, appeal is possible when the arbitration award is rejected. The court takes into account the following while enforcing a foreign arbitral award:

- if the party against whom it is invoked furnishes proof to the court that a party to the arbitration agreement was under some incapacity;
- the arbitration agreement is not valid under the law to which the parties have subjected it;
- the party against whom the award is invoked was not given proper notice of the appointment of the arbitrator

or of the arbitral proceedings or was otherwise unable due to some reasonable causes to present his case;

- the concerned foreign arbitral award contains decisions on matters beyond the scope of the submission to arbitration; provided that, if the decisions on matters submitted to arbitration can be separated from those not so submitted, that part of the award which contains decisions on matters submitted to arbitration may be recognized and enforced;
- the composition of the arbitral tribunal or the arbitral procedure was not in accordance with the agreement of the parties or, in absence of such agreement was not in accordance with the law of the country where the arbitration took place;
- the award has not yet become binding on the parties, or has been set aside or suspended by a competent authority of the country in which, or under the law of which, that award was made;
- the court in which recognition or execution of the foreign arbitral award is sought, finds that the subject matter of the dispute is not capable of settlement by arbitration under the law for the time being in force in Bangladesh; or
- the recognition and execution of the foreign arbitral award is in conflict with the public policy of Bangladesh.

IX. Non-Competition Provisions

If the franchise agreement prohibits the master franchisee from engaging in certain competitive activities during the term of the agreement, and for a 12-month period after the termination or expiration of the agreement, please comment on the enforceability of non-competition covenants in your country.

Restraint of trade (i.e., non-compete) provisions are often included in employment contracts, but are also used in the franchising context. They are valid in principle. However, when the franchisor seeks to enforce such restraint provisions, the courts retain discretion as to whether to enforce the restraint in question. Courts will not enforce the restraint where it may considered contrary to the public interest or is unreasonable. The courts will consider the merits of the enforceability of each restraint on a case-by-case basis, and the reasonableness of the restraint is assessed with reference to a number of factors.

The decision whether to uphold a restraint of trade consists of an analysis of the broad interests of the public and the interests of the contracting parties themselves. With regard to the interests of the public, the tension lies between two competing interests: (i) agreements solemnly entered into should be upheld and enforced, and, (ii) persons should generally be free to engage in economic activity, and should not be rendered unenforceable. Reasonableness as between the parties themselves depends on many factors, the most important of which are:

- □ whether the franchisor has a "proprietary" interest that may legitimately be protected by means of a restraint agreement;
- □ the geographical area of the restraint;
- □ the duration of the restraint; and
- □ whether adequate consideration has been given for the restraint.

X. Language Requirements

Does the law in your country require that a franchise agreement be translated into the local language in order to be enforceable between the parties?

Bangladesh law stipulates that a franchise agreement should be in either Bengali or English.

XI. Other Significant Matters

Please advise as to whether there are any significant matters not addressed above of which a franchisor should be aware in

connection with its entering into a franchise agreement in your country.

In addition to the royalty, the franchisee can apply for an additional payment of consultancy fee, which can be a maximum of 1% of the revenue it earned in the preceding year.

The government of Bangladesh is considering an increase in the withholding tax applicable to royalty fees. However, such an increase over the rate of withholding tax shall not impact franchisors which belong to a country that has a DTA with Bangladesh as all of these DTAs stipulate a withholding tax of 10% for royalty fees.

Bangladesh

Annex 1

See Chapter 10	Para 25

APP. 5	59

APPLICATION FOR REMITTANCE OF ROYALTY/TECHNICAL FEES

Name and address of the applicant Company	Name and address of the beneficiary to whom Royalty/ Technical feesis payable	No. & date of BOI Permission letter (where needed)	Ex-factory /net sales value on which Royalty/ Tehcnical fee is calculated.	Rate of Royalty/ Technical fee.	Amount Remittable (In Taka)		Refundable Surcharge, if any, payable	Net amount remittable (In Taka)	Remarks
					Gross amount	Income tax, if any, payable			
1	2	3	4	5	6	7	8	9	10

CERTIFICATE

Certified that the amount of royalty/technical fee payable for the period .... to the beneficiary mentioned in column 2 is the net amount payable to them after deduction of tax liability, if any, payable thereon as certified by the auditors and has been calculated strictly in accordance with the terms of the Govt./Bangladesh Bank's approval mentioned in column 3 above.

We undertake that if any discrepancy is subsequently found in the amount of remittance made by us, we shall arrange for repatriation of the amount remitted in excess by us forthwith on receipt of instruction from Bangladesh Bank and shall also render ourselves liable for action under Foreign Exchange Regulation Act, 1947.

Authorised Signature of the applicant Company

Name and address of the Company

............*Contd.* *P/2*

Page-2

See Chapter 10	Para 25

APP. 5	59

AUDITOR'S CERTIFICATE

Certified that we have verified the information furnished in the above statement found them to be correct

AUDITORS

AUTHORISED DEALER'S CERTIFICATE

Date of remittance	Amount of remittance allowed		Rate of foreign exchange applied for conversion of Taka into foreign currency	Code Number	Remarks
	Foreign currency	Taka equivalent			

Certified that the above remittance has been allowed after due verification from relevant documents that (*i) no tax is payable and therefore no provision for payment of tax with regard to this remittance has been made, (*ii) due provision for payment of tax in respect of this remittance has been made.

*Delete whichever is not applicable

Date:

Seal & Signature of the Authorised Dealer

Bangladesh

Annex 2

-2-

<table>
<tr><td>16.</td><td>Percentage of Total Remittances for the year (14 + 15) in respect of Sl. 11 or 12(a)</td><td></td><td></td></tr>
<tr><td>17.</td><td>Brief Statement of Benefits received /to be received by the Local Company/ Firm under the Agreement</td><td></td><td>(1
)
(2
)</td></tr>
<tr><td>18.</td><td>Brief Background of the Foreign Service Provider</td><td></td><td></td></tr>
<tr><td>19.</td><td>Statement of Remittances of such fees for the last 3(three) years</td><td></td><td><table><tr><td>Year of remittanc</td><td>BOI's Approval No. & date</td><td>Amount in million Tk.</td><td>%</td><td>Type of fees</td></tr><tr><td></td><td></td><td></td><td></td><td></td></tr><tr><td></td><td></td><td></td><td></td><td></td></tr><tr><td></td><td></td><td></td><td></td><td></td></tr></table></td></tr>
<tr><td>20.</td><td>Statement of Actual Production/Services for</td><td></td><td><table><tr><td>Year</td><td>Items of products/service</td><td>Qty</td><td>Sales Value/Revenue</td></tr><tr><td></td><td></td><td></td><td></td></tr><tr><td></td><td></td><td></td><td></td></tr><tr><td></td><td></td><td></td><td></td></tr></table></td></tr>
<tr><td>21.</td><td>Statement of Export Earning (if any)</td><td></td><td><table><tr><td>Yr. of Expo</td><td>Items of Export</td><td>Qty</td><td>C&F/CIF value</td></tr><tr><td></td><td></td><td></td><td></td></tr><tr><td></td><td></td><td></td><td></td></tr><tr><td></td><td></td><td></td><td></td></tr></table></td></tr>
<tr><td>22.</td><td>Name & address of the nominated local Bank through which remittance to be effected</td><td></td><td></td></tr>
</table>

Signature of the Managing Director/Managing Partner/Proprietor and Official Seal.

Documents to be Enclosed:

(1) A copy of Registration letter issued by the Board of Investment (BOI);
(2) A copy of Technology Transfer Agreement(Royalty/Technical Know-how/Technical Assistance Agreement);
(3) Filled-in Prescribed Application Form supplied by BOI signed by the Managing Director/Managing Partner/Proprietor;
(4) Resolution of the Board of Directors of the company/ Partners of the Firm regarding remittance of fees/showing amount, due year of remittance and name & address of the foreign service provider as per Agreement;
(5) A copy of Annual Report of the company/Firm comprising Audited Balance Sheet along with the Profit and Loss Accounts (in case of the project in operation) or Bill of Entry/Invoices of the Imported Machinery (in case of under implementation project);
(6) Income Tax Return certified/authenticated/attested by Chartered Accountant Firm for the concerned Assessment Year along with Computation Sheet for taxable income for the same period and Tax Clearance Certificate issued by Deputy Commissioner of Taxes of the concerned Tax Circle;
(7) A copy of Memorandum & Articles of Association and Certificate of Incorporation of the company (if not submitted earlier);
(8) Invoice(s) in support of fees to be remitted;
(9) Authenticated Banking documents showing Export Earning (if any);
(IO)Attested copy of Patent Right/Trade Mark/Brand Name Registration in Bangladesh (if any).

(All documents other than Original must be certified by the authorized signatory of the Company/Firm).

Franchising in China

Kelly F. Xiang

NIXON PEABODY LLP

Shanghai, China

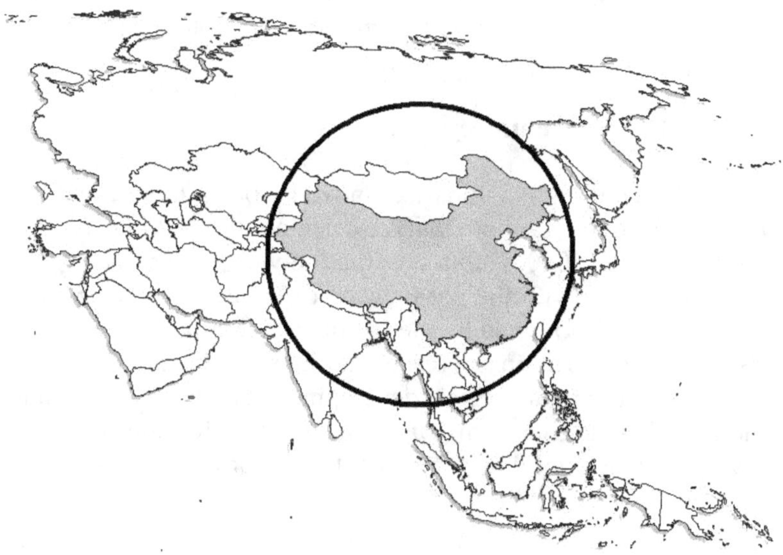

China

I. Introduction

A. Historical Background of the Country

After World War II, the communists under Mao Zedong established an autocratic socialist system that, while ensuring China's sovereignty, imposed strict controls over everyday life. After 1978, Mao's successor Deng Xiaoping and other leaders focused on market-oriented economic development and by 2000 output had quadrupled. For much of the population, living standards have improved dramatically and the room for personal choice has expanded, yet political controls remain tight. Since the early 1990s, China has increased its global outreach and participation in international organizations.

B. Economy of the Country

Since the late 1970s China has moved from a closed, centrally planned system to a more market-oriented one that plays a major global role. In 2010, China became the world's largest exporter. Reforms began with the phasing out of collectivized agriculture, and expanded to include the gradual liberalization of prices, fiscal decentralization, increased autonomy for state enterprises, growth of the private sector, development of stock markets and a modern banking system, and opening to foreign trade and investment. China has implemented reforms in a gradualist fashion.

In recent years, China has renewed its support for state-owned enterprises in sectors considered important to "economic security," explicitly looking to foster globally competitive industries. After keeping its currency tightly linked to the U.S. dollar for years, in July 2005, China moved to an exchange rate system that references a basket of currencies. From mid-2005 to late-2008, cumulative appreciation of the renminbi against the U.S. dollar was more than 20%, but the exchange rate remained virtually pegged to the dollar from the onset of the global financial crisis until June 2010, when Beijing allowed resumption of a gradual appreciation and expanded the daily trading band within which the RMB is permitted to fluctuate. The restructuring of the economy and resulting efficiency gains have contributed to a more than tenfold increase in GDP since 1978. Measured on a purchasing power parity (PPP) basis that adjusts for price differences, China in 2013 stood as the second-largest economy in the world after the U.S., having surpassed Japan in 2001. The dollar values of China's agricultural and industrial output each exceed those of the U.S.; China is second to the U.S. in the value of services it produces. Still, per capita income is below the world average.

The Chinese government faces numerous economic challenges, including: (a) reducing its high domestic savings rate and correspondingly low domestic consumption; (b) facilitating higher-wage job opportunities for the aspiring middle class, including rural migrants and increasing numbers of college graduates; (c) reducing corruption and other economic crimes; and (d) containing environmental damage and social strife related to the economy's rapid transformation.

Economic development has progressed further in coastal provinces than in the interior, and by 2011 more than 250 million migrant workers and their dependents had relocated to urban areas to find work. One consequence of population control policy is that China is now one of the most rapidly aging countries in the world.

Deterioration in the environment (notably air pollution, soil erosion, and the steady fall of the water table, especially in the North) is another long-term problem. China continues to lose arable land because of erosion and economic development. The Chinese government is seeking to add energy production capacity from sources other than coal and oil, focusing on nuclear and alternative energy development.

Several factors are converging to slow China's growth, including debt overhang from its credit-fueled stimulus program, industrial overcapacity, inefficient allocation of capital by state-owned banks, and the slow recovery of China's trading partners. The government's 12th Five-Year Plan, adopted in March 2011 and reiterated at the Communist Party's "Third Plenum" meeting in November 2013, emphasizes continued economic reforms and the need to increase domestic consumption in order to make the economy less dependent in the future on fixed investments, exports, and heavy industry. However, China has made only marginal progress toward these rebalancing goals. The new government of President Xi Jinping has signaled a greater willingness to undertake reforms that focus on China's long-term economic health, including giving the market a more decisive role in allocating resources.

C. Franchise Legal Overview

In China, franchise transactions are regulated specifically by the *Regulations on the Administration of Commercial Franchise* (the "2007 Regulations")—effective as of May 1, 2007; *Administrative Measures for Archival Filing of Commercial Franchises*—effective as of February 1, 2012 (the "Archival Filing Measures"); and the *Administration Measures for the Information Disclosure of Commercial Franchises*—effective as of April 1, 2012 (the "Disclosure Measures"). The applicable laws do not provide for any exclusions, exceptions, or exemptions.

II. Regulatory Requirements

A. Pre-Sale Disclosure

Please describe any pre-sale franchise disclosure or similar requirements that may apply to franchise transactions.

The 2007 Regulations and the Disclosure Measures mandate prior disclosure before the signing of the franchise agreement.

A franchisor in China is required to provide a franchisee with accurate information on specified matters concerning the franchise system and the proposed franchise contract at least 30 days before the franchise contract is executed, except that the franchisor and the franchisee are renewing a contract on terms identical to that of their existing franchise contract. However, the 2007 Regulations and the Disclosure Measures are silent on whether disclosure is required on the transfer of a franchise.

There are no specific provisions in the 2007 Regulations that apply to letters of intent related to any part of a franchise business transaction. According to the 2007 Regulations, if a franchisor requires a franchisee to pay expenses before conclusion of the franchising contract, the franchisor shall explain in written form to the franchisee about the application of these expenses and the conditions and methods for the refund of these expenses.

In addition, the franchisor is required to inform the franchisee promptly of any significant change in the information provided in the disclosure document.

B. Government Approvals, Registrations, Filing Requirements

Please describe any necessary government approvals, registrations, or filing requirements that may apply to franchise transactions.

Under the 2007 Regulations, a franchisor must be an enterprise, but it does not require that the franchisor be an enterprise incorporated in China. In order to become a franchisor, the enterprise must have a mature operation method and the ability to provide continuous guidance, technical support, and business training to the franchisee. The enterprise must own at least two stores that it operates directly and have been in operation for more than one year ("Qualification and 2+1 Rule").

Within 15 days of the execution of its first franchise agreement, the franchisor is required to file with the Ministry of Commerce ("MOFCOM") or its local counterpart at the provincial level:

1. Copy of its incorporation certificate or business license;

2. Standard form of its franchise agreement;
3. Franchise operation manual;
4. Marketing plan;
5. Written commitment to meet the requirements of Qualification and 2+1 Rule and related supporting documents;[100] and
6. If the product or service under the franchise requires special approval, the related approval documents.

If the franchisor engages in franchising within one province, it must file the above documents with MOFCOM's local counterpart at the provincial level; if the franchisor engages in franchising in more than one province, it shall file those documents with MOFCOM, but in practice, MOFCOM normally authorizes its local counterpart at provincial level to handle this matter. A foreign franchisor engaging in cross-border franchising in China must file those documents with MOFCOM.

C. Limits on Fees and Typical Term of Franchise Agreement

Please describe any limits upon the nature and extent of fees and the term of a typical franchise agreement.

The parties may freely agree on the nature, amount, or payment of fees. Initial fees and royalties are common in China. The franchise term specified in the franchise agreement shall not be less than three years, unless the franchisee agrees otherwise. This provision shall not apply when the franchisor and franchisee renew the franchise agreement.

[100] If a franchisor has been engaging in franchising activities in China since before May 1, 2007, then this requirement shall not apply.

III. Currency

If all payments under a franchise agreement must be made in immediately available U.S. Dollars, please advise as to any restrictions, reporting requirements, or regulations concerning the exchange, repatriation or remittance of U.S. Dollars.

At present, China maintains general foreign exchange control and RMB is not freely convertible. Payment of fees to a foreign franchisor is deemed as current account transactions under Chinese law. The parties may freely agree on the nature, amount, or payment of fees. For payments for trade in services, when a single receipt or payment is over US$ 50,000, the applicant shall submit transaction documents to the bank for its review, for example, for royalties for use of proprietary rights and franchise fees, the applicant shall submit relevant contract (agreement) and invoice (payment notice) to the bank for its review.

IV. Taxes, Tariffs, and Duties

Please do not provide any in-depth comments on tax structuring. However, please provide your general comments on the typical amount of withholding tax that would apply and whether a "gross-up" provision contained in a franchise agreement would be enforceable in your country.

China has strict regulations and procedures regarding withholding tax from non-tax resident enterprises for their China-sourced income. In China, franchisees are required to withhold income tax on payments to a U.S. franchisor at a rate of 10%, subject to the double taxation treaty with the U.S. and value-added tax at a rate of 6%.

V. Trademarks

Please advise us as to whether there are any special requirements for granting a valid trademark license, including the use of a registered user agreement or a short trademark license agreement and any required filing of such an agreement with the trademark authorities.

In China, the 2007 Regulations specify that the patent or trademark licenses related to the franchised operations are to be implemented according to the laws and administrative regulations on patent or trademarks. Given this, franchisors shall file the license agreement at the patent bureau or trademark office in the People's Republic of China.

VI. Restrictions on Transfer

Please advise as to whether there are any restrictions (1) on a franchisor to restrict transfers by a master franchisee, any interest in a master franchisee, or the assets of the master franchisee or (2) the ability of a master franchisee to control and/or restrict transfers of a subfranchisee's rights under a master franchise agreement, interest in the subfranchisee, or the assets of the subfranchisee.

Pursuant to 2007 Regulations, a franchisee may not assign its franchise rights to a third party without the consent of the franchisor.

VII. Termination

Please advise us as to any laws relating to termination in your country, such as agency laws, required indemnity provisions, notice or "good cause" requirements, or other laws affecting termination of a franchise agreement. Please describe.

According to the 2007 Regulations, a franchisor and the franchisee shall specify in the franchising contract that the franchisee may unilaterally terminate the contract within a certain term after the conclusion of such franchising contract. In addition, if a franchisor conceals relevant information or provides false information to a franchisee, the franchisee can terminate the franchising contract. Other than the abovementioned provisions, there is no known special provision regarding termination of a franchise agreement.

VIII. Governing Law, Jurisdiction, and Dispute Resolution

A. Choice of Law of Foreign Jurisdiction

Please confirm whether the choice of law of a foreign jurisdiction would likely to be upheld under the law of the country, except for certain matters such as trademarks, bankruptcy and competition matters, which we assume would be governed by the law in your country.

There are no restrictions on the applicable governing law of the franchising contract with foreign elements. Foreign elements refer to one or more following factors: one or more parties to the contract are foreign natural parties, stateless persons, or foreign legal persons; the subject matter is located in a foreign territory and the legal facts which give rise to, modify, or extinguish private rights and civil obligations occur outside China.

B. International Arbitration Dispute Resolution

Please confirm that a court in your country would honor an election of international arbitration dispute resolution, and therefore refuse to hear any disputes arising under a franchise agreement.

According to Chinese law, parties to a contract with a foreign element may apply to a Chinese arbitral institution or another arbitral institution for arbitration on the basis of their arbitration agreement. Therefore, depending on the parties' choice, the disputes arising out of or in relation to a franchise contract with a foreign element can be arbitrated by a Chinese arbitral institution or another arbitral institution located outside China.

Further, China is a signatory to the *Convention on the Recognition and Enforcement of Foreign Arbitral Awards* (the "New York Convention"). Generally, the arbitral awards rendered by an arbitral institution located outside China but a member of New York Convention can be enforced in China, and vice versa. It is common for franchisors to require the parties engage in mediation or arbitration to resolve disputes.

IX. Non-Competition Provisions

If the franchise agreement prohibits the franchisee from engaging in certain competitive activities during the term of the agreement, and for a 12-month period after the termination or expiration of the agreement, please comment on the enforceability of non-competition covenants in your country.

Generally, in China, there are no legal restrictions on non-compete clauses so long as they are reasonable.

X. Language Requirements

Does the law in your country require that a franchise agreement be translated into the local language in order to be enforceable between the parties?

There is no mandatory requirement to use Chinese in contracting, so English is an acceptable language. However, in any court proceedings in China, the court requires Chinese translations of all documents, whether pleadings or documentary evidence. Also, for governmental filing purposes, the Chinese governmental agencies normally require a Chinese version of any document to be filed. In addition, banks normally require a Chinese translation of the supporting documents (e.g., franchise agreement) to transfer royalties outside China. Normally, the Chinese translation should be provided by a Chinese licensed translation company.

XI. Other Significant Matters

Please advise as to whether there are any significant matters not addressed above of which a franchisor should be aware in connection with its entering into a franchise agreement in your country.

Each year by March 31, a franchisor shall report to the record filing authority information on its entry into, and rescission, termination and renewal of, franchisee contracts during the preceding year. China Franchising Association is the local franchise association in China. There is no legal requirement that a franchisor must become a member of such association.

Franchising in Hong Kong

David Allison

BIRD & BIRD

Hong Kong, China

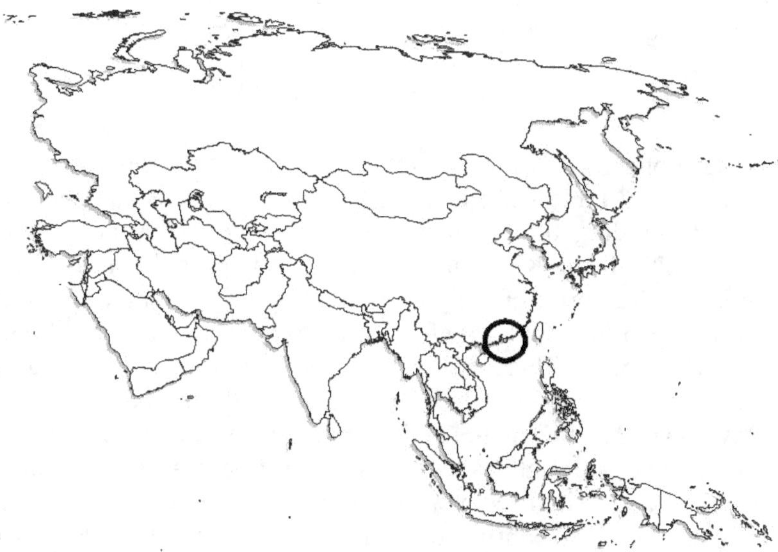

Hong Kong

I. Introduction

A. Historical Background of the Country

Pursuant to an agreement signed by China and the United Kingdom on December 19, 1984, Hong Kong became the Hong Kong Special Administrative Region (SAR) of the People's Republic of China on July 1, 1997. In this agreement, China promised that, under its "one country, two systems" formula, China's socialist economic system would not be imposed on Hong Kong and that Hong Kong would enjoy a "high degree of autonomy" in all matters except foreign and defense affairs for the subsequent 50 years.

B. Economy of the Country

Hong Kong has a free market economy, highly dependent on international trade and finance—the value of goods and services trade, including the sizable share of re-exports, is about four times GDP. Hong Kong has no tariffs on imported goods, and it levies excise duties on only four commodities, whether imported or produced locally: hard alcohol, tobacco, hydrocarbon oil, and methyl alcohol. There are no quotas or dumping laws. Hong Kong's open economy left it exposed to the global economic slowdown that began in 2008. Although increasing integration with China—through trade, tourism, and financial links—helped it to make an initial recovery more quickly than many observers anticipated, its continued reliance on foreign trade and investment leaves it vulnerable to renewed global financial market volatility or a slowdown in the global economy.

The mainland has long been Hong Kong's largest trading partner, accounting for about half of Hong Kong's total trade by value. Hong Kong's natural resources are limited, and food and raw materials must be imported. As a result of China's easing of travel restrictions, the number of mainland tourists to the territory has surged from 4.5 million in 2001 to 34.9 million in 2012, outnumbering visitors from all other countries combined.

Hong Kong

Hong Kong has also established itself as the premier stock market for Chinese firms seeking to list abroad. In 2012 mainland Chinese companies constituted about 46.6% of the firms listed on the Hong Kong Stock Exchange and accounted for about 57.4% of the Exchange's market capitalization. During the past decade, as Hong Kong's manufacturing industry moved to the mainland, its service industry has grown rapidly. Credit expansion and tight housing supply conditions have caused Hong Kong property prices to rise rapidly; consumer prices increased by more than 4% in 2013. Lower and middle income segments of the population are increasingly unable to afford adequate housing.

Hong Kong continues to link its currency closely to the U.S. dollar, maintaining an arrangement established in 1983. In 2013, Hong Kong and China signed new agreements under the Closer Economic Partnership Agreement, adopted in 2003 to forge closer ties between Hong Kong and the mainland. The new measures, effective from January 2014, cover services and trade facilitation, and will improve access to the mainland's service sector for Hong Kong-based companies.

C. Franchise Legal Overview

Although a part of the People's Republic of China, Hong Kong has its own distinct legal system which has its base in English common law. It has no franchise-specific law.

II. Regulatory Requirements

A. Pre-Sale Disclosure

Please describe any pre-sale franchise disclosure or similar requirements that may apply to franchise transactions.

Hong Kong has no specific legislation or set of regulations that deal with franchising. Accordingly, the ordinary principles of contract and the common law will apply to franchises in Hong Kong.[101]

B. Governmental Approvals, Registrations, Filing Requirements

Please describe any necessary government approvals, registrations, or filing requirements that may apply to franchise transactions.

There are no government approvals, registrations, or filing requirements that apply to franchise transactions in Hong Kong.

C. Limits on Fees and Typical Term of Franchise Agreement

Please describe any limits upon the nature and extent of fees and the term of a typical franchise agreement.

No limit has been prescribed on the nature and rate of the franchise fees and the term of a typical franchise agreement.

III. Currency

If all payments under a franchise agreement must be made in immediately available U.S. Dollars, please advise as to any restrictions, reporting requirements, or regulations concerning the exchange, repatriation or remittance of U.S. Dollars.

---

[101] *Editor's Note:* Although there are no disclosure requirements mandated under the laws of Hong Kong, the Hong Kong Franchise Association ("HKFA") has established a Code of Ethics, which provides that a franchisor should issue to the prospective franchisee full and accurate written disclosure of all information material to the franchise relationship within a reasonable time prior to the execution of the agreement. The Hong Kong General Chamber of Commerce established HKFA to monitor and promote the development of franchising. Membership in HKFA is voluntary.

Hong Kong maintains no restrictions in terms of currency. Parties are free to use whichever currency they wish in relation to their franchise and there are no exchange controls or restrictions in place. It is common to find agreements in Hong Kong being denominated in Hong Kong Dollars, U.S. dollars, or sometimes Chinese renminbi.

IV. Taxes, Tariffs and Duties

Please do not provide any in-depth comments on tax structuring. However, please provide your general comments on the typical amount of withholding tax that would apply and whether a "gross-up" provision contained in a franchise agreement would be enforceable in your country.

Hong Kong maintains a relatively straightforward tax system operating under the *Inland Revenue Ordinance (Cap. 112).* Key features include a simple flat tax rate based on all profits arising in or derived from Hong Kong. Because only Hong Kong based profits are taxed, companies will not be subject to tax on income they receive from sources outside Hong Kong. There are in any event a number of bi-lateral double tax treaties in place with various foreign jurisdictions.[102]

While Hong Kong does not impose withholding tax on dividends or interest, withholding tax may be imposed in relation to royalty payments made to a non-resident in respect of use of intellectual property.

V. Trademarks

Please advise us as to whether there are any special requirements for granting a valid trademark license, including the use of a registered user agreement or a short trademark

[102] *Editor's Note:* The list of countries and territories that have double taxation treaties with Hong Kong are provided on the following site, see http://www.ird.gov.hk/eng/tax/dta_inc.htm (last visited June 7, 2015).

license agreement and any required filing of such an agreement with the trademark authorities.

Trademarks in Hong Kong are governed by the *Trade Marks Ordinance* (Cap. 559) ("Ordinance"). Under the Ordinance, a trademark license may be either "general" or "limited." The license must be in writing and must be duly executed by the licensor either by signature or by affixing the corporate seal.

A license agreement is a registrable transaction in Hong Kong and must be registered with the Hong Kong Intellectual Property Department ("IPD").[103] Failure to do so will deprive the licensee with rights under the Ordinance, including rights in relation to infringement and taking action to enforce the trademark.

Recordal of the license is made by filing the relevant forms with the IPD and paying the recordal fee (currently HK$800—approximately US$ 100). It is not necessary to produce a copy of the license when filing for recordal of the license unless specifically requested by the IPD.

Recordal of a license with the IPD is essentially a procedural matter and recordal is almost always granted unless the application is deficient in terms of basic information required on the application form or if the application has not been signed by the licensor.

---

103 *Editor's Note:* The IPD maintains a database of trademarks, patents, and registered designs that enables individuals to search for intellectual property currently registered with the IPD. See http://ipsearch.ipd.gov.hk/index.html (last visited June 7, 2015).

VI. Restrictions on Transfer

Please advise as to whether there are any restrictions (1) on a franchisor to restrict transfers by a master franchisee, any interest in a master franchisee, or the assets of the master franchisee or (2) the ability of a master franchisee to control and/or restrict transfers of a subfranchisee's rights under a master franchise agreement, an interest in the subfranchisee, or the assets of the subfranchisee.

There are no specific restrictions on transfer in Hong Kong. These are matters for the parties to agree between themselves.

VII. Termination

Please advise us as to any laws relating to termination in your country, such as agency laws, required indemnity provisions, notice or "good cause" requirements, or other laws affecting termination of a franchise agreement. Please describe.

There are no special restrictions on termination of a franchise agreement in Hong Kong. Ordinary common law principles of contract will apply.

VIII. Governing Law, Jurisdiction and Dispute Resolution

A. Choice of Law of Foreign Jurisdiction

Please confirm whether the choice of law of a foreign jurisdiction would likely to be upheld under the law of the country, except for certain matters such as trademarks, bankruptcy and competition matters, which we assume would be governed by the law in your country.

Parties are generally free to choose the laws of a foreign jurisdiction to apply when interpreting their franchise agreement or for the purpose of dispute resolution. The courts in Hong Kong will generally respect party choice regarding jurisdiction subject only to the usual common law rules relating to conflict of laws.

B. International Arbitration Dispute Resolution

Please confirm that a court in your country would honor an election of international arbitration dispute resolution, and therefore refuse to hear any disputes arising under a franchise agreement.

Hong Kong can be described as a very pro-international arbitration jurisdiction. Arbitration matters are regulated by the *Arbitration Ordinance (Cap. 609)*, which draws heavily upon the UNCITRAL Model Law. With very few exceptions, Hong Kong courts would honor parties' election of international arbitration for dispute resolution.

Hong Kong is a signatory to the *Convention on the Recognition and Enforcement of Foreign Arbitral Awards* (the "New York Convention").[104]

IX. Non-Competitive Provisions

If the franchise agreement prohibits the franchisee from engaging in certain competitive activities during the term of the agreement, and for a 12-month period after the termination or expiration of the agreement, please comment on the enforceability of non-competition covenants in your country.

As there is no specific legislation dealing with franchising in Hong Kong, parties are at liberty to agree on their own non-competition covenants.

---

[104] *Editor's Note:* Arbitral awards made in Hong Kong are also enforceable in mainland China under the *Arrangement Concerning Mutual Enforcement of Arbitral Awards*, which is between mainland China and Hong Kong.

There are, however, common law restrictions that will apply to any non-competition provisions that parties may wish to insert in employees' contracts of employment. It is broad public policy that an employee should be entitled to work for whomever they wish after termination of employment. This is subject only to an employer's right to protect identifiable business interests by restricting the ability of an employee to work for direct competitors upon termination. In general, the post-termination restriction should not be termed as a "non-compete" provision *per se* but rather it should be addressed at a specific, identifiable threat and should be no wider than is reasonably necessary, both in terms of time and geography, to protect the employer's legitimate business interest.

Outside the employment sphere, Hong Kong does not currently have in force any specific competition or anti-trust legislation. However, the recently enacted *Competition Ordinance* (Cap. 619) ("Competition Ordinance") may have an impact in the future for franchises whose conduct has the object or effect of restricting competition in Hong Kong either through anti-competitive agreements between undertakings or through the abuse of substantial market power. The Competition Ordinance has not yet come into effect in Hong Kong.

X. Language Requirements

Does the law in your country require that a franchise agreement be translated into the local language in order to be enforceable between the parties?

There is no requirement that franchise agreements be translated into the local language in Hong Kong and a franchise agreement may be concluded in any language.

It should be noted however, that Hong Kong has two official languages, Chinese and English, for the purposes of any communications with the Government or court proceedings (see *Official Languages Ordinance* Cap. 5). Accordingly, in practice most franchise agreements in Hong Kong are drawn up in either English or Chinese.

XI. Other Significant Matters

Please advise as to whether there are any significant matters not addressed above of which a franchisor should be aware in connection with its entering into a franchise agreement in your country.

As previously noted, the key body dealing with franchising in Hong Kong is the Hong Kong Franchising Association—see www.franchise.org.hk. This is a body organized within the Hong Kong General Chamber of Commerce.[105]

---

[105] *Editor's Note:* Although there is no official record of the total number of franchise operators in Hong Kong, records of the Hong Kong Franchising Association indicate that there were about 55 franchise operators in 1992. The number of franchise operators grew to 95 in 1997, and ultimately reached 124 in 1999. At present, there are approximately 75 franchise operators in Hong Kong. Of these franchise operators, 56% are local franchises. 42.7% of the franchises in Hong Kong are in catering businesses, 37.3% in services, and 20% in retailing.

Franchising in India

Preeti Mehta

Kanga & Co.

Mumbai, India

India

I. Introduction

A. Historical Background of Country

By the 19th century, Great Britain had become the dominant political power on the subcontinent. The British Indian Army played a vital role in both World Wars. Nonviolent resistance to British rule, led by Mohandas Gandhi and Jawaharlal Nehru, eventually brought about independence from Britain in 1947.

Communal violence led to the subcontinent's bloody partition, which resulted in the creation of two separate states, India and Pakistan. The two countries have fought three wars since independence, the last of which in 1971 resulted in East Pakistan becoming the separate nation of Bangladesh. India's nuclear weapons tests in 1998 caused Pakistan to conduct its own tests that same year. In November 2008, terrorists originating from Pakistan conducted a series of coordinated attacks in Mumbai, India's financial capital.

In January 2011, India assumed a nonpermanent seat in the UN Security Council for the 2011–12 term.

Despite pressing problems such as significant overpopulation, environmental degradation, and extensive poverty, rapid economic development is fueling India's rise on the world stage.

B. Economy of Country

India is developing into an open-market economy, yet traces of its past policies remain. Economic liberalization, including industrial deregulation, privatization of state-owned enterprises, and reduced controls on foreign trade and investment, began in the early 1990s and has served to accelerate the country's growth, which has averaged more than 7% per year since 1997.

India's diverse economy encompasses traditional village farming, modern agriculture, handicrafts, a wide range of modern industries, and a multitude of services. Slightly more than half of the work force is in agriculture, but services are the major source of economic growth, accounting for nearly two-thirds of India's output, with less than one-third of its labor force. India has capitalized on its large educated English-speaking population to become a major exporter of information technology services and software workers.

In 2010, the Indian economy rebounded robustly from the global financial crisis—in large part because of strong domestic demand—and growth exceeded 8% year-on-year in real terms. However, India's economic growth began slowing in 2011 because of a tight monetary policy, intended to address persistent inflation, and a decline in investment, caused by investor pessimism about domestic economic reforms and about the global situation.

In late 2012, the Indian Government announced reforms and deficit reduction measures to reverse India's slowdown. The outlook on India's medium-term growth is positive due to a young population and corresponding low dependency ratio, healthy savings and investment rates, and increasing integration into the global economy.

India has many long-term challenges that it has not yet fully addressed, including poverty, inadequate physical and social infrastructure, limited non-agricultural employment opportunities, inadequate availability of quality basic and higher education, and accommodating rural-to-urban migration.

C. Franchise Legal Overview

Franchising in India is at an early stage and there is no franchise specific legislation that regulates the license or sale of franchise rights. It is governed by a number of statutes, rules, and regulations, e.g. *The Indian Contract Act, 1872, the Trademark Act, 1999 etc.*

India

II. Regulatory Requirements

A. Pre-Sale Disclosure

Please describe any pre-sale franchise disclosure or similar requirements that may apply to franchise transactions.

Laws of India do not require any pre-sale franchise disclosure or other requirements in respect of franchise transactions.

B. Government Approvals, Registrations, Filing Requirements

Please describe any necessary government approvals, registrations, or filing requirements that may apply to franchise transactions.

There is no approval, registration, or filing requirement for entering into or carrying out franchise transactions under Indian law other than the reporting and registration requirements (*See* Section III (Currency)) as mentioned below. A domestic franchisee is permitted to make payments to a foreign franchisor without obtaining any approval from the government or the Reserve Bank of India. However, such payments are required to be made through an authorized dealer (i.e., a bank). See Section III for the requirements of submitting an application-cum-declaration with an authorized dealer for the purpose of remittance and see also Section V of this chapter for information about the registrations required for trademarks.

Personal and corporate guarantees by a resident in favor of a non-resident are permitted without the approval of the Reserve Bank in very limited situations, which would normally not cover franchise or other commercial transactions. Accordingly, the issue of corporate or personal guarantees by a resident in favor of a non-resident franchisor would require prior approval of the Reserve Bank of India. The Reserve Bank of India can take two to three months to approve such guarantees.

C. Limits on Fees and Typical Term of Franchise Agreement

Please describe any limits upon the nature and extent of fees and the term of a typical franchise agreement.

Indian law does not set any limits or caps on the types or amounts of fees and the tenure of a franchise agreement. In this regard, the parties may contractually agree upon the desired terms and conditions in the franchise agreement.

III. Currency

If all payments under a franchise agreement must be made in immediately available U.S. Dollars, please advise as to any restrictions, reporting requirements, or regulations concerning the exchange, repatriation or remittance of U.S. Dollars.

The purchase of, or the payment for use of, a trademark or franchise, is a current account transaction under the Foreign *Exchange Management (Current Account Transaction) Rules, 2000*, and does not require any prior approval from the government or the Reserve Bank of India.[106] Payment can be made in freely convertible currency including U.S. Dollars, Euros, and British Pound Sterling. There are no further restrictions with respect to which currency can be used to make payments, provided payments are made using any freely convertible currency. However, any payment by a resident to a non-resident would be required to be made through an authorized dealer.

In this regard, standard procedures are prescribed for the resident franchisee to follow whereby the franchisee is required to designate a branch of an authorized dealer through which it would make remittances to the non-resident franchisor. The

---

[106] The Reserve Bank of India was established in 1935 pursuant to the *Reserve Bank of India Act, 1934*. The bank is India's central banking institution and its responsibilities include formulating monetary policy among other duties.

franchisee is also required to furnish an application-cum-declaration to the authorized dealer in the specified format providing the purpose of the payment.

IV. Taxes, Tariffs, and Duties

Please do not provide any in-depth comments on tax structuring. However, please provide your general comments on the typical amount of withholding tax that would apply and whether a "gross-up" provision contained in a franchise agreement would be enforceable in your country.

The income generated by the franchisor and franchisee in India would be subject to tax under the *Income Tax Act, 1961*. A franchisee is required to withhold tax on the payments to be made to the franchisor. The applicable rate of withholding tax for payment towards royalties and technical services is the lesser of (i) 10% and (ii) the rate prescribed in the double tax avoidance agreement between India and the relevant country to which remittance has to be made.

Further, a gross up provision contained in a franchise agreement is enforceable in India.

India has entered into double tax avoidance agreements with a number of countries,[107] including the United States, which

[107] India has double taxation avoidance treaties inter-alia with: Albania, Armenia, Austria, Australia, Bangladesh, Belarus, Belgium, Botswana, Brazil, Bulgaria, Canada, China, Colombia, Cyprus, Czech Republic, Denmark, Estonia, Ethiopia, Finland, Fiji, France, Georgia, Germany, Greece, Hungary, Iceland, Indonesia, Ireland, Israel, Italy, Japan, Jordan, Kazakhstan, Kenya, Korea, Kuwait, Kyrgyz Republic, Latvia, Lithuania, Luxembourg, Libya, Malaysia, Malta, Magnolia, Mauritius, Montenegro, Morocco, Mozambique, Myanmar, Namibia, Netherlands, Nepal, New Zealand, Norway, Oman, Philippines, Poland, Portuguese Republic, Qatar, Romania, Russia, Saudi Arabia, Serbia, Singapore, Slovenia, South Africa, Spain, Sri Lanka, Sudan, Sweden, Switzerland, Syria, Tajikistan, Tanzania, Thailand, Trinidad and Tobago, Turkey, Turkmenistan, Uganda, Ukraine, United Arab Emirates, United Kingdom, United Mexican States, United States, Uruguay, Uzbekistan, Vietnam, and Zambia.

provides relief from the double taxation of income derived from cross border transactions on which tax has been paid in India under the *Income Tax Act, 1961* and the income tax laws of the other country involved, respectively.

V. Trademarks

Please advise us as to whether there are any special requirements for granting a valid trademark license, including the use of a registered user agreement or a short trademark license agreement and any required filing of such an agreement with the trademark authorities.

In India, trademarks are governed by the *Trade Marks Act, 1999.* A registered trademark is one that is registered in the Register of Trade Marks under the *Trade Marks Act, 1999*. In the case of the infringement of a registered trademark, the owner of such trademark can take an action of infringement available under the statute. Whereas, in the case of infringement of an unregistered trademark, remedy is only available under the common law tort of "passing-off."

Trade Marks Act, 1999 does not provide for the licensing of trademarks. However, it deals with the appointment of a "registered user." A registered user does not have any right of assignment or transfer, but can institute infringement proceedings. To appoint a person as the registered user of trademark, a joint application by the owner of the trademark and the proposed registered user is required to be filed with the Registrar of Trade Marks. So long as an application is filed properly, it cannot be rejected by the Registrar of Trade Marks. However, there is no time specified for grant of approval by the Registrar of Trade Marks. It is important to note that a person cannot be made registered user of a trademark that is not registered under the *Trade Marks Act, 1999.*

Parties can contractually agree about the licensing of an unregistered trademark and there is no requirement to file or report under the law. However, under such licensing, the rights of the licensor and the licensee shall be only contractual and not under the *Trade Marks Act, 1999*.

VI. Restrictions on Transfer

Please advise as to whether there are any restrictions (1) on a franchisor to restrict transfers by a master franchisee, any interest in a master franchisee, or the assets of the master franchisee or (2) the ability of a master franchisee to control and/or restrict transfers of a subfranchisee's rights under a master franchise agreement, interest in the subfranchisee, or the assets of the subfranchisee.

There are no restrictions under Indian law (a) on a franchisor's ability to restrict transfer by a master franchisee of any interest in the master franchisee or the assets of the master franchisee, or (b) on the ability of a master franchisee to control and/or restrict transfer of a sub-franchisee's rights under (i) a master franchise agreement, (ii) an interest in the sub-franchisee, or (iii) the assets of the sub-franchisee. Hence, parties can contractually agree to such restrictions and the same would be enforceable by Indian Courts.

VII. Termination

Please advise us as to any laws relating to termination in your country, such as agency laws, required indemnity provisions, notice or "good cause" requirements, or other laws affecting termination of a franchise agreement. Please describe.

There are no specific laws that govern the termination of a franchise agreement and such action is governed by the contract between the parties. The *Indian Contract Act*, 1872 provides the freedom to parties to the contract to decide the terms thereof, including the termination.

VIII. Governing Law, Jurisdiction, and Dispute Resolution

A. Choice of Law of Foreign Jurisdiction

Please confirm whether the choice of law of a foreign jurisdiction would likely to be upheld under the law of the country, except for certain matters such as trademarks, bankruptcy and competition matters, which we assume would be governed by the law in your country.

The choice of law of a foreign jurisdiction under a franchise agreement between a resident franchisee and a non-resident franchisor is permitted under Indian law. However, in matters such as bankruptcy and liquidation, the governing law would be the law of the land of the party undergoing bankruptcy proceedings or liquidation. The Indian courts recognize and enforce the judgment/decree of the courts of another country that the Government of India has notified to be a reciprocating territory under Section 44A of the *Civil Procedure Code, 1908*. However, if the decree has been passed by a court of a country that is not notified under Section 44A of the *Civil Procedure Code, 1908*, then such a decree cannot be enforced by the Courts in India and in such a situation, the party seeking relief will have to file a suit before the Court in India to obtain the appropriate relief.

B. International Arbitration Dispute Resolution

Please confirm that a court in your country would honor an election of international arbitration dispute resolution, and therefore refuse to hear any disputes arising under a franchise agreement.

Arbitration and Conciliation Act, 1996 (of India) recognizes arbitration by a foreign/international dispute resolution body. India is also a signatory to the *Convention on the Recognition and Enforcement of Foreign Arbitral Awards* (the "New York

Convention") and an arbitration award passed in a foreign arbitration is enforceable in India. However, in light of a recent judgment of the Supreme Court of India in the case of *Bharat Aluminium Company and Ors. vs. Kaiser Aluminium Technical Service, Inc. and Ors.*,[108] where parties have agreed to international arbitration at a venue outside India, then Part 1 of *Arbitration and Conciliation Act, 1996* (which among other things, provides for recourse to Indian courts for injunctive relief) shall not be applicable. Hence, if in an international arbitration, an injunctive relief is required to be obtained from a Court in India, then the venue for the arbitration should be in India.

IX. Non-Competition Provisions

If the franchise agreement prohibits the franchisee from engaging in certain competitive activities during the term of the agreement, and for a 12-month period after the termination or expiration of the agreement, please comment on the enforceability of non-competition covenants in your country.

Non-competition provisions are governed by Section 27 of the *Indian Contract Act, 1872,* which states that an agreement in restraint of trade is void. The scope and application of Section 27 has been explained by judicial pronouncements of Indian Courts, which decide the legitimacy of such negative covenants on the principle of reasonableness. Under this emerging principle, the contractual provisions of non-competition would normally be upheld by the Courts in India beyond the expiration of the term of the agreement provided such restrictions are reasonable in scope and are found to be necessary to protect the bona fide interest of the aggrieved party. Imposition of a non-competition restriction under a franchise agreement that prohibits a master franchisee from engaging in competitive activities during the term of that such franchise agreement and for a period of twelve

[108] Reported as: *(2012) 9 SCC 552.*

months after the expiration of the agreement would be upheld by the Courts in India.

X. Language Requirements

Does the law in your country require that a franchise agreement be translated into the local language in order to be enforceable between the parties?

There is no mandatory requirement under Indian law with regards to any particular language; therefore, English language may be used without the need for translation into a local language.

XI. Other Significant Matters

Please advise as to whether there are any significant matters not addressed above of which a franchisor should be aware in connection with its entering into a franchise agreement in your country.

The issues discussed above constitute the significant issues relating to franchising in India. In addition thereto, we may briefly mention that if the consumer is not satisfied with the quality of goods he had purchased, he can approach the consumer dispute redressal forums established under the *Consumer Protection Act, 1986*. The said Act also provides the remedy in case of the deficiency in services. The remedies may vary from case to case, in the form of compensation, injunction, etc. The question may arise in a franchise chain as to who would be liable for the defect in products or deficiency in service; the consumers may make both the franchisor and the franchisee liable in respect of consequences of sale or consumption of defective goods.

The Franchising Association of India is a leading franchise association whose principal contact is Mr. C.Y. Pal.

Barista, Costa Coffee, McDonalds, Mothercare, Next, Papa John, Pizza Hut, Subway, Wetzel Pretzel etc. are some of the international franchise brands that operate in India. Some of the Indian brands are Aptech, Café Coffee Day, Jawed Habib, Mainland China, Lakme, etc.

Franchising in Indonesia

*Nurdin Adiwibowo, Freddy Karyadi,
and Gustaaf Reerink*

ABNR LAW

Jakarta, Indonesia

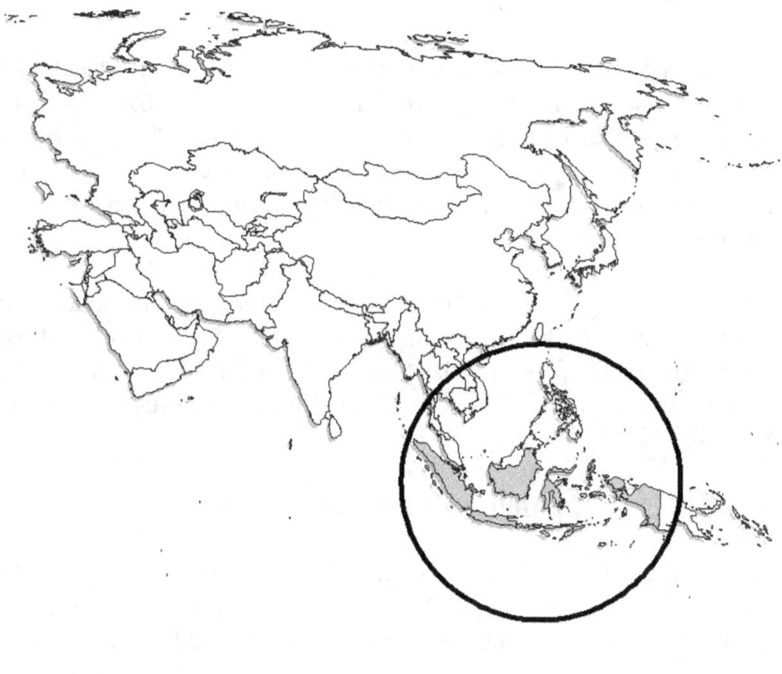

Indonesia

I. Introduction

A. Background

Since 1998, Indonesia has been developing into a modern democracy in which the rule of law is increasingly observed. Recent reforms in the field of, among others, foreign investment law, corporate law, intellectual property law, and antitrust law have contributed to Indonesia becoming an attractive country for investment. Despite these promising developments, corruption is still a major issue, which also has a negative impact on the possibilities to legally enforce franchising agreements and related rights.

B. Economy

Indonesia is the largest economy of Southeast Asia. Due to its robust annual economic growth rate of more than 6% in recent years, Indonesia just recently became a member of the G-20. A major driver for Indonesia's economic success is domestic consumption, which has increased significantly as a result of an emerging consumer class.

The franchising sector is one of the sectors that is benefiting from the above developments. For 2015, the Department of Trade (the DOT, formerly the Department of Trade and Industry) expects the number of domestic franchise businesses to increase by 15–20%.[109]

C. Franchise Legal Overview

Franchising in Indonesia is governed by *Government Regulation No. 42 of 2007* ("GR 42"), which was enacted and became effective on July 23, 2007. GR 42 is implemented by *Regulation of the Minister of Trade No. 53/M-DAG/PER/8/2012 dated*

[109] Bisnis Waralaba Diproyeksikan Naik 15-20 Persen Tahun Ini, *Kompas*, 21 January 2015.

August 24, 2012 ("Regulation 53"), which revoked the previous implementing regulation issued on August 21, 2008, and which was amended by *Regulation of the Minister of Trade No.57/M-DAG/PER/9/2014 dated September 17, 2014* ("Regulation 57"), *Regulation of the Minister of Trade No. 68/M-DAG/PER/10/2012 dated 29 October 2012* ("Regulation 68"), *Regulation of the Minister of Trade No. 07/M-DAG/PER/2/2013 dated 11 February 2013* ("Regulation 07"), *Regulation of the Minister of Trade No. 60/M-DAG/PER/9/2013 dated September 30, 2013* ("Regulation 60"), and *Decree of the Director General of Domestic Trade No. 138/PDN/KEP/10/2008 dated October 31, 2008* ("Decree 138").

The above regulations apply to franchisors and franchisees. A franchisor is a private individual or a business entity that grants a right to benefit from or use a franchise that is owned by the franchisor. The franchisor can be a domestic or foreign franchisor or subsequent franchisor. A franchisee is a private individual or business entity that receives a right from a franchisor to benefit from or use a franchise that is owned by the franchisor. A franchisee can be a domestic or foreign franchisee or subsequent franchisee. A franchise is a special right that is owned by a private individual or a business entity in relation to a business system with distinct characteristics in marketing products or services that has been proven profitable and may be used or applied by another party on the basis of a franchising agreement.

A franchise should:

- have unique business characteristics,
- be proven profitable,
- have written standards regarding the service and the goods/services offered,
- be easy to teach and apply,

- offer continuous support from the franchisor to the franchisee, and

- have registered intellectual property rights.

The Department of Trade is the governmental agency regulating franchising. It has delegated part of its authorities to the provincial and/or regency/municipal level.

In principle, Indonesian laws and regulations have a territorial effect, which means that they (i) only regulate activities undertaken within the Indonesian territorial boundaries, (ii) can only be enforced in Indonesia, and (iii) are only applicable to entities formally established or factually doing business in Indonesia.

II. Regulatory Requirements

A. Pre-Sale Disclosure

Please describe any pre-sale franchise disclosure or similar requirements that may apply to franchise transactions.

Under GR 42 and Regulation 53, there is an obligation to disclose the franchise offer prospectus and the franchise agreement to prospective franchisees no later than two weeks prior to the execution of the agreement.

The franchise offer prospectus and the franchise agreement should not only be disclosed to franchisees, but also to subsequent franchisees, which all fall under the definition of "franchisee" (see under Section I(C) above).

Although Regulation 53 does not contain any provisions relating to a transferee franchisee, it is common practice to disclose the franchise offer prospectus and the franchise agreement to a transferee franchisee no later than two weeks prior to signing the agreement.

In practice, a franchisor is not required to disclose the franchise offer prospectus and the franchise agreement to a renewing franchisee, unless material changes to the franchise or the rights and obligations of the parties are made.

As with a franchise renewal situation, local practice suggests that the franchise offer prospectus and the franchise agreement need not be disclosed to an existing franchisee planning to execute an agreement for an additional franchise.

B. Government Approvals, Registrations, Filing Requirements

Please describe any necessary government approvals, registrations or filing requirements that may apply to franchise transactions.

GR 42 and Regulation 53 require both a franchisor and a franchisee to hold a Franchise Registration Letter (*Surat Tanda Pendaftaran Waralaba* ("STPW") for the franchising business they are engaged in.

In order to obtain an STPW, a franchisor from abroad, franchisor from Indonesia, a subsequent franchisor of a foreign franchise, or a franchisor of a domestic franchise is required to register the franchise offer prospectus at the Department of Trade. The franchise offer prospectus that is registered by a franchisor from abroad should be legalized by a public notary with an accompanying explanation letter from the Trade Attaché or an official of a representative office of the Republic of Indonesia in the franchisor's country of origin.

The franchise offer prospectus should contain information on:

- The identity of the franchisor, including a copy of the identity card of the franchisor (in case the franchisor is a private person), the identity cards of the shareholders, the members of the board of directors, and the board of directors (in case the franchisor is a company (*Perseroan Terbatas* or PT));

- The legality of the franchisor business, including the Trade Business License (*Surat Izin Usaha Dagangan* or SIUP), the Tourism Business License (*Izin tetap Usaha Pariwisata*), the Permit for the Establishment of an Education Unit (*Surat Izin Pendidikan Satuan Pendidikan*);
- The history of business activities of the franchisor;
- The organizational structure of the franchisor;
- The financial statements of the last two years;
- The number of business units;
- The franchisees involved in the franchising business; and
- The rights and obligations of the franchisor and the franchisees.

If the prospectus is written in a foreign language, it should be translated into the Indonesian language.

Based on Regulation 57, a franchisor from abroad, franchisor from Indonesia, a subsequent franchisor of a foreign franchise, or a franchisor of a domestic franchise is now also required to submit a copy of the master franchise agreement to the Department of Trade. An official of the Department of Trade will review the master franchise agreement within a period of maximum 20 working days. If the master franchise agreement is not in contradiction with prevailing laws and regulations, the applicant franchisor may submit additional documents to complete the process of obtaining an STPW.

In order to obtain an STPW, a franchisee or a foreign franchise is required to register the franchise agreement to which it is a party at the Department of Trade, while a franchisee of a domestic franchise, a subsequent franchisee of a foreign franchise, and a franchisee of a domestic franchise is required to register the franchise agreement at the Trade Bureau of the Province of Jakarta Special Capital Region, the regency or municipal level or the local One Roof Services Office.

The competent authorities must issue an STPW within two business days after the submission of all required forms and documents. If the forms and documents are incomplete and not in order, the competent authorities must reject the application within two business days. In practice, it takes about two to three weeks to obtain an STPW.

Before the STPW is issued, the competent authorities may request the applicant to give a presentation about the franchising activities to the Evaluation Team, which consists of the Director General of Domestic Trade and others members as needed. The evaluation by the Evaluation Team constitutes a recommendation for the approval of the issuance of the STPW.

An STPW is valid for five years and may be extended for another five years. The STPW is no longer valid upon the lapse of the validity period, the termination of the Franchising Agreement or the franchisor and/or franchisee ceasing its business activities.

A franchisor and franchisee may only conduct business within the scope of their business license. In certain cases, the franchisor or franchisee may sell products supporting their main business, provided that these products do not exceed 10% of the total products that are being sold.

A franchisor or franchisee who fails to obtain an STPW may be imposed with an administrative sanction in the form of maximum three written warnings and a maximum Rp. 100,000,000 fine.

A franchisor or franchisee that has already obtained an STPW is required to submit an annual report regarding the Franchise activities to the Department of Trade on March 31 of the following year at the latest.

Franchisees from Indonesia, Subsequent franchisees of a foreign Franchise, and Subsequent franchisees of a domestic Franchise that have already obtained an STPW are required to submit a report regarding the franchise activities to the head of the Trade Bureau of the Province of Jakarta Special Capital Region or the regency or municipal level.

A franchisor or franchisee who fails to submit a report may be imposed with an administrative sanction in the form of maximum three written warnings, if following these warnings no report has been submitted, the suspension of the STPW for a maximum period of two months, and if after this period still no report has been submitted, a revocation of the STPW.

C. Limits on Fees and Typical Term of Franchise Agreement

Please describe any limits upon the nature and extent of fees and the term of a typical franchise agreement.

According to GR 42, a franchise agreement should contain at least the following provisions:

- □ name and address of the parties;
- □ type of intellectual property rights;
- □ business activities;
- □ rights and obligations of the parties;
- □ assistance, facilities, operational guidance, supervision, and marketing that will be provided by the franchisor to the franchisee;
- □ the business area;
- □ the term of the agreement;

- manner of payment of invoices;
- ownership, change of ownership, and inheritance rights;
- dispute resolution;
- the method to extend, cancel, and terminate the agreement.

Please note that GR 42 also puts a limit on choice of law (see under Section VII (A) below).

Apart from the above, *Article 1338 of the Indonesian Civil Code* recognizes the principle of freedom of contract. On the basis of this principle, parties are free to determine the content of the agreement made between them, as long as the agreement has fulfilled the requirements for an agreement to be valid as stipulated in *Article 1320 of the Indonesian Civil Code* (i.e., consent of the parties, capacity of the parties to enter into an agreement, certain subjects, and permissible cause (e.g., the agreement does not contravene prevailing regulations and principles of public order and morality)).

III. Currency

If all payments under a franchise agreement must be made in immediately available U.S. Dollars, please advise as to any restrictions, reporting requirements, or regulations concerning the exchange, repatriation or remittance of U.S. Dollars.

There is no foreign exchange control in Indonesia. However, the transfer of funds in foreign currencies to and from abroad is subject to a reporting obligation to Indonesia's central bank, Bank of Indonesia. The reporting obligation is on the side of the Indonesian party.

IV. Taxes, Tariffs, and Duties

Please do not provide any in-depth comments on tax structuring. However, please provide your general comments on the typical amount of withholding tax that would apply and whether a "grossup" provision contained in a franchise agreement would be enforceable in your country.

Indonesian tax law imposes a withholding tax upon the royalty payable by a franchisee. If the franchisor is an Indonesian tax resident or a non-Indonesian tax resident, the rate of withholding tax is 15%. If the franchisor is a non-resident, the rate of the withholding tax depends on whether the country where the franchisor resides or has it domicile has a tax avoidance arrangement with Indonesia. The 20% withholding tax upon the royalty paid by a franchisee is withheld if the franchisor's country does not have a double taxation arrangement with Indonesia. The relevant applicable tax treaty may reduce the withholding tax rate if the recipient can fulfill certain administrative documentations and beneficial ownership tests for passive income (in case the payment to non-resident franchisor falls under royalty clause in the tax treaty).

In addition to the withholding tax to be paid by the franchisor, a franchisee is required to pay Value Added Tax (VAT). The standard VAT rate is 10 percent. Certain goods and services, such as food and beverages served in restaurants and catering services, are not subject to VAT. The franchisee can request the tax authorities to refund the excess of input VAT over output VAT.

If the franchisee is active in a certain industry, such as restaurant, regional taxes may be imposed as well. The percentage of tax imposed may vary in each region.

As discussed under Section C above, *Article 1338 of the Indonesian Civil Code* recognizes the principle of freedom of contract. This also means that a gross up provision on withholding tax contained in a franchise agreement should in principle be enforceable in Indonesia.

V. Trademarks

Please advise us as to whether there are any special requirements for granting a valid trademark license, including the use of a registered user agreement or a short trademark license agreement and any required filing of such an agreement with the trademark authorities.

According to the Indonesian Trademark Law, trademark license agreements are to be recorded at the Trademark Office. However, to date regulations implementing the law have not yet been issued. In practice, a trademark license agreement may be recorded in the Indonesia Trademark Office (ITO), which will subsequently issue a receipt of submission of the agreement. However, the ITO will not process the registration until the issuance of implementing legislation.

VI. Restrictions on Transfer

Please advise as to whether there are any restrictions (1) on a franchisor to restrict transfers by a master franchisee, any interest in a master franchisee, or the assets of the master franchisee or (2) the ability of a master franchisee to control and/or restrict transfers of a subfranchisee's rights under a master franchise agreement, interest in the subfranchisee, or the assets of the subfranchisee.

If a franchise agreement is unilaterally terminated or dissolved by the franchisor before the expiry of the agreement, the franchisor is not permitted to appoint a new franchisee for the same region before the parties have reached agreement over the settlement of disputes (clean break) or there is a binding court ruling. The Department of Trade will not issue an STPW to the new franchisee until the clean break statement is obtained from the relevant franchisee. The clean break statement should indicate that the franchisor and the franchisee have settled all issues arising as a result of the termination. In practice a clean break statement is also required if an existing franchisee transfers its business to a new franchisee.

VII. Termination

Please advise us as to any laws relating to termination in your country, such as agency laws, required indemnity provisions, notice or "good cause" requirements, or other laws affecting termination of a franchise agreement. Please describe.

As discussed under Section II(C) above, each franchising agreement should contain provisions regarding the termination of the agreement. Parties can regulate that the franchising agreement may be terminated for convenience and/or for cause. A franchising agreement can only be terminated for cause if certain conditions for termination specified in the agreement have been fulfilled.

Under the Indonesian Civil Code, an agreement may be dissolved in case of a serious breach of contract. Other than in case of termination, dissolution has a retroactive effect.

Unless agreed otherwise between parties, the party wishing the agreement to be dissolved should request the court to do so. The court has the discretionary power to set a term within which the defaulting party can remedy the breach of contract. This term should be no longer than 30 days. If parties have waived *Article 1266 and Article 1267 of the Indonesian Civil Code*, a party wishing to dissolve the agreement, may need to give notice and equally set a term for the defaulting party to remedy the breach of contract.

Depending on the circumstances, in addition to terminating or requesting for dissolution of / dissolving the agreement, the non-defaulting party may claim damages for loss.

As discussed above, if a franchise agreement is unilaterally terminated or dissolved by the franchisor before the expiry of the agreement, the franchisor is not permitted to appoint a new franchisee for the same region before the parties have reached agreement over the settlement of disputes (clean break) or there is a binding court ruling. The Department of Trade will not issue an STPW to the new franchisee until the clean break statement is obtained from the relevant franchisee. The clean break statement should indicate that the franchisor and the franchisee have settled all issues arising as a result of the termination.

VIII. Governing Law, Jurisdiction, and Dispute Resolution

A. Choice of Law of Foreign Jurisdiction

Please confirm whether the choice of law of a foreign jurisdiction would likely to be upheld under the law of the country, except for certain matters such as trademarks, bankruptcy and competition matters, which we assume would be governed by the law in your country.

GR 42 requires that franchise arrangements are based on a franchise agreement that is governed by the laws of the Republic of Indonesia.

B. International Arbitration Dispute Resolution

Please confirm that a court in your country would honor an election of international arbitration dispute resolution, and therefore refuse to hear any disputes arising under a franchise agreement.

An election of international arbitration dispute resolution will generally be honored by the Indonesian courts. Please note:

(i) Indonesia is a signatory to the *1958 New York Convention on the Recognition of and Enforcement of Foreign Arbitral Awards* (the "New York Convention") and has adopted such convention into Indonesian law by way of *Presidential Decree No. 34 of 1981*.

(ii) Any final award rendered against any of the parties in the relevant documents by an arbitration panel duly appointed and empowered in accordance with the terms of the relevant documents would be recognized and enforced against each such party by the competent courts of the Republic of Indonesia without re-examination of the merits pursuant to *Law number 30 of 1999* and the New York Convention. However, enforcement of an arbitral award with respect to the relevant documents against any relevant party may be denied if:

(a) the award is issued by an arbitrator or arbitration tribunal in a foreign country which is not a signatory to an international convention on the recognition of foreign arbitral awards to which Indonesia is a signatory, or does not have a bilateral arrangement with the Republic of Indonesia for the recognition of arbitral awards on a reciprocal basis,

(b) the award is not on commercial law matters, or

(c) the award is against the public policy of the Republic of Indonesia.

The procedure for enforcement of foreign arbitral awards in Indonesia is regulated by *Law number 30 of 1999* and *Indonesian Supreme Court Regulation No. 1 of 1990* regarding the Procedure for the Enforcement of Foreign Arbitral Awards, which applies both to arbitral awards made in States bound by the 1958 New York Convention and to arbitral awards from States having a relevant bilateral agreement with Indonesia. In addition, to enforce the award it is necessary to register the award with the Clerk of Central Jakarta District Court, obtain a writ of execution (known as an *Exequatur*) from the Chairman of the Central Jakarta District Court or, in case the award which involves the Republic of Indonesia as one of the parties in dispute, from the Supreme Court of the Republic of Indonesia (through the Central Jakarta District Court). With respect to this matter, we draw your attention, however, that there have been a number of instances where Indonesian Courts have refused to give effect to the enforcement of arbitration agreements or foreign arbitration awards for other specified or unspecified reasons.

IX. Non-Competition Provisions

If the franchise agreement prohibits the master franchisee from engaging in certain competitive activities during the term of the agreement, and for a 12-month period after the termination or expiration of the agreement, please comment on the enforceability of non-competition covenants in your country.

In 2009, the Indonesian Commission for the Supervision of Business Supervision (*Komisi Pengawasan Persaingan Usaha* or KPPU) enacted *Regulation of the KPPU No. 6 of 2009*. The regulation gives guidelines regarding provisions that, by exemption to applicable general antitrust rules, may be used in franchising agreements and provisions that are in violation with general antitrust rules.

The principle of exemption with regard to franchising agreements is based on the idea that in principle certain provisions in franchise agreements that are essential to protect the common identity and the reputation of the franchising network or to protect the confidentiality of intellectual property rights that are part of the franchising concept may be exempt from applicable general antitrust rules. Based on this principle, a franchise agreement may contain provisions that create certain obligations on the part of the franchisee in order to protect the franchising concept and intellectual property rights that are owned by the franchisor. Such provisions for example create an obligation on the part of the franchisee to use a business method that is determined by the franchisor, a prohibition to change the franchising location without informing the franchisor or the prohibition to share information regarding intellectual property rights with third parties, even after the expiry of the franchising agreement.

Indonesia

In principle, a limitation of business activities by the franchisor within an agreed area and a limitation of business activities of the franchisee with this area is also permissible. However, this may not result in an absolute protection of the area of sales, for instance by directly or indirectly hindering customers to obtain products or services for the reason that they reside outside the agreed area and effectively dividing the market. In other words, a limitation of the area in which the franchisee may undertake business activities that is not create to form a franchising network but instead is meant to limit the market and customers is in violation with antitrust rules.

Provisions in franchising agreements regarding the obligation to obtain certain products from the franchisor or a certain third party are usually meant to protect the quality standard of franchising products. This protection of the minimum quality of products is important in a franchising business in order to uphold the identity of the franchising concept itself. However, the obligation to obtain certain products is not permissible as far as it does not relate to products of which the intellectual property rights are essential to the franchising concept. Equally, it is not allowed for a franchisor to prohibit a franchisee to acquire products and/or services from third parties which products and/or services fulfill the quality standards determined by the franchisor.

Franchising agreements commonly contain provisions which aim to maintain resale prices. These provisions are usually meant to prevent that franchisees sell their products at a price that would harm the franchising identity/image. According to the guidelines, a recommended (and thus non-binding) resale price would be permissible. However, provisions regarding resale prices which would lead to a price cartel, so that there can be no competition on price would be in violation with antitrust rules.

Provisions that oblige franchisees to acquire various sorts of products from the franchisor to guarantee the quality standard of the franchising concept would not be contradictory to business competition principles. However, such an obligation may limit product substitution and thus hinder competition. Therefore, an obligation for the franchisee to acquire products that are not related to the franchising concept, creating to an entry barrier for other entrepreneurs, is not permissible.

Provisions that prohibit franchisees to undertake business activities that could compete with the franchising business network can be justified. Such an prohibition is usually meant to protect the intellectual property rights of the franchisor and guarantee the identity and reputation of the franchising network, particularly if the franchisor has already transferred certain knowhow. However, the long term hindering of equal business activities may hinder competition and technological progress, this negatively influencing economic efficiency. Therefore, provisions that prohibit franchisees to undertake equal business activities for a long period after the expiry of the franchising agreement should be avoided. In determining the term which does not limit business competition the KPPU will take various aspects into consideration, including the franchising technology, the investments made and the nature of the franchising products. If the franchising technology is already part of the public domain, the term that equal business activities may not be undertaken by franchisees is usually one year.

The guidelines explicitly state that franchise agreements containing provisions which may hinder or put a limit on franchisees in doing business, potentially resulting in a monopoly or unhealthy business competition, are not exempt from applicable general antitrust rules. This means that franchising agreements containing provisions that lead to price fixing, limitation of supplies, tying of franchise products with products outside the franchising concept, market division, and non-competition clauses that remain applicable after the expiry of the agreement are potentially in violation with general antitrust principles.

X. Language Requirements

Does the law in your country require that a franchise agreement be translated into the local language in order to be enforceable between the parties?

On the basis of GR 42, if a franchise agreement is written in a foreign language, the agreement must be translated into the Indonesian language.

XI. Other Significant Matters

Please advise as to whether there are any significant matters not addressed above of which a franchisor should be aware in connection with its entering into a franchise agreement in your country.

Regulation 53 and in particular Regulations 68 and 7 contains provisions which aim to support and protect local small and medium enterprises.

Regulation 53 prohibits a franchisor to appoint a direct or indirect subsidiary or an affiliated company as a franchisee.

In addition, Regulation 53 requires a franchisor and a franchisee to use and display a franchise logo in their central office and all outlets in accordance with Ministerial Regulation 60.

Regulation 53 requires a franchisor and franchisee to use raw materials, business equipment and sell products that are at least 80% domestically produced. In certain cases, the Department of Trade may give permission, upon recommendation by the Evaluation Team, to use raw materials, business equipment and sell products that are less than 80% domestically produced.

The same regulation also requires a franchisor to give support to the franchisee in the form of education and training in the management of franchising, regular guidance in operational management, support in developing business through promotion (advertising, leaflets/catalogues/brochures or exhibitions) and research on and development of business and products that can be traded.

A franchisor or franchisee who fails to conduct business within the scope of their business license, submit an annual report regarding the franchise activities to the Department of Trade, use and display a franchise logo in their central office and all outlets, use raw materials, business equipment and sell products that are at least 80% domestically produced or a franchisor who fails to give support to the franchisee may be imposed with an administrative sanction in the form of maximum three written warnings, if following these warnings no report has been submitted, the suspension of the STPW for a maximum period of two months, and if after this period still no report has been submitted, a revocation of the STPW.

Finally, the regulation requires a franchisor to cooperate with local small and medium entrepreneurs in the local area as franchisees or goods/service supplier as long as they meet the requirements set by the franchisor. Regulation 53 does not stipulate what will be the sanction if a franchisor fails to meet this requirement.

Regulation 68 creates specific obligations for franchisors and franchisees that own outlets of so-called Modern Shops. A Modern Shop is a shop with an independent service system, which sells various types of retail products, for instance minimarkets, supermarkets, department stores, hypermarkets or wholesale grocery stores. Most importantly, Regulation 68 limits the number of outlets of so-called Modern Shops that may owned by franchisors and franchisees to 150. In the event the franchisors or franchisees owns 150 outlets and want to open more outlets, at least 40% of these extra outlets should be franchised to local small and medium business partners. This obligation only applies to Modern Shops of, in case of mini markets, less than 400 m2, in case of supermarkets, less than 1,200 m2, and in case of department stores, less than 2,000 m2. Furthermore, this obligation does not apply to franchisors and franchisees (i) who have not yet made any profit, as evidenced by financial statements audited by a registered accountant, (ii) following an evaluation by the Evaluation Team, are deemed to be unable to find a local business partner who can become a franchisee.

Franchisors and franchisees must meet the above obligation within five years after the enactment of the regulation (so before October 29, 2017) by each year releasing at least 20% of the outlets that are required to be franchised by the franchisor or franchisee.

The Regulation creates obligations similar to those based on Regulation 53, namely that a franchisor should sell products that are at least 80% domestically produced and is required to give support to the franchisee in the form of training and guidance in the management and in meeting services standards and quality of products that are being traded. The same sanctions may be imposed as those which may be imposed on the basis of Regulation 53.

Regulation 7 creates specific obligations for franchisors and franchisees that own food and beverage outlets, such as restaurants, bars and cafes. Most importantly, Regulation 68 limits the number of food and beverage outlets that may be owned by franchisors and franchisees to 250. In the event the franchisors or franchisees owns 250 outlets and want to open more outlets, these extra outlets should be franchised or a collaboration with capital participation should be entered into. If franchisors or franchisees opt for a collaboration with capital participation, the other party should invest, in case of an investment of Rp 10 billion or less, at least 40% and in case of an investment of more than Rp. 10 billion, at least 30%. Priority should be given to franchising to or entering into a collaboration with local small or medium business partners.

Franchisors and franchisees must meet the above obligation within five years after the enactment of the regulation (so before February 14, 2018).

Indonesia

Regulation 7 creates obligations similar to those based on Regulations 53 and 68, namely that franchisors and franchisees should use raw materials and business equipment that are at least 80% domestically produced. In certain cases, the Department of Trade may give permission, upon recommendation by the Evaluation Team, to use raw materials, business equipment and sell products that are less than 80% domestically produced. Furthermore, franchisors are required to give support to the franchisee in the form of training and guidance in the management and in meeting services standards and quality of products that are being traded. The same sanctions may be imposed as those which may be imposed on the basis of Regulations 53 and 68.

Franchising in Japan

Kakuji Mitani

MOMO-O, MATSUO & NAMBA

Tokyo, Japan

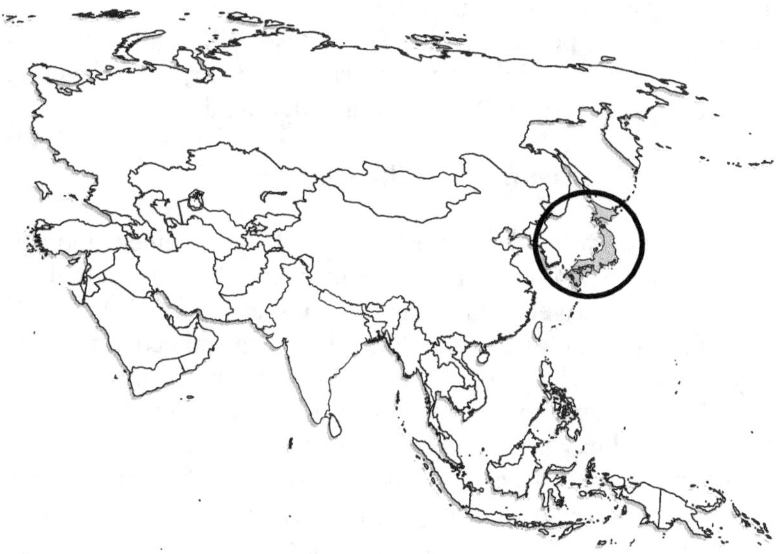

Japan

I. Introduction

A. Historical Background of the Country

After Japan's defeat in World War II, it recovered to become an economic power and an ally of the U.S. While the emperor retains his throne as a symbol of national unity, elected politicians hold actual decision-making power. Following three decades of unprecedented growth, Japan's economy experienced a major slowdown starting in the 1990s, but the country remains a major economic power. In March 2011, Japan's strongest-ever earthquake, and an accompanying tsunami, devastated the northeast part of Honshu island, killing thousands and damaging several nuclear power plants. The catastrophe had a negative impact on the country's economy and its energy infrastructure, and tested its ability to deal with humanitarian disasters.

B. Economy of the Country

In the years following World War II, government-industry cooperation, a strong work ethic, mastery of high technology, and a comparatively small defense allocation (1% of GDP) helped Japan develop a technologically advanced economy. Two notable characteristics of the post-war economy were the close interlocking structures of manufacturers, suppliers, and distributors, known as *keiretsu*, and the guarantee of lifetime employment for a substantial portion of the urban labor force. Both features are now eroding under the dual pressures of global competition and domestic demographic change.

Japan's industrial sector is heavily dependent on imported raw materials and fuels. A tiny agricultural sector is highly subsidized and protected, with crop yields among the highest in the world. Usually self-sufficient in rice, Japan imports about 60% of its food on a caloric basis. Japan maintains one of the world's largest fishing fleets and accounts for nearly 15% of the global catch.

Japan

For three decades, overall real economic growth had been spectacular - a 10% average in the 1960s, a 5% average in the 1970s, and a 4% average in the 1980s. Growth slowed markedly in the 1990s, averaging just 1.7%, largely because of the after effects of inefficient investment and an asset price bubble in the late 1980s that required a protracted period of time for firms to reduce excess debt, capital, and labor. Modest economic growth continued after 2000, but the economy has fallen into recession three times since 2008.

A sharp downturn in business investment and global demand for Japan's exports in late 2008 pushed Japan into recession. Government stimulus spending helped the economy recover in late 2009 and 2010, but the economy contracted again in 2011 as the massive 9.0 magnitude earthquake in March disrupted manufacturing. Recovery spending helped boost GDP in early 2012, but slower global economic growth began weakening Japan's export-oriented economy by mid-year. Electricity supplies became tight after Japan tentatively shut down almost all of its nuclear power plants after the Fukushima Daiichi nuclear reactors were crippled by the earthquake and resulting tsunami. In 2015, there are huge social debates regarding resuming nuclear power plants.

Prime Minister Shinzo Abe, who was elected again in the end of 2012, has declared the economy his government's top priority; he has said he will increase stimulus spending and press the Bank of Japan to loosen monetary policy. Measured on a purchasing power parity (PPP) basis that adjusts for price differences, Japan in 2012 stood as the fourth-largest economy in the world after second-place China, which surpassed Japan in 2001, and third-place India, which edged out Japan in 2012. The new government will continue a longstanding debate on restructuring the economy and reining in Japan's huge government debt, which exceeds 200% of GDP. Persistent deflation, reliance on exports to drive growth, and an aging and shrinking population are other major long-term challenges for the economy.

Japan

C. Franchise Legal Overview

Franchises are regulated as a "qualified chain-store business" under the *Small and Medium-sized Retail Business Promotion Act* ("Act"),[110] supplemented by the *Ministerial Order to Implement the Act* ("Ministerial Order"); concurrently, *Guidelines on Franchising under the Antimonopoly Act* ("JFTC Guidelines")[111] issued by Japan Fair Trade Commission (JFTC) are also applicable.[112]

---

[110] The Act defines a "chain-store business" as "a business in which, according to standard contract, goods are continually sold, directly or by a designated third party, and assistance over the operation is continually given, principally to medium- or small-sized retailers." (Article 4.(5)) According to Article 2.(1) of the Act, a retailer is "medium- or small-sized if (a) its amount of the stated capital is 50 million yen or less, (b) the number of its permanent employees is 50 or less, or (c) it is an individual or a cooperative." The regulation set forth in the Act shall apply only to the transaction with such "medium- or small-sized" retailers.

[111] The JFTC Guidelines are available online in English. See http://www.jftc.go.jp/en/legislation_gls/imonopoly_guidelines.files/franchise.pdf (last visited June 7, 2015).

[112] The JFTC Guidelines speculate as follows concerning the definition of "franchise system": "The franchise system is defined in many ways. However, the franchise system is generally considered to be a form of business in which the head office provides the member with the rights to use a specific trademark and trade name, and provides coordinated control, guidance, and support for the member's business and its management. The head office may provide support in relation to the selling of commodities and the provision of services. In return, the member pays the head office . . . . This document is intended for businesses that fit this definition and that have the characteristics mentioned . . . below, irrespective of what the business is called . . . . [1.(1)] The basis of the trading relationship for the franchise system is a franchise agreement between the head office and the member. This agreement is a standardized agreement that generally includes the following provisions: (a) A provision that grants the member permission to use the trademark and trade name of the head office; (b) A provision for the head office to provide the member with control and guidance to ensure there is a unified corporate identity for the business and to ensure that the member can maintain their business; (c) A provision for the member to pay the head office for the services mentioned in the

(Footnote continued on next page)

II. Regulatory Requirements

A. Pre-Sale Disclosure

Please describe any pre-sale franchise disclosure or similar requirements that may apply to franchise transactions.

Under the Act, a franchisor is required to deliver a disclosure document before concluding a contract that falls into the category of "qualified chain-store business" with a franchisee.[113] The disclosure document shall include terms and conditions concerning the initial fee or development fee at the commencement of business, sales of goods/products by a franchisee, franchisor's management of business operation, trademark, store name, renewal and termination of the agreement, etc.

Further, the Ministerial Order sets forth the matters to be contained in a disclosure document in more detail. These include, for instance, the names of franchisor's directors, the number of franchisor's employees, franchisor's balance sheet and income statement for the past three years, the number of franchisees for the past three years, the number of lawsuits concerning the franchise agreement, non-competition obligation, the amount of penalties, etc.

The Japan Franchise Association[114] ("JFA"), a trade association certified by the Ministry of Economy, Trade and Industry and comprised of major companies operating franchise businesses, has established voluntary principles and rules, although a franchisor is not required to join the JFA under the Act. As a

(Footnote continued from previous page)

previous two provisions; and (d) A provision concerning the termination of a franchise agreement." (1.(3))

113 Article 11.1

114 http://www.jfa-fc.or.jp.e.ek.hp.transer.com/ (last visited June 7, 2015).

practical matter, a major franchisor often submits to the JFA its disclosure document and obtains JFA's certification. The JFA's voluntary rule on disclosure requires that the prospective franchisee must be given seven days or more for consideration of the disclosure document before concluding the franchise agreement.

Concurrently, the JFTC Guidelines require a franchisor to disclose the information concerning its franchising system, including but not limited to, matters relating to the supply of products, the cost of guidance to a franchisee, royalties for the use of the trademark and trade name and for guidance in management, and loans extended to a franchisee. In addition, the JFTC Guidelines provide that, "from the viewpoint of the Antimonopoly Act," a disclosure document must be delivered sufficiently in advance so that the prospective franchisee can make an informed decision.[115]

B. Government Approvals, Registrations, Filing Requirements

Please describe any necessary government approvals, registrations, or filing requirements that may apply to franchise transactions.

There are no legal requirements concerning government approvals, registrations or filings that may apply to franchise transactions. As a practical matter, however, a franchisor often registers its disclosure document with the JFA and obtains the JFA's certification.

---

[115] The JFTC Guidelines, Section 2.(2).A. *Editor's note*: As a practical matter, to comply with this voluntary rule it is recommended that the prospective franchisee be given seven days or more to review the disclosure document before executing the franchise agreement.

C. Limits on Fees and Typical Term of Franchise Agreement

Please describe any limits upon the nature and extent of fees and the term of a typical franchise agreement.

There is no specific restriction regarding the nature and extent of fees and the term of a franchise agreement under the franchise law. However, an excessively "unilateral" franchise agreement may be deemed in violation of the Antimonopoly Act as an unfair trade practice. The JFTC Guidelines provide that "when a franchise agreement or the actions of the head office [franchisor] are considered to exceed the boundaries for the conduct of proper business based on the franchise system, thereby providing the member [franchisee] with undue disadvantage regarding normal commercial practice, Item 14 (abuse of dominant bargaining position) of the General Designation[116] may be applied. In addition, where the restrictions placed on a member are illegal, Item 10 (Tie-in sale) or Item 13 (Dealing on restrictive terms) of the General Designation may be applied."[117] In terms of the JFTC Guidelines, a franchisor shall consider carefully the legality of the following conditions of the franchise agreement: (1) restriction on suppliers, (2) mandatory purchasing quotas, (3) restrictions on bargain sales, (4) revisions to the franchise agreement after it has been signed, (5) restrictions on trade after termination of an agreement, (6) tie-in sales and dealing on restrictive terms, and (7) restrictions on the sales price.

---

[116] "General Designation" is published by the JFTC as a category of an unfair trade practice under the Antimonopoly Act (Fair Trade Commission Public Notice No. 15 of June 18, 1982). *See* http://www.jftc.go.jp/en/legislation_gls/unfairtradepractices.html (last visited June 7, 2015).

[117] After the amendment in 2009, the Antimonopoly Act itself stipulates both "abuse of dominant bargaining position" and "dealing on restrictive terms" as a category of "Unfair Trade Practices" which could be subject to penalty surcharge. At the same time, the terms of "General Designation" are slightly revised.

III. Currency

If all payments under a franchise agreement must be made in immediately available U.S. Dollars, please advise as to any restrictions, reporting requirements, or regulations concerning the exchange, repatriation or remittance of U.S. Dollars.

There is no restriction on the payment under a franchise agreement being made in U.S. Dollars. If the payment (both inbound and outbound) exceeds certain thresholds under the *Foreign Exchange and Foreign Trade Control Act*, a party is required to report it to the Bank of Japan.

IV. Taxes, Tariffs, and Duties

Please do not provide any in-depth comments on tax structuring. However, please provide your general comments on the typical amount of withholding tax that would apply and whether a "gross-up" provision contained in a franchise agreement would be enforceable in your country.

A withholding tax of 20% will be imposed on royalties paid to non-residents or foreign entities pursuant to the *Income Tax Act*, in principle. However, Japan has a double taxation treaty with more than sixty countries, including the United States, and a withholding tax is exempted or reduced depending upon such treaty. The exemption may be obtained on an application-basis to the competent Japanese tax authority.

The "gross-up" provision is enforceable in Japan, in principle. Please take notice that the "gross-up" provision may affect the total amount to be paid by a franchisee to a franchisor, and therefore a franchisor is required to explain the impact of the provision very carefully and let a franchisee fully understand it, or the provision will possibly be declared invalid by courts in Japan.

V. Trademarks

Please advise us as to whether there are any special requirements for granting a valid trademark license, including the use of a registered user agreement or a short trademark license agreement and any required filing of such an agreement with the trademark authorities.

There are no special requirements for granting a valid trademark license in Japan,[118] although it is very important for a franchisor to register its trademark(s) at the Patent Office before entering into the market because Japan adopts the registration principle (first-to-file rule) under the Trademark Act. As long as certain criteria are met, the trademark can be registered even if the trademark is not currently in use, while the registered trademark is broadly protected under the Trademark Act.

The license of the registered trademark is usually a part of the franchise agreement. Thus, a franchisor must register its trademark(s) at the Patent Office in order to exercise its trademark rights. If the same or similar trademark is already registered by a third party at the Patent Office, the use of the trademark could be prohibited by an injunctive order claimed by the trademark owner.

VI. Restrictions on Transfer

Please advise as to whether there are any restrictions (1) on a franchisor to restrict transfers by a master franchisee, any interest in a master franchisee, or the assets of the master franchisee or (2) the ability of a master franchisee to control and/or restrict transfers of a subfranchisee's rights under a

[118] The license agreement is not required to be registered, but an exclusive license can be registered under the Trademark Act. If there is a registration of an exclusive license, a trademark owner is not able to exercise the right as a trademark owner, unless such registration has expired. Practically speaking, the registration of an exclusive license is not common.

master franchise agreement, an interest in the subfranchisee, or the assets of the subfranchisee.

There are no special provisions regarding transfer of the franchise agreement. However, in the event that the provision proscribing such transfer is unreasonably and unilaterally in favor of a franchisor and against the public order and morality under the Civil Law of Japan, the provision will be deemed invalid by courts in Japan. The JFTC could also consider the provision against the JFTC Guidelines.

VII. Termination

Please advise us as to any laws relating to termination in your country, such as agency laws, required indemnity provisions, notice or "good cause" requirements, or other laws affecting termination of a franchise agreement. Please describe.

There are no special provisions regarding the termination of the franchise agreement; provided, however, the terms and conditions concerning termination must be fully explained to the franchisee before the signing of the agreement under the Act.

In addition, as well as the transfer provision above, in the event that the provision concerning the termination is unreasonably and unilaterally in favor of a franchisor and against the public order and morality under the Civil Law, the provision will be deemed invalid by courts in Japan. As well, the JFTC could consider the provision against the JFTC Guidelines.

Further, it should be noted that, as a general rule, when two parties are in a continuous relationship of distribution, court precedents in Japan tend to protect the interests of the terminated party, and to restrict the right of the terminating party to terminate the contract, without any notice or compensation, provided that the terminated party has not breached the contract or has not acted in bad faith. Thus, if a franchisor intends to terminate the agreement, caution should be exercised and the franchisor should act in full compliance with the procedures set forth in the agreement.

VIII. Governing Law, Jurisdiction, and Dispute Resolution

A. Choice of Law of Foreign Jurisdiction

Please confirm whether the choice of law of a foreign jurisdiction would likely to be upheld under the law of the country, except for certain matters such as trademarks, bankruptcy and competition matters, which we assume would be governed by the law in your country.

Under the *Act on General Rules for Application of Laws*, the parties may select the governing law at the conclusion of the agreement.[119]

B. International Arbitration Dispute Resolution

Please confirm that a court in your country would honor an election of international arbitration dispute resolution, and therefore refuse to hear any disputes arising under a franchise agreement.

If the franchise agreement contains a provision under which any dispute shall be resolved by arbitration, a court in Japan is required to dismiss a filed lawsuit under the *Arbitration Act*.[120]

---

119 Article 7 stipulates as follows: "The formation and effect of a juridical act shall be governed by the law of the place chosen by the parties at the time of the act."

120 Article 14. Provided, however, that this principle shall not apply (i) when the arbitration agreement is null and void, cancelled, or for other reasons invalid; (ii) when arbitration proceedings are inoperative or incapable of being performed based on the arbitration agreement; or (iii) when the request is made by the defendant subsequent to the presentation of its

(Footnote continued on next page)

Japan is a signatory to the *Convention on the Recognition and Enforcement of Foreign Arbitral Awards* (the "New York Convention").

IX. Non-Competition Provisions

If the franchise agreement prohibits the franchisee from engaging in certain competitive activities during the term of the agreement, and for a 12-month period after the termination or expiration of the agreement, please comment on the enforceability of non-competition covenants in your country.

A non-competition provision in a franchise agreement is generally permitted in terms of the purpose of the franchise system; provided, however, that unreasonable restrictions on the franchisee's business might be deemed illegal by the JFTC under the Antimonopoly Act.

As for non-competition obligations of a franchisee after the termination, the JFTC Guidelines stipulate that the obligations that are not necessary to protect its franchise business or know-how may violate the Antimonopoly Act. Although it depends on each case, as a general rule, a 12-month period after the termination of the agreement may be considered reasonable under current business conditions.

X. Language Requirements

Does the law in your country require that a franchise agreement be translated into the local language in order to be enforceable between the parties?

(Footnote continued from previous page)

statement in the oral hearing or in the preparations for argument proceedings on the substance of the dispute. Id.

The Act provides no requirement on the language used for the disclosure documents or franchise agreement, nor is a language requirement explicitly mentioned in the JFTC Guidelines.

Thus, there is no legal limitation on the disclosure to a potential franchisee being made in a foreign language. However, the disclosure must be fully understood by a franchisee under the Act and the JFTC Guidelines. As a practical matter, a disclosure document and a franchise agreement is prepared in Japanese for a franchisee's understanding.

XI. Other Significant Matters

Please advise as to whether there are any significant matters not addressed above of which a franchisor should be aware in connection with its entering into a franchise agreement in your country.

Although there is no legal requirement that a franchisor must become a member of the official franchise trade association, the JFA, many major franchisors and franchisees are JFA members. The JFA reviews disclosure documents and certifies their creation in accordance with the Act. The JFA operates the website "*The Franchise*"[121] for a franchisee, where disclosure documents of major franchisors, including but not limited to 7-Eleven Japan, McDonald's Japan, and 31 Ice Cream (Baskin-Robbins), are available to the public.

---

[121] http://frn.jfa-fc.or.jp/ (Japanese only) (last visited June 7, 2015).

Franchising in Kazakhstan

Saule Akhmetova

GRATA LAW FIRM

Almaty, Kazakhstan

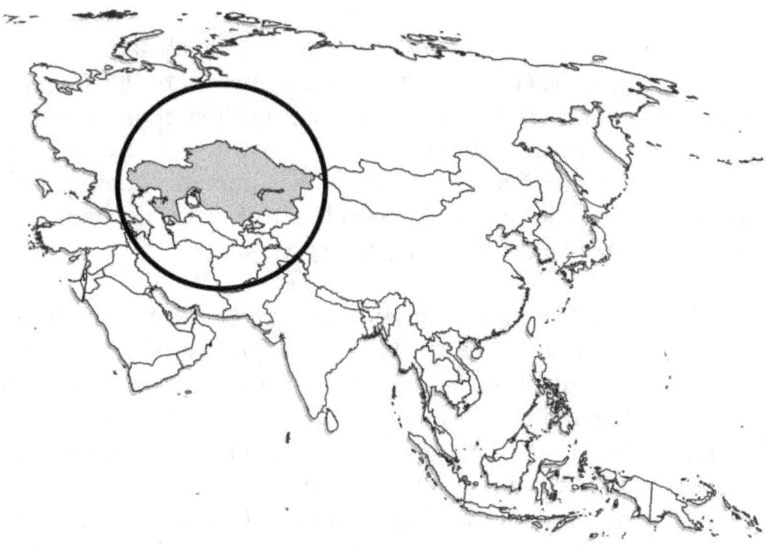

Kazakhstan

I. Introduction

A. Historical Background of Country

Ethnic Kazakhs, a mix of Turkic and Mongol nomadic tribes, migrated to the region in what is now Kazakhstan by the 13th century. The area was conquered by Russia in the 18th century, and Kazakhstan became a Soviet Republic in 1936. During the 1950s and 1960s agricultural "Virgin Lands" program, Soviet citizens were encouraged to help cultivate Kazakhstan's northern pastures. This influx of immigrants (mostly Russians, but also some other deported nationalities) skewed the ethnic mixture and enabled non-ethnic Kazakhs to outnumber natives.

Non-Muslim ethnic minorities departed Kazakhstan in large numbers from the mid-1990s through the mid-2000s and a national program has repatriated about a million ethnic Kazakhs back to Kazakhstan. These trends have allowed Kazakhs to become the titular majority again. This dramatic demographic shift has also undermined the previous religious diversity and made the country more than 70 percent Muslim.

Kazakhstan's economy is larger than those of all the other Central Asian states largely due to the country's vast natural resources. Current issues include: developing a cohesive national identity; managing Islamic revivalism; expanding the development of the country's vast energy resources and exporting them to world markets; diversifying the economy outside the oil, gas, and mining sectors; enhancing Kazakhstan's economic competitiveness; developing a multiparty parliament and advancing political and social reform; and strengthening relations with neighboring states and other foreign powers.

B. Economy of Country

Kazakhstan, geographically the largest of the former Soviet republics, excluding Russia, possesses enormous fossil fuel reserves and plentiful supplies of other minerals and metals, such as uranium, copper, and zinc. It also has a large agricultural sector featuring livestock and grain. In 2002 Kazakhstan became the first country in the former Soviet Union to receive an investment-grade credit rating.

Extractive industries have been and will continue to be the engine of Kazakhstan's growth, although the country is aggressively pursuing diversification strategies. Landlocked, with restricted access to the high seas, Kazakhstan relies on its neighbors to export its products, especially oil and grain. Although its Caspian Sea ports, pipelines, and rail lines carrying oil have been upgraded, civil aviation and roadways continue to need attention. Telecoms are improving, but require considerable investment, as does the information technology base. Supply and distribution of electricity can be erratic because of regional dependencies, but the country is moving forward with plans to improve reliability of electricity and gas supply to its population.

At the end of 2007, global financial markets froze up and the loss of capital inflows to Kazakhstani banks caused a credit crunch. The subsequent and sharp fall of oil and commodity prices in 2008 aggravated the economic situation, and Kazakhstan plunged into recession. While the global financial crisis took a significant toll on Kazakhstan's economy, it has rebounded well, helped by prudent government measures. Rising commodity prices have helped the recovery. Despite solid macroeconomic indicators, the government realizes that its economy suffers from an overreliance on oil and extractive industries, the so-called "Dutch disease." In response, Kazakhstan has embarked on an ambitious diversification program, aimed at developing targeted sectors like transport, pharmaceuticals, telecommunications, petrochemicals and food processing. In 2010, Kazakhstan joined the Belarus-Kazakhstan-Russia Customs Union in an effort to boost foreign investment and improve trade relationships.

C. Franchise Legal Overview

The relationship between franchisor and franchisee in Kazakhstan is mainly regulated by *Civil Code* and the specific

Law on Franchising. Significant changes were introduced to the legislation in April 2015 to harmonize local laws with international legislation.

II. Regulatory Requirements

A. Pre-Sale Disclosure

Please describe any pre-sale franchise disclosure or similar requirements that may apply to franchise transactions.

1. Initial Disclosure

Article 18 of *the Law of the Republic of Kazakhstan 'On Complex Entrepreneurial Licenses (Franchise)' No.330-II, dated June 24, 2002* ("Law on Franchising") states that, prior to the execution of a franchise agreement the franchisor to a potential franchisee information about the exclusive rights that are given to the franchise when entering into a franchise agreement. In practice, depending on the situation, this provision can be interpreted as a franchisor's right as well as a franchisor's obligation. However, the franchisor is obliged to warn the potential franchisee about the confidential commercial nature of such information.

B. Government Approvals, Registrations, and Filing Requirements

Please describe any necessary government approvals, registrations or filing requirements that may apply to franchising transactions.

Civil Code of the Republic of Kazakhstan requires the registration of the franchise agreement with Kazakh Patent Office (*Патентное ведомство Республики Казахстан*), if the agreement provides for the transfer of intellectual property registered in Kazakhstan. Failure to comply with the registration requirements invalidates the franchise agreement.

According to the Law on Franchising, if intellectual property is not registered in the Republic of Kazakhstan, its registration and transfer under the franchise agreement is carried out at the discretion of the parties.

If the parties to the franchise agreement decide to register the agreement in Kazakhstan (see Section V below), it is necessary to note that the regulatory authority (Kazakh Patent Office *(Патентное ведомство Республики Казахстан)*) has the discretion to reject the registration of a franchise agreement if the intellectual property is not registered or protected (through international registration under the *Madrid Agreement*) in Kazakhstan.[122]

In practice the procedure for registering a franchise agreement takes about 3-6 months.

C. Limits of Fees and Typical Term of Franchise Agreement

Please describe any limits upon the nature and extent of fees and the term of a typical franchise agreement.

Kazakh Law does not provide any limits regarding the nature and extent of fees for the franchise agreement. Parties are free to choose the nature and extent of fees. Please note, that in accordance with the *Law on Franchising*, the franchise agreement can be concluded for a definite term, as well as for indefinite term.

[122] *Editor's note* - The Madrid system (officially the Madrid system for the international registration of marks) is the primary international system for facilitating the registration of trademarks in multiple jurisdictions around the world. Its legal basis is the multilateral treaty *Madrid Agreement Concerning the International Registration of Marks* of 1891, as well as the *Protocol Relating to the Madrid Agreement* (1989).

Kazakhstan

III. Currency

If all payments under a franchise agreement must be made in immediately available US Dollars, please advise as to any restrictions, reporting requirements, or regulations concerning the exchange, repatriation or remittance of US Dollars.

For the purposes of Kazakhstan currency regulation, a franchise agreement is considered as an export (import) of services operation.

Please note that according to Article 20 of the *Law of the Republic of Kazakhstan on Currency Regulation and Control, dated June 13, 2005 No. 57-III* and the *Rules of Performing Currency Operations in the Republic of Kazakhstan, dated April 28, 2012 No. 154* ("Rules"), payment from residents to non-residents of Kazakhstan under export (import) of services contracts (i) for a period of more than 180 days and (ii) for an amount exceeding US$ 100,000 and payments from non-residents of Kazakhstan to residents under (export (import) of services contracts (i) for a period of more than 180 days and (ii) for and amount exceeding US$ 500,000 require notification to the National Bank of the Republic of Kazakhstan (*Национальный банк Республики Казахстан*) ("National Bank").

Therefore, if payments under a franchise agreement are not of the above nature, no notification and other filings are required.

If payments under the franchise agreement, however, meet the above requirements then such notification of the National Bank shall be performed by the Kazakh servicing bank of the resident of Kazakhstan by way of submission of reports to the National Bank (i.e., no notifications required by the parties of the franchise agreement).

Other than that, there are, generally, no special restrictions or requirements regarding exchange, repatriation or remittance of US Dollars applicable to the payments under a franchise agreement (repatriation requirements will be applicable only if goods (if any) cross the border of Kazakhstan).

IV. Taxes, Tariffs and Duties

Please do not provide any in-depth comments on tax structuring. However, please provide your general comments on the typical amount of withholding tax that would apply and whether a "gross-up" provision contained in a franchise agreement would be enforceable in your country.

Under the Kazakhstan national tax law, the applicable withholding tax rate depends on the type of income to be paid to a non-resident entity. Payments under franchise agreements are considered royalties or other incomes depending on the provisions of the agreements. The rate of withholding income tax for royalties is 15%. Royalty paid to resident in a "blacklisted" jurisdiction are taxed at 20%.

A non-resident may apply provisions of an applicable double taxation treaty to enjoy a tax exemption or a tax rate reduction. Kazakhstan has entered into 47 double taxation treaties with other countries, including the U.S. and most European countries.

Since 2009, grossing up income payable to a non-resident entity in terms of the amount of withholding tax to be paid to the Kazakh government is allowed under Kazakhstani tax law.

V. Trademarks

Please advise us as to whether there are any special requirements for granting a valid trademark license, including the use of a registered user agreement or a short trademark license agreement and any required filing of such an agreement with the trademark authorities.

The granting of a trademark license in Kazakhstan is regulated by the *Civil Code and the Law of the Republic of Kazakhstan 'On Trademarks, Service Marks and Appellation of Origin of*

Goods' ("Law on Trademarks"). According to Kazakhstani law, trademark license agreements must be registered with the Patent Office. Failure to register will invalidate the agreement.

Trademark license registration procedure is carried out under Law on Trademarks or *Singapore Treaty* if one of the trademark license parties is a member of this Treaty. However there is no practice of application of Singapore Treaty in Kazakhstan at the moment.

According to Law on Trademarks, all documents for registration, including the agreement, should be submitted in the Kazakh and Russian languages. Documents in a language other than Russian and Kazakh should be translated and notarized.

The regulatory authority, RGKP National Institute of IP of the Committee of IP rights of the Ministry of Justice of the Republic of Kazakhstan *(РГКП «Национальный институт интеллектуальной собственности» Комита по правам интеллектуальной собственности Министерства юстиции Республики Казахстан),* may refuse to register a license agreement for any of the following reasons:

1) Expiration of a trademark certificate in respect of which the agreement is concluded and it is impossible to renew it;

2) Failure to provide all the necessary documents and information required for registering licensing agreements within three months;

3) Parties lack the rights necessary to conclude the agreement;

4) Licensee lacks the authority in the license agreement to register the sublicense agreement and there is not a license agreement registered with the competent authority.

The registration process takes approximately 2 months from the date of application to the Kazakh Patent Office *(Патентное ведомство Республики Казахстан)*. A license agreement should be submitted for registration with the Kazakh Patent Office no later than six months after the date of signing the agreement.

VI. Restrictions on Transfer

Please advise as to whether there are any restrictions (1) on a franchisor to restrict transfers by a master franchisee, any interest in a master franchisee, or the assets of the master franchisee or (2) the ability of a master franchisee to control and/or restrict transfers of a subfranchisee's rights under a master franchise agreement, interest in the subfranchisee, or the assets of the subfranchisee.

Law on Franchising provides the pre-emptive right of the franchisor in case of alienation by the franchisee its enterprise or share in enterprise. Since the Kazakh legislation does not contain other restrictions the parties can agree and include any such restrictions in the agreement if they wish. According to the *Law on Franchising*, a franchise agreement may include restrictive (exclusive) conditions, particularly, the obligation of the franchisor not to grant other similar franchises on the territory in question or to refrain from immediate self-employment in that territory. In addition, a franchise agreement may stipulate the right of the franchisee to allow the use of some or all of the exclusive rights given to him to others under the terms agreed with the franchisor or as defined in the agreement.

VII. Termination

Please advise us as to any laws relating to termination in your country, such as agency laws, required indemnity provisions, notice or "good cause" requirements, or other laws affecting termination of a franchise agreement. Please describe.

According to *Article 908* of *the Civil Code of the Republic of Kazakhstan No. 409-I, dated July 1, 1999* ("Civil Code"), a franchise agreement concluded with a specified term can be terminated in accordance with the regulations of the Civil Code (*Chapter 24)*, (i.e. by the parties' mutual agreement, in case of material breach or in other cases provided by the agreement). The Civil Code provides an indemnity in case of material breach of agreement.

Please also note that according to the *Civil Code (Article 908.2, Articles 374 and 404)*, a party to the agreement has the right to refuse an agreement for an indefinite-term by giving six months prior notice to terminate, unless the agreement stipulates a longer period of notice.

VIII. Governing Law, Jurisdiction and Dispute Resolution

A. Choice of Law of Foreign Jurisdiction

Please confirm whether the choice of law of a foreign jurisdiction would likely to be upheld under the law of the country, except for certain matters such as trademarks, bankruptcy and competition matters, which we assume would be governed by the law in your country.

Kazakh law does not prevent the parties from choosing a foreign governing law. In accordance with *Articles 1120* and *1112 of the Civil Code of the Republic of Kazakhstan*, agreements regulating intellectual property rights shall be governed by the law chosen by the parties, unless otherwise provided by the laws of the Republic of Kazakhstan. Kazakh Law applies to title to and protection of IP rights according to *Articles 1109* and *1111 of the Civil Code* in case of registration of IP rights with the Kazakh Patent Office *(Патентное ведомство Республики Казахстан)* and the inclusion of IP objects into the Kazakh IP Rights Registers.

Please also note that in accordance with *Article 1120 of the Civil Code* and the international private law principle of territoriality, if the a party seeks to protect its intellectual property rights in

Kazakhstan, then the law of Kazakhstan shall apply to the intellectual property rights.

B. International Arbitration Dispute Resolution

Please confirm that a court in your country would honor an election of international arbitration dispute resolution, and therefore refuse to hear any disputes arising under a franchise agreement.

We confirm the above statement; however, the following should be noted:

As a matter of law, Kazakh courts should stay proceedings and refer parties to arbitration, if: (i) there is a prima facie arbitration agreement between the parties, and/or (ii) the defendant filed a jurisdictional objection against hearing the case in the court *prior to* consideration of the case on its merits.

As per recent amendments, courts have the powers to dismiss claims at the filing stage if there is an arbitration agreement between the parties. However, if the court assumes jurisdiction over a dispute despite arbitration agreement, a defendant has the right to raise jurisdictional objection before the court proceeds to hear the case on merits. In this case, the court must stay the proceedings and refer parties to arbitration, unless the court finds that the arbitration agreement is not valid or incapable of being performed.

Kazakhstan is a signatory to the 1958 *New York Convention on the Recognition and Enforcement of Foreign Arbitral Awards* ("New York Convention").

IX. Non-Competition Provisions

If the franchise agreement prohibits the master franchisee from engaging in certain competitive activities during the term of the agreement, and for a 12-month period after the termination or expiration of the agreement, please comment on the enforceability of non-competition covenants in your country.

In accordance with the *Law on Franchising and Civil Code*, a franchise agreement may set restrictive covenants. For example a commitment from the franchisee not to compete with the franchisor in respect of business carried out in the territory in question by the franchisee is permissible. Additionally, an agreement may also set the condition whereby the franchisee promises not to obtain other franchise opportunities from competitors (or potential competitors) of the franchisor.

X. Language Requirements

Does the law in your country require that a franchise agreement be translated into the local language in order to be enforceable between the parties?

The Law of the Republic of Kazakhstan "On Languages in Kazakhstan" No 151-I, dated July 11, 1997 requires that all agreements be made in Kazakh language and in a language acceptable for the parties. In practice, many agreements in Kazakhstan are executed in English and in Russian, However, Kazakh versions of the text are being used increasingly often in Kazakhstan. In order to avoid risk, some Agreements are executed in three languages: Kazakh, Russian and English. The parties may contractually agree which version shall prevail if there are inconsistencies among these texts.

XI. Other Significant Matters

Please advise as to whether there are any significant matters not addressed above of which a franchisor should be aware in connection with its entering into a franchise agreement in your country.

The Franchise Union of the Republic of Kazakhstan *(Ассоциация франчайзинга Республики Казахстан)* operates to develop and support franchising in Kazakhstan.

Kazakhstan

There are 150 partner franchising networks and more than 1,000 operating franchised facilities in Kazakhstan. This market is filled with national brands, imports are also growing and there has been an expansion of franchise companies from neighboring countries. In recent years, Russian franchising proposals have increased in Kazakhstan. Major international franchise brands such as Coca-Cola, KFC, Hardee's, Pizza Hut, Baskin Robbins, Adidas, InterContinental, Marriott and Hyatt hotel chains are concentrated in the Kazakhstani cities of Almaty and Astana.

Franchising in Malaysia

Wong Sai Fong and Michelle C.Y. Loi

SHEARN DELAMORE & CO.

Kuala Lumpur, Malaysia

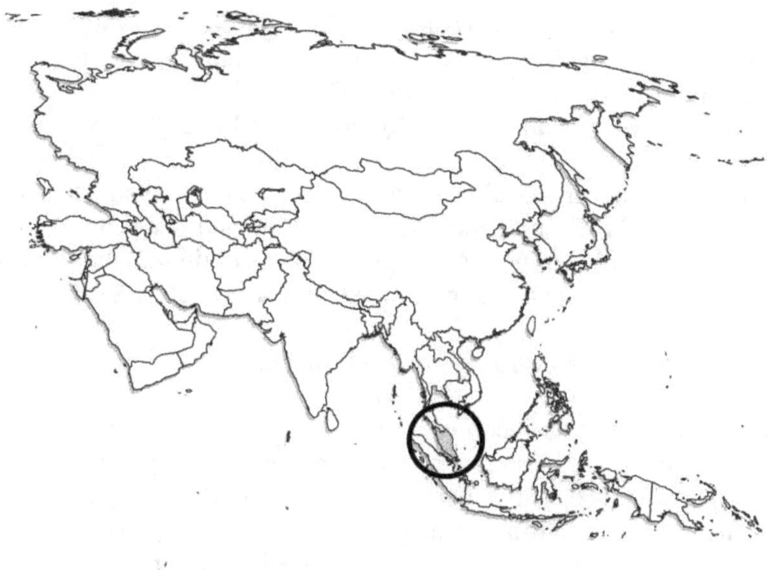

Malaysia

I. Introduction

A. Historical Backgound of the Country

In 1948, the British-ruled territories on the Malay Peninsula, except Singapore, formed the Federation of Malaya, which became independent in 1957. Malaysia was formed in 1963 when the former British colonies of Singapore, as well as Sabah and Sarawak on the northern coast of Borneo, joined the Federation. The first several years of the country's independence were marred by a communist insurgency, Indonesian confrontation with Malaysia, Philippine claims to Sabah, and Singapore's withdrawal in 1965. During the 22-year term of Prime Minister Mahathir bin Mohamad (1981-2003), Malaysia was successful in diversifying its economy from dependence on exports of raw materials to the development of manufacturing, services, and tourism. Prime Minister Mohamed Najib bin Abdul Razak (in office since April 2009) has continued these pro-business policies and has introduced some civil reforms.

B. Economy of the Country

Malaysia, a middle-income country, has transformed itself since the 1970s from a producer of raw materials into an emerging multi-sector economy. Under current Prime Minister Najib, Malaysia is attempting to achieve high-income status by 2020 and to move farther up the value-added production chain by attracting investments in Islamic finance, high technology industries, biotechnology, and services. Najib's Economic Transformation Program (ETP) is a series of projects and policy measures intended to accelerate the country's economic growth. The government has also taken steps to liberalize some services sub-sectors. The Najib administration also is continuing efforts to boost domestic demand and reduce the economy's dependence on exports. Nevertheless, exports - particularly of electronics, oil and gas, palm oil and rubber - remain a significant driver of the economy.

Malaysia

As an oil and gas exporter, Malaysia has profited from higher world energy prices, although the rising cost of domestic gasoline and diesel fuel, combined with sustained budget deficits, has forced Kuala Lumpur to begin to address fiscal shortfalls, through initial reductions in energy and sugar subsidies and the announcement of the 2015 implementation of a 6% goods and services tax. The government is also trying to lessen its dependence on state oil producer Petronas. The oil and gas sector supplies about 32% of government revenue in 2013. Bank Negara Malaysia (central bank) maintains healthy foreign exchange reserves, and a well-developed regulatory regime has limited Malaysia's exposure to riskier financial instruments and the global financial crisis.

Nevertheless, Malaysia could be vulnerable to a fall in commodity prices or a general slowdown in global economic activity because exports are a major component of GDP. In order to attract increased investment, Najib earlier raised possible revisions to the special economic and social preferences accorded to ethnic Malays under the New Economic Policy of 1970, but retreated in 2013 after he encountered significant opposition from Malay nationalists and other vested interests. In September 2013 Najib launched the new Bumiputra Economic Empowerment Program (BEEP), policies that favor and advance the economic condition of ethnic Malays.

C. Franchise Legal Overview

All franchise businesses in Malaysia are governed by the *Franchise Act 1998* (hereafter referred to as "the Act"). The Act was gazetted on December 31, 1998 and came into operation on October 8, 1999. The Act was amended by the Franchise (Amendment) Act 2012, which came into force on January 1, 2013.

A foreign franchisor must have its franchise registered with the Franchise Development Division of the Ministry of Domestic Trade, Cooperatives and Consumerism before it may license its franchise business to a Malaysian franchisee. The Malaysian franchisee must also obtain a license and register with the same government agency before it can operate its franchise business or sub-license another subfranchisee to do so. A local franchisor of a local franchise business must be similarly registered before it can license the franchise business to a franchisee.

An offer of a license for a franchise business whether by a foreign or local franchisor is only permissible upon the registration of the franchise.

II. Regulatory Requirements

A. Pre-Sale Disclosure

Please describe any pre-sale franchise disclosure or similar requirements that may apply to franchise transactions.

It is a compulsory requirement that a franchisor submit to a franchisee a copy of the franchise agreement and completed disclosure documents at least ten days before the franchisee signs the agreement with the franchisor. The object is to enable the prospective franchisees to evaluate the franchise business and the system under which it is to be operated before making any commitment.

The disclosure document is a legally binding document and must be read together with the franchise agreement. The requisite prescribed particulars and information for completion of the disclosure document are set out in the Act. If any of the information and particulars noted in the disclosure documents submitted changed materially during the application process, the processing officer must be informed of such material changes.

The essential terms for the franchise agreement are also set out in the Act. Prevailing government policies on specific business sectors sometimes play a part in the consideration of an application for registration of a franchise. As a result, particulars of the franchise business, the franchisor and franchisee, their financial standing, identity and designation of officers having charge of the franchisor's franchise business, payment computations and terms and royalties to be paid by franchisee to franchisor upfront and during the course of the franchise business and how such payments are to be treated upon termination of the franchise license may need more specificity and clarification.

Both the disclosure document and the intended franchise agreement together with such other required documents as identified below must be submitted with the application. The application is to be accompanied by a formal letter of application requesting for registration of the franchise. The disclosure document including any subsequent updated or amended versions provided to the franchisee prior to execution of the franchise agreement must be identical to the disclosure documents submitted to the Franchise Registry.

B. Governmental Approvals, Registrations, Filing Requirements

Please describe any necessary government approvals, registrations or filing requirements that may apply to franchise transactions.

In Malaysia, it is an offense for any foreign or local franchisor to offer or license its franchise without having its franchise registered first with the Registrar. A franchisor can be exempted from registration only if it has secured an exemption from the Minister of Domestic Trade, Cooperatives and Consumerism. Exemptions are usually not granted.

Any one who submits false or misleading information or documents for purposes of registration of the franchise commits an offense. In the application process, the processing officer may in writing require the applicant or the director or manager of the applicant to provide additional information, documents or make amendments to the proposed disclosure document or franchise agreement to better comply with the requirements of the Act and government policy.

The application may be approved or rejected and if rejected, the Registrar need not provide any reasons for the rejection. The Registrar is only required to notify the applicant of the rejection. An appeal to the Minister against the Registrar's rejection must be lodged within one month of the date the Registrar's notification of the rejection. The decision of the Minister is final on appeal. Approval, if granted, may be on such terms and conditions as may be imposed by the Registrar. If certain particulars requested by the processing officer were not provided, the application is deemed withdrawn. Sector specific businesses may be subject to prevailing government policies. The applicant is at liberty to submit a new application.

The franchise, once registered, continues to be effective as of the date of the Registrar's notification of the approval unless the Registrar issues an order in writing to the franchisor to suspend, terminate or cancel the registration of the franchise. The nature of and grounds for taking such a course of action will be provided and the franchisor is given an opportunity to make a written representation on the matter within fourteen days from the date of such written notification of the grounds.

Processing of an application takes on average three to four months; but if a case for expedited examination can be made, there is a possibility that the application process may be hastened.

In addition to the intended franchise agreement and the disclosure document, the following additional documents and particulars must be submitted with the application:

- Franchisor's incorporation details such as its share capital and equity structure and the extent of its franchise business operations;
- Particulars and professional designation of the board members of the franchisor;

- □ Franchisor's background and a description of its franchise concept. The uniqueness of any given aspects of the franchise business ought to be highlighted;
- □ Description of the franchisor's experience in the franchise business;
- □ Information on the number of prevailing outlets listed by country and the number of franchise outlets in each of these countries;
- □ Franchisor's audited accounts for the last three years;
- □ The identity of the franchisee or master franchisee if available;
- □ Certified registration particulars or applications of the trade and service marks licensed for use with the franchise business;
- □ Company brochure of the franchisor containing general information on the business of the the franchisor and on the franchise business;
- □ Photographs of or brochures and other printed materials on franchisor's existing franchise business outlets identified by location; and
- □ If requested, forward financial forecast for the franchise business and estimated detailed initial investment for the first franchise outlet.

Occasionally, the operations and training manual may be requested by the processing officer for review. Ordinarily, no copies are submitted with the application.

C. Limits on Fees and Typical Term of Franchise Agreement

Please describe any limits upon the nature and extent of fees and the term of a typical franchise agreement.

There are no limits on the nature and extent of the fees, royalties and payments that may be imposed on the franchisee for the franchise business provided they are within the requirements of the Act. The current application processing fee is a nominal RM50.00 (approximately US$ 13.97). The following are essential terms that must be provided in the franchise agreement:

Malaysia

- □ In the event there is a conflict between the provisions of the Act and the provisions of other written laws, the provisions of the Act shall prevail; even if such a provision is absent from the franchise agreement.
- □ The franchisee cannot be required by agreement to contract out of the requirements of the Act.
- □ The franchise business is to be operated in accordance with the the franchise system as determined by the franchisor.
- □ The franchisor shall grant to the franchisee the right to use its trade or service mark or any confidential information or intellectual property for the conduct of the franchise business.
- □ The franchisor shall have the right to administer continuous control over the franchise business conducted by the franchisee to ensure its compliance with the franchise system.
- □ The franchisor is obliged to provide assistance to the franchisee including any assistance relating to the provision or supply of materials and services, training, marketing including business and technical assistance whether pending the execution of, during and post-termination of the franchise agreement.
- □ In return for the rights and license granted, the franchisor is entitled to be paid a fee or other form of consideration including royalty.
- □ The franchisee is to operate the franchise business separately from the franchisor and the relationship of the franchisee with the franchisor shall not be regarded as a partnership, service contract or agency pending the execution, during and post-termination of the franchise agreement.
- □ The franchisee is further obliged to give a written guarantee that the franchisee and its employees shall not disclose to any person any information contained in the operation manual or obtained while undergoing training and for two years after the expiration or earlier termination of the franchise agreement.

- The franchisee is further obliged to give a written guarantee to the franchisor that the franchisee and his employees shall not be involved in any business similar to the franchise business during the franchise term and for two years after the expiration or earlier termination of the franchise agreement.
- The conditions under which the franchisor and franchisee may assign the rights under the franchise business.
- The duration of the initial term of the franchise and the terms for renewal.
- Post-termination or expiration effect of the franchise agreement including how monies already paid by the franchisee are to be treated and the obligations and actions to be taken by franchisor and franchisee.
- Treatment of any monies paid by the franchisee before execution of the franchise agreement. The purpose of the payment and the conditions for use and refund of the monies must be spelt out.
- There shall be a cooling off period to be determined by the franchisor and franchisee which shall not be less than seven working days during which the franchisee has the option to terminate the agreement. Upon termination, an amount to cover the reasonable expenses incurred by the franchisor to prepare the franchise agreement may be retained from any fees already paid and all other monies shall be refunded to the franchisee.
- Except in limited circusmstances, the franchise agreement must not unreasonably and materially discriminate between franchisees operating a franchise business in the charges offered or made for franchise fees, royalties, goods, services, equipment, rentals, training or advertisng services.
- The method for computation of any payments or royalties to be paid by the franchisee including the terms for timely and payments made out of time.
- A promotion fund may be established. The fund is to be managed under a separate account any payment the franchisee is required to make for purposes of promotion

of the franchisebusiness must be paid and managed under this separate account.

- The initial franchise terms must not be less that five years.
- An opportunity to cure or remedy a breach of any of the terms of the franchise agreement must be given to the franchisee. The opportunity given to remedy the breach must not be less than fourteen days of the date of written notification by the franchisor.
- The franchise agreement cannot be terminated before the termination date except for good cause. "Good cause" would include the failure of a franchisee to comply with any term of the franchise agreement and such failure is not remedied within the period accorded to the franchisee to make good the breach.
- It would also constitute "good cause" and the franchise agreement may be terminated without any requirement for notice or an opportunity to remedy the breach if the franchisee makes an assignment of the franchise rights for the benefit of creditors or a similar disposition of the assets of the franchise business to any other person or becomes bankrupt or insolvent or voluntarily abandons the franchise business or any of its key personnel is convicted of a criminal offense which impairs the goodwill associated with the franchisor or the franchisor's trade or service marks or other intellectual property or where the franchisee repeatedly fails to comply with the terms of the franchise agreement.
- The franchise agreement may also be terminated before the expiration of the initial term if the franchisor and franchisee agree to terminate or where the court decides that there are certain terms and conditions in the franchise agreement which merits and permits the franchise agreement to be terminated earlier.
- At any time before the expiration of the initial term, a franchisee shall have the right and option to give notice to the franchisor to extend the franchise term, and, unless the franchisee has breached the terms of the then current agreement or if such breach is not cured, the

franchisor shall extend the franchise term for a extended term on terms and conditions which are similar or not less favorable than those prevailing in the then current franchise agreement.

III. Currency

If all payments under a franchise agreement must be made in immediately available U.S. Dollars, please advise as to any restrictions, reporting requirements, or regulations concerning the exchange, repatriation or remittance of U.S. Dollars.

Payments may be freely made by a Malaysian resident franchisee to a foreign franchisor up to a maximum sum of Malaysian Ringgit 200,000 (approximately US$ 57,000) per remittance. Any payment in excess of said amount or its foreign currency equivalent requires notification to the Central Bank (Bank Negara). The notification procedure merely involves completing a specified form at the commercial bank from which the remittance is made.

IV. Taxes, Tariffs and Duties

Please do not provide any in-depth comments on tax structuring. However, please provide your general comments on the typical amount of withholding tax that would apply and whether a "gross-up" provision contained in a franchise agreement would be enforceable in your country.

Withholding tax is an amount withheld by the Malaysian franchisee on income earned by the non-resident foreign franchisor and paid to the Inland Revenue Board of Malaysia.

The *Income Tax Act 1967* provides that where a Malaysian franchisee payer is liable to make payment to a non-resident foreign franchisor payee, it shall deduct withholding tax at the prescribed rate from such payment and pay such tax to the Director General of Inland Revenue within one month after such payment has been paid or credited to the non-resident foreign franchisor payee.

Royalties paid to non-resident foreign franchisor payee is subject to withholding tax.

"Royalty" is defined as "any sums paid as consideration for the use of or the right to use (a) copyrights, artistic or scientific works, patents, designs or models, plans, secret processes or formulae, trademarks or tapes for radio or television broadcasting, motion picture films, films or video tapes or other means of reproduction where such films or tapes have been or are to be used or reproduced in Malaysia or other like property or rights; (b) know-how or information concerning technical, industrial, commercial or scientific knowledge, experience or skill; and (c) income derived from the alienation of any property, know-how or information mentioned in above paragraph of this definition.

"Gross up" provisions providing for the treatment of withholding tax in a franchise agreement are enforceable as a contractual term.

V. Trademarks

Please advise us as to whether there are any special requirements for granting a valid trademark license, including the use of a registered user agreement or a short trademark license agreement and any required filing of such an agreement with the trademark authorities.

At the time the franchise application is submitted, the franchisor is required to provide proof that it has registrations for the trade or service marks to be licensed for use by the franchisee or has applied to the Malaysian Intellectual Property Corporation ("MyIPO") for its trade or service mark to be registered in accordance with the *Trade Marks Act 1976*. A registration certificate issued by the Registrar of Trademarks is prima facie evidence of trade mark ownership. A registered trade marks owner has an exclusive right to use its registered marks in the course of the franchise business. The owner also has the right to take legal action for infringement under the Trade Marks Act 1976 or passing off under the common law against others who use their marks without consent.

If the franchise agreement is exclusive to the franchisee or where the franchisor does not in any way use its registered trade or service mark in relation to the franchise business or goods in Malaysia, then, the franchisee must be recorded as the permittted or authorized user of the registered marks. A short form registered user agreement may be used for purposes of the recordation instead of the franchise agreement. Where the trade or service marks are pending registration, recordation of the franchisee as the permitted or authorized user is not possible and exercising control and supervision of such use as will be the case of the franchise business, are sufficient. Recordation of the franchisee as the permitted or authorized user of the registered trade or service marks is a permitted unilateral step the franchisor is entitled to take under the Trade Marks Act 1976. Unless the recordation is completed, the registered marks are at risk of being expunged from the Register on grounds of non use by the franchisor who is the registered owner. An official written confirmation of the recordation from MyIPO can be expected within three months of the filing for recordation.

VI. Restrictions on Transfer

Please advise as to whether there are any restrictions (1) on a franchisor to restrict transfers by a master franchisee, any interest in a master franchisee, or the assets of the master franchisee or (2) the ability of a master franchisee to control and/or restrict transfers of a subfranchisee's rights under a master franchise agreement, interest in the subfranchisee, or the assets of the subfranchisee.

The franchisor is free to transfer and assign any of its rights and interest in the franchise agreement, or assets of the franchise business, but the franchisee must obtain the prior written consent of the franchisor in order to do so. The franchisor should not unreasonably withhold consent and consent may be given subject to terms. Similar restrictions are imposed by the master franchisee with a subfranchisee. The franchise agreement between the franchisor and the master franchisee will oblige the master franchisee to impose such restrictions on its subfranchisee.

VII. Termination

Please advise us as to any laws relating to termination in your country, such as agency laws, required indemnity provisions, notice or "good cause" requirements, or other laws affecting termination of a franchise agreement. Please describe.

See comments and response above in Section II.C. (Limits on Fees and Typical Term of Franchise Agreement).

VIII. Governing Law, Jurisdiction and Dispute Resolution

A. Choice of Law of Foreign Jurisdiction

Please confirm whether the choice of law of a foreign jurisdiction would likely to be upheld under the law of the country, except for certain matters such as trademarks, bankruptcy and competition matters, which we assume would be governed by the law in your country.

It is a requirement that Malaysian law governs the franchise agreement although Malaysian courts need not have exclusive jurisdiction. Disputes are encouraged to be settled internally through mediation or arbitration before turning to the Malaysian courts. Unless a case can be made for certain exceptions, arbitration shall be conducted under the auspices of the Kuala Lumpur Regional Centre for Arbitration in Kuala Lumpur under its own rules or any other commercial arbitartion rules of the disputing parties' choice.

B. International Arbitration Dispute Resolution

Please confirm that a court in your country would honor an election of international arbitration dispute resolution, and therefore refuse to hear any disputes arising under a franchise agreement.

Malaysia is a signatory to the 1958 New York Convention on the Recognition and Enforcement of Foreign Arbitral Awards. Malaysian courts will generally respect an international arbitration dispute resolution clause in the franchise agreement and will not hear the dispute if it were brought before the Malaysian courts.

IX. Non-Competition Provisions

If the franchise agreement prohibits the master franchisee from engaging in certain competitive activities during the term of the agreement, and for a 12-month period after the termination or expiration of the agreement, please comment on the enforceability of non-competitioncovenants in your country.

See comments and response above in Section II.C. (Limits on Fees and Typical Term of Franchise Agreement).

X. Language Requirements

Does the law in your country require that a franchise agreement be translated into the local language in order to be enforceable between the parties?

No, there is no requirement in the Act that a franchise agreement be translated into the local language in order to be enforceable between the parties. Normally, agreements are drafted either in English or Malay language.

Malaysia

XI. Other Significant Matters

Please advise as to whether there are any significant matters not addressed above of which a franchisor should be aware in connection with its entering into a franchise agreement in your country.

The franchisor must, within six months from the end of each financial year of the franchise business, submit a report to the Registrar containing certain prescribed particulars including any material changes to the information and particulars provided in the disclosure document submitted at the time of application. The annual report must also be accompanied by a financial statement as to how the monies in the promotion fund are utilized and disbursed. The registration of the franchise may be cancelled if the annual report is not submitted for five consecutive years.

The Malaysian Franchise Association ("MFA") was formed in 1994 to support the implementation of the government programme to promote entrepreneurship through franchising. The MFA serves as a resource center for both current and prospective franchisors and franchisees, as well as for media and the public.

Address: 1st Floor, Wisma Motor, 339 Jalan Tuanku Abdul Rahman, 50100 Kuala Lumpur, Malaysia.
Tel: 603-26971557
Fax: 603-26971559

Franchising in Nepal

Devendra Pradhan and Shirshak Ghimire
PRADHAN & ASSOCIATES

Kathmandu, Nepal

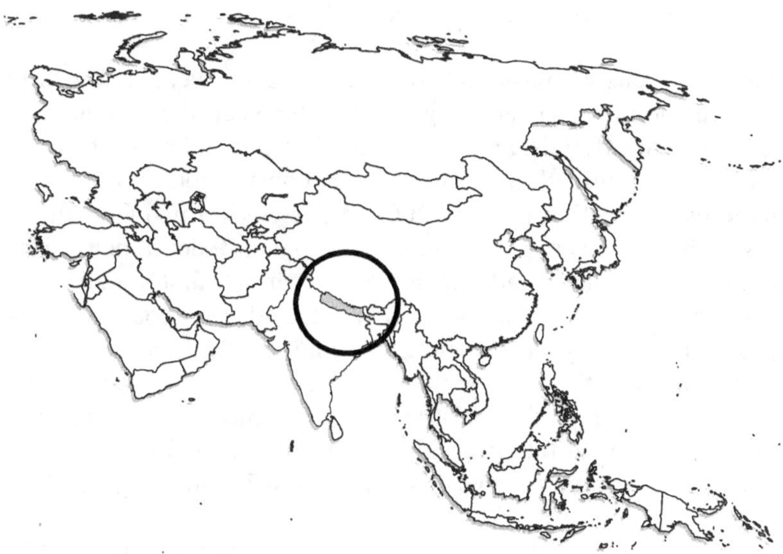

Nepal

I. Introduction

A. Historical Background of the Country

In 1951, the Nepali monarch ended the century-old system of rule by hereditary premiers and instituted a cabinet system of government. Reforms in 1990 established a multiparty democracy within the framework of a constitutional monarchy. An insurgency led by Maoists broke out in 1996. The ensuing 10-year civil war between Maoist and government forces witnessed the dissolution of the cabinet and parliament and assumption of absolute power by the king in 2002.

Several weeks of mass protests in April 2006 were followed by several months of peace negotiations between the Maoists and government officials, and culminated in a late 2006 peace accord and the promulgation of an interim constitution. Following a nationwide election in April 2008, the newly formed Constituent Assembly ("Assembly") declared Nepal a federal democratic republic and abolished the monarchy at its first meeting the following month. The Assembly elected the country's first president in July. Between 2008 and 2011 there were four different coalition governments, led twice by the United Communist Party of Nepal-Maoist, which received a plurality of votes in the 2008 Assembly election, and twice by the Communist Party of Nepal-United Marxist-Leninist ("UML").

After the Assembly failed to draft a constitution by the May 2012 deadline set by the Supreme Court, then Prime Minister Baburam Bhattarai dissolved the Assembly. Months of negotiations ensued until March 2013 when the major political parties agreed to create an interim government headed by then Chief Justice Khil Raj Regmi with a mandate to hold elections for a new Assembly. Elections were held in November 2013, in which the Nepali Congress won the largest share of the seats in the Assembly. In February 2014, a coalition government with the second place UML was formed and with Nepali Congress President Sushil Koirala as prime minister.

Nepal

B. Economy of the Country

Nepal is heavily dependent on remittances, which amounts to as much as 22-25% of GDP. Agriculture is the mainstay of the economy, providing a livelihood for more than 70% of the population and accounting for a little over one-third of GDP. Industrial activity mainly involves the processing of agricultural products, including pulses, jute, sugarcane, tobacco, and grain. Nepal has considerable scope for exploiting its potential in hydropower, with an estimated 42,000 MW of commercially feasible capacity. Additional challenges to Nepal's growth include its landlocked geographic location, persistent power shortages, underdeveloped transportation infrastructure, civil strife and labor unrest, and its susceptibility to natural disaster. The lack of political consensus in the past several years has delayed national budgets and prevented much-needed economic reform, although the government passed a full budget in 2013.

C. Franchise Legal Overview

Though Nepal does not have franchise specific legislation, a number of laws, regulations, procedures and directives are applicable in franchise agreements, notably– (i) *Agency Act 1957*, (ii) *Agency Rules 1963*, (iii) *Contract Act 2000*, (iv) *Foreign Investment and Technology Transfer Act 1992*, (v) *Income Tax Act 2002*, (vi) *Value Added Tax Act 1996*, (vii) *Customs Act 2007*, (viii) *Foreign Exchange Regulation Act 1962*, (ix) *Arbitration Act 1999*, (x) *Patent Design Trademark Act 1965* and (xi) the *Procedural Manual for Foreign Investment in Nepal 2012*.

II. Regulatory Requirements

A. Pre-Sale Disclosure

Please describe any pre-sale franchise disclosure or similar requirements that may apply to franchise transactions.

There are no pre-sale franchise disclosure requirements applicable to the franchise agreements in Nepal.

B. Governmental Approvals, Registrations, Filing Requirements

Please describe any necessary government approvals, registrations, or filing requirements that may apply to franchise transactions.

In the context of Nepal, franchising can be seen as the equivalent of a "technology transfer" under the *Foreign Investment and Technology Transfer Act 1992* ("FITTA"), which is the primary law governing technology transfer in Nepal. A technology transfer under the FITTA constitutes an agreement between a local industry and a foreign investor on the following matters:

- □ use of any technological right, specialization, formula, process, patent or technical know-how of foreign origin;
- □ use of any trademark of foreign ownership; or
- □ acquiring any foreign technical, consultancy, management and marketing service.[123]

Licensing of the intellectual property rights, its business model and know-how by a foreign entity to a local entity will fall under the definition of "technology transfer" under the FITTA. Any kind of technology transfer from a foreign entity to a local entity requires the approval of the Department of Industry ("DOI").[124] In case the patent, design or trademark is already registered in Nepal, the owner of such intellectual property may assign the rights to or license the usage of such intellectual property under the *Patent Design Trademark Act 1965* ("PDTA") with approval

[123] *FITTA*, §2(c).

[124] *Id.*, §3(1).

from DOI.[125] For obtaining such approval, the DOI must be provided with:

- □ Technology Transfer Agreement, Licensing Agreement or the Deed of Assignment;
- □ Corporate Documents of the franchisor, Licensor or Assignor; and
- □ Industry Registration Certificate of the franchisee, Licensee or Assignee.

Generally, the approval is granted within a month after the application for approval is made.[126]

Franchising may cover the use of technological rights, intellectual property rights or distribution of products. In the event a local entity is involved solely in the distribution of a foreign entity's products, then the provision of the *Agency Act 1957* ("Agency Act") shall be applicable. The definition of an agent includes a distributor or representative.[127] Where an agency agreement has been entered into, the agent is required to be registered with the Department of Commerce after submitting necessary information about the nature of the agency including the agreement between the two entities, the price list, tax registration certificate and the applicable incorporation documents, along with certain registration fees as collateral.[128]

C. Limits on Fees and Typical Term of Franchise Agreement

Please describe any limits upon the nature and extent of fees and the term of a typical franchise agreement.

---

125 *PDTA*, §21D.

126 *FITTA*, §3(3).

127 *Agency Act*, §2(a).

128 *Id.*, §4.

No limit has been prescribed on the nature and rate of the franchise fees and the term of a typical franchise agreement. The approval of the terms and conditions of the franchise agreement by the DOI will depend upon the nature of the technology and other technical expertise being transferred.

III. Currency

If all payments under a franchise agreement must be made in immediately available U.S. Dollars, please advise as to any restrictions, reporting requirements, or regulations concerning the exchange, repatriation or remittance of U.S. Dollars.

The franchisee can apply to the DOI for the repatriation of franchise fees as per the agreement. To do so, the franchisee has to submit the calculation of the amount due to the franchisor certified by the auditor along with the certificate of payment of income tax on royalty as per the prevailing tax rate.[129]

According to the *Foreign Exchange Regulation Act 1962* ("FERA"), any kind of foreign currency transaction including payment of royalty in foreign exchange requires the approval of the Central Bank, i.e. the *Nepal Rastra Bank* ("NRB").[130] Foreign currency transaction includes any payment made in foreign exchange.[131] A franchisor is allowed to repatriate the franchise fees due under the technology transfer agreement.[132]

IV. Taxes, Tariffs, and Duties

Please do not provide any in-depth comments on tax structuring. However, please provide your general comments on the typical

[129] *Procedural Manual for Foreign Investment in Nepal 2012* ("PMFIN"), Para 3.2.4.

[130] *Foreign Exchange Regulation Act 1962* ("FERA"), §3.

[131] *Id.*, §2(d1).

[132] *Id.*, §10C(5).

amount of withholding tax that would apply and whether a "gross-up" provision contained in a franchise agreement would be enforceable in your country.

The *Income Tax Act 2002* ("ITA") defines "royalty" as the payment for the conferment of rights in any intangible property including usage or licensing of intellectual property rights, technology transfer and other know-how.[133] A withholding tax of 15% is levied upon any payment of royalty on an intangible property for which Nepal is its source.[134] The ITA also allows for a 50% tax concession on income derived from a service charge or a royalty for a technology transfer provided by a franchisor for the industries established in any special economic zone.[135] The ITA also provides a 25% exemption on the income tax levied on the royalty earned from the export of intellectual property and a 50% concession on income tax levied upon the income earned from the transfer of assignment of intellectual property in a franchise agreement.[136]

The *Value Added Tax Act 1996* ("VAT Act") imposes Value Added Tax ("VAT") over goods and services supplied, imported to, or exported from Nepal.[137] The VAT Act defines goods as any moveable or immoveable property,[138] and services as anything other than goods.[139] The services provided by a foreign entity to a Nepalese entity including conferment of rights pertaining to copyright, patent, license, trademark and other such intellectual property rights are considered as providing service under the purview of the VAT Act.[140] The VAT Act imposes

133 *ITA*, §2(ak).

134 *Id.*, §88(1).

135 *Id.*, §11 (3A) (d) as added by Finance Act of 2014-15.

136 *Id.*, §§11(3I), 11(3J) as added by Finance Act of 2014-15.

137 *VAT Act*, §5(1).

138 *Id.*, §2(e).

139 *Id.*, §2(f).

140 *Id.*, §8(2) as added by Finance Act of 2014-15.

VAT at the rate of 13% on all goods and services including franchise services.[141] Any goods exported from Nepal and any service provided to a person not having a business or legal presence in Nepal is charged VAT at the rate of zero per cent.[142]

According to the Customs Act, the customs value of goods to be imported are determined on the basis of the transaction value of such goods based on the rules on customs valuation, annexes and explanatory notes set forth in the *Agreement on Implementation of Article VII of the General Agreement on Tariffs and Trade 1994.*[143] Therefore, the payments regarding patents, trademarks and copyrights are added to the price actually paid or payable for the imported goods in determining their customs value.

Nepal has signed double taxation agreements with India, Qatar, China, Austria, Republic of Korea, Mauritius, Norway, Pakistan, Sri Lanka and Thailand.

No restrictions have been placed upon "gross up" clauses which shall be guided by the franchise agreement.

V. Trademarks

Please advise us as to whether there are any special requirements for granting a valid trademark license, including the use of a registered user agreement or a short trademark license agreement and any required filing of such an agreement with the trademark authorities.

Trademarks registered in Nepal can be licensed or assigned through a joint application by both the franchisor and the franchisee to the DOI.[144] The rights of the franchise shall be as

---

[141] *Id.*, §7(1) as added by Finance Act of 2014-15.

[142] *Id.*, Schedule 2.

[143] *Customs Act*, §13(1).

[144] *PDTA*, §21D.

stated in the agreement. However, the statutory rights granted to the owner of a trademark can only apply when the trademark is registered within Nepal.[145] DOI will register the license/assignment only after all the requisite procedures have been met.

VI. Restrictions on Transfer

Please advise as to whether there are any restrictions (1) on a franchisor to restrict transfers by a master franchisee, any interest in a master franchisee, or the assets of the master franchisee or (2) the ability of a master franchisee to control and/or restrict transfers of a subfranchisee's rights under a master franchise agreement, an interest in the subfranchisee, or the assets of the subfranchisee.

There are no restrictions on a franchisor to restrict (i) transfers by a master franchisee, (ii) any interest in a master franchisee, (iii) the assets of the master franchisee, (iv) the ability of a master franchisee to control and/or restrict transfers of a subfranchisee's rights under a master franchise agreement, (v) interest in the subfranchisee, or (vi) the assets of the subfranchisee.

VII. Termination

Please advise us as to any laws relating to termination in your country, such as agency laws, required indemnity provisions, notice or "good cause" requirements, or other laws affecting termination of a franchise agreement. Please describe.

There are no specific laws regulating termination of franchise agreements in Nepal. The general law of contract under the *Contract Act 2000* ("Contract Act") shall apply to franchise agreements. The parties to a contract are granted freedom to

[145] *Id.*, §21B.

choose the terms and conditions of the contract, including the termination provisions.[146]

In the event the violation of the terms of the franchise agreement also results in the violation of the terms of the registered agency under the Agency Act, the agent may be subject to a fine and a five year ban from engaging in agency business.[147]Agency may be transferred through an application with a deed of consent from the registered agent and that of the principal company.[148]

VIII. Governing Law, Jurisdiction, and Dispute Resolution

A. Choice of Law of Foreign Jurisdiction

Please confirm whether the choice of law of a foreign jurisdiction would likely to be upheld under the law of the country, except for certain matters such as trademarks, bankruptcy and competition matters, which we assume would be governed by the law in your country.

In any dispute arising between a franchisor and franchisee, the parties are required, first, to attempt to resolve their rights amicably, in the presence of the DOI. If that fails, the parties shall settle such dispute through arbitration under the prevailing arbitration rules of the United Nations Commission on International Trade Law ("UNCITRAL"). In such case, Kathmandu must be the venue of arbitration and the arbitration proceedings are subject to the laws of Nepal.[149] For industries with fixed assets above NPR500 million (approximately US$ 5,261,500), disputes may be settled as mentioned in the franchise agreement where the parties may select the choice of

[146] *Contract Act*, §4.

[147] *Agency Act*, §7.

[148] *Agency Rules*, Rule 7.

[149] *FITTA*, §7

law and jurisdiction of their choice.[150] Therefore, industries with investments up to NPR500 million (approximately US$ 5,261,500) or less must choose Nepalese law as the choice of law.

B. International Arbitration Dispute Resolution

Please confirm that a court in your country would honor an election of international arbitration dispute resolution, and therefore refuse to hear any disputes arising under a franchise agreement.

Nepalese courts will honor selection of international arbitration as the method of resolving dispute provided the parties have attempted to amicably resolve the disputes in the presence of the DOI. Nepal is a signatory to the *Convention on the Recognition and Enforcement of Foreign Arbitral Awards* (the "New York Convention"). According to the *Arbitration Act 1999* ("Arbitration Act") foreign arbitral awards are enforceable in Nepal on reciprocal basis, if the following conditions are met:

- □ the arbitrator has been appointed and the award has been made according to the laws and procedure mentioned in the agreement;
- □ the parties had been notified about the arbitration proceedings in time;
- □ the decision is according to the conditions mentioned in the agreement or confined only to the subject matters referred to the arbitrator;
- □ the decision has become final and binding on the parties according to the laws of the country where the decision was decided;
- □ the laws of the country of the petitioner or the laws of the country where arbitration proceedings have been conducted do not contain any provisions stating that

---

150 *PMFIN*, Pg. 63

arbitration award taken in Nepal cannot be implemented; and

- the application has been filed for the implementation of the award within 90 days from the date of award.[151]

However, a foreign arbitral award will not be enforced (i) when the dispute is of such a nature which could not have been resolved through arbitration under Nepalese laws, or (ii) when the enforcement of the foreign arbitral award would be contrary to the public policy of Nepal.

IX. Non-Competition Provisions

If the franchise agreement prohibits the franchisee from engaging in certain competitive activities during the term of the agreement, and for a 12-month period after the termination or expiration of the agreement, please comment on the enforceability of non-competition covenants in your country.

Pertaining to any contractual provisions under franchise agreements, the following would not be considered as being restrictive of trade:

- a clause preventing the seller of the business and goodwill associated with it from engaging in a similar business or trade at a specified time and place; or
- a clause preventing any individual from receiving the service of any other entity for a specified period of time after the termination of services from the particular entity.[152]

Therefore, a provision of the agreement prohibiting the master franchisee from engaging in certain competitive activities during the term of the agreement, or for a 12-month period after the termination or expiration of the agreement, will be enforceable.

---

[151] *Arbitration Act*, §34(2).

[152] *Contract Act*, §13(a).

X. Language Requirements

Does the law in your country require that a franchise agreement be translated into the local language in order to be enforceable between the parties?

The laws of Nepal do not require that a franchise agreement must be translated into the local language to make it enforceable. For the purpose of approval from DOI, the franchise agreement can either be in Nepalese or English.[153]

XI. Other Significant Matters

Please advise as to whether there are any significant matters not addressed above of which a franchisor should be aware in connection with its entering into a franchise agreement in your country.

There are no franchise associations in Nepal to date. There is no franchised brands specific legislation that has been proposed to be enacted. Some of the notable franchised brands operating in Nepal are Pizza Hut, KFC, Hyatt, Radisson, Crowne Plaza, etc.

[153] *PMFIN*, Pg. 63.

Franchising in the Philippines

Maria Teresa D. Mercado-Ferrer

SYCIP SALAZAR HERNANDEZ & GATMAITAN

Manila, Philippines

Philippines

I. Introduction

A. Historical Background of the Country

On July 4, 1946, the Republic of the Philippines attained its independence. A 20-year rule by Ferdinand Marcos ended in 1986, when a "people power" movement in Manila forced him into exile and installed Corazon Aquino as president. Her presidency was hampered by several coup attempts that prevented a return to full political stability and economic development. Fidel Ramos was elected president in 1992. His administration was marked by increased stability and by progress on economic reforms. In 1992, the U.S. closed its last military bases on the islands.

Joseph Estrada was elected president in 1998. He was succeeded by his vice-president, Gloria Macapagal-Arroyo, in January 2001, after Estrada's stormy impeachment trial on corruption charges broke down and another “people power” movement demanded his resignation. Macapagal-Arroyo was elected to a six-year term as president in May 2004. Her presidency was marred by several corruption allegations but the Philippine economy was one of the few to avoid contraction following the 2008 global financial crisis, expanding each year of her administration. Benigno Aquino III was elected to a six-year term as president in May 2010.

B. Economy of the Country

The economy has weathered global economic and financial downturns better than its regional peers due to minimal exposure to troubled international securities, lower dependence on exports, relatively resilient domestic consumption, large remittances from overseas Filipino workers, and a rapidly expanding business process outsourcing industry. The current account balance had recorded consecutive surpluses since 2003; international reserves are at record highs; the banking system is stable; and the stock market was Asia's second best-performer in 2012.

Efforts to improve tax administration and expenditure management have helped ease the Philippines' tight fiscal situation and reduce high debt levels. The Philippines has received several credit rating upgrades on its sovereign debt, and has had little difficulty tapping domestic and international markets to finance its deficits. Economic growth in the Philippines averaged 4.5% during the Macapagal-Arroyo administration, but poverty worsened during her term. Growth has accelerated under the Aquino government, but with limited progress thus far in bringing down unemployment, which hovers around 7%, and improving the quality of jobs. Underemployment is nearly 20% and more than 40% of the employed are estimated to be working in the informal sector.

The Aquino administration has been working to boost the budgets for education, health, cash transfers to the poor, and other social spending programs, and is relying on the private sector to help fund major infrastructure projects under its public-private partnership program. Long term challenges include reforming governance and the judicial system, building infrastructure, improving regulatory predictability, and the ease of doing business, attracting higher levels of local and foreign investments. The Philippine Constitution and the other laws continue to restrict foreign ownership in important activities/sectors, such as land ownership and public utilities.

C. Overview of the Legal Framework

Agreements covering the sale of franchise rights are generally considered technology transfer agreements ("TTAs"), the execution of which in the Philippines are governed by the *Intellectual Property Code of the Philippines* (the "IP Code"), particularly Chapter IX, which covers provisions on voluntary licensing.[154] A TTA is defined as a contract or agreement involving the transfer of systematic knowledge for the manufacture of a product, the application of a process, or

[154] Rep. Act No. 8293 (1998), secs. 85 to 92.

rendering of a service including management contracts, and the transfer, assignment or licensing of all forms of intellectual property rights.[155]

Section 87 of the IP Code prohibits the following clauses in a TTA:

- □ those that impose upon the licensee the obligation to acquire from a specific source capital goods, intermediate products, raw materials, and other technologies, or of permanently employing personnel indicated by the licensor;
- □ those pursuant to which the licensor reserves the right to fix the sale or resale prices of the products manufactured on the basis of the license;
- □ those that contain restrictions regarding the volume and structure of production;
- □ those that prohibit the use of competitive technologies in a non-exclusive TTA;
- □ those that establish a full or partial purchase option in favor of the licensor;
- □ those that obligate the licensee to transfer for free to the licensor the inventions or improvements that may be obtained through the use of the licensed technology;
- □ those that require payment of royalties to the owners of patents for patents which are not used;
- □ those that prohibit the licensee from exporting the licensed product unless justified for the protection of the legitimate interests of the licensor, such as exports to countries where exclusive licenses to manufacture and/or distribute the licensed product(s) have already been granted;
- □ those which restrict the use of the technology supplied after the expiration of the TTA, except in cases of early termination of the TTA due to reason(s) attributable to the licensee;

[155] *Id*, sec. 4.2.

- those that require payments for patents and other industrial property rights after their expiration or termination;
- those that require that the technology recipient shall not contest the validity of any of the patents of the technology supplier;
- those that restrict the research and development activities of the licensee designed to absorb and adapt the transferred technology to local conditions or to initiate research and development programs in connection with new products, processes or equipment;
- those that prevent the licensee from adapting the imported technology to local conditions, or introducing innovation to it, as long as it does not impair the quality standards prescribed by the licensor;
- those that exempt the licensor from liability for non-fulfillment of its responsibilities under the TTA and/or liability arising from third party suits brought about by the use of the licensed technology; and
- other clauses with equivalent effects.

Section 88 of the IP Code, on the other hand, mandates that the following provisions be included in the TTA:

- that the laws of the Philippines shall govern the interpretation of the TTA and in the event of litigation, the venue shall be the proper court in the place where the licensee has its principal office;
- continued access to improvements in techniques and processes related to the technology shall be made available during the period of the TTA;
- in the event the TTA shall provide for arbitration, the procedure of arbitration of the Arbitration Law of the Philippines or the Arbitration Rules of the United Nations Commission on International Trade Law (UNCITRAL) or the Rules of Conciliation and Arbitration of the International Chamber of Commerce (ICC) shall apply and the venue of arbitration shall be the Philippines or any neutral country; and

- ☐ Philippine taxes on all payments relating to the TTA shall be borne by the licensor.

II. Regulatory Requirements

A. Pre-Sale Disclosure

Please describe any pre-sale franchise disclosure or similar requirements that may apply to franchise transactions.

Under Philippine laws and regulations, no pre-sale franchise disclosure or similar requirements apply to franchise transactions.

B. Government Approvals, Registrations, Filing Requirements

Please describe any necessary government approvals, registrations, or filing requirements that may apply to franchise transactions.

There is no requirement for registration of a TTA with any government agency. However, as discussed under Section I.C. above, a TTA must comply with Sections 87 (prohibited clauses) and 88 (required clauses) of the IP Code. Otherwise, the agreement will be deemed automatically unenforceable, unless the agreement is approved by and registered, as an exceptional case, with the Documentation, Information, and Technology Transfer Bureau ("DITTB") of the Intellectual Property Office ("IPO").[156]

Exemptions from the requirements of Sections 87 and 88 may be allowed in exceptional or meritorious cases where substantial benefits will accrue to the economy, such as high technology content, increase in foreign exchange earnings, employment generation, regional dispersal of industries and/or substitution

[156] Rep.Act No. 8293 (1998), sec. 92,

with or use of local raw materials, or in the case of Board of Investments-registered companies with pioneer status.[157] Evaluation, for the purposes of granting an exemption, is made on a case-to-case basis. Such evaluation is based on the adverse effects of the terms and conditions of the TTA on competition and trade.

To claim such exemption, the following procedures must be followed:

1. A party to a TTA or its duly authorized representative may file a sworn application for exemption with the Director of the DITTB, stating the exemption(s) being requested, the justification for the exemption(s), and that the agreement is not subject to any judicial, administrative or other proceeding. The application should be accompanied by two original notarized agreements, payment of the appropriate fees, and other documents that may be required by the DITTB to support and establish the merits of the request. The application should be filed in accordance with the following schedule:

    a. New Agreements—within thirty days from the date of execution or effectivity, whichever is earlier;

    b. Renewal Agreements—any time prior to the expiration of the term of the existing TTA; and

[157] *Id.* sec. 91.

c. Amendatory Agreements—within thirty days from the date of effectivity of such amendment or modification.

The date on which the applicant complies with the requirements of the DITTB is considered the filing date, which shall be recorded in the Filing Date Entry Book. The DITTB shall issue a Notice of Filing Date to the applicant, which is the date when the evaluation of the request shall commence.

2. Should the DITTB find that the documents submitted are incomplete or insufficient, the DITTB shall issue a notice to the applicant within six days from the filing date, requiring the applicant to submit additional documents. The failure of the applicant to comply with any of the requirements within a period of fifteen days from the date of receipt of the notice shall be construed as an abandonment of the application (without prejudice to refiling a new application). However, if the applicant needs additional time to comply with the requirements, a final extension of fifteen days will be granted upon payment of the required fee.

3. The DITTB shall decide whether or not to grant the application within thirty-five days from the filing date.

4. The DITTB shall issue the Certificate of Registration within two days from the approval of the application.

5. After the issuance of the Certificate of Registration, the title of the TTA and parties thereto, its registration number, and the date of registration shall be entered in the Certificate Registry Book.[158]

Although the registration of a TTA with the DITTB is not mandatory, provided the TTA complies with the IP Code, if a party wishes to avail of preferential tax rates under tax treaties entered into by the Philippines with other countries, it is advisable that the parties secure from the DITTB a Certificate of Compliance (if the agreement complies with the IP Code provisions) or Certificate of Registration (if the agreement does not fully comply with the IP Code provisions but is granted an exemption from compliance) to facilitate its application for availment of preferential tax treatment with the Philippine Bureau of Internal Revenue.

C. Limits on Fees and Typical Term of Franchise Agreement

Please describe any limits upon the nature and extent of fees and the term of a typical franchise agreement.

The parties to a franchise agreement may freely determine the nature and extent of applicable fees, as well as the term of the agreement.

If the agreement does not provide for a term, the courts are empowered to fix the duration of the obligation if from its nature and the circumstances, it can be inferred that a period was intended. In doing so, the courts shall determine such period as may under the circumstances have been probably contemplated

[158] *Intellectual Property Office, Rules and Regulations on Voluntary Licensing, Rules 4 to 16* (hereafter, "IPO Rules").

by the parties. Once fixed by the courts, the period cannot be changed by the parties.[159]

III. Currency

If all payments under a franchise agreement must be made in immediately available U.S. Dollars, please advise as to any restrictions, reporting requirements, or regulations concerning the exchange, repatriation, or remittance of U.S. Dollars.

In case payments to a non-resident franchisor are required to be made in foreign currency, the resident franchisee may freely purchase foreign exchange from Authorized Agent Banks ("AABs") and AAB-subsidiary or affiliate foreign exchange corporations without need of prior approval from the Philippine central monetary authority, the *Bangko Sentral ng Pilipinas* or "BSP," subject to the presentation and submission of the following documents to the foreign exchange selling institution:

1. for the sale of foreign currency not exceeding US$ 120,000 or its equivalent in other foreign currency, a duly accomplished application to purchase foreign exchange; and

2. for the sale of foreign currency exceeding US$ 120,000 or its equivalent in other foreign currency, a duly accomplished application to purchase foreign exchange, supported by (i) a statement or computation of the royalty, franchise, or licensing fees, and (ii) a copy of the contract or agreement.[160]

---

[159] New Civil Code of the Philippines, art. 1197.

[160] *Bangko Sentral ng Pilipinas Manual of Regulations on Foreign Exchange Transactions, sec. 2, as amended by Bangko Sentral ng Pilipinas Circular No. 794 (2013).*

The BSP requires that all foreign exchange purchases for non-trade current account transactions shall be directly remitted to the intended non-resident beneficiary's account (whether offshore or onshore).[161]

The ability of a franchisee to make payments in foreign currency is subject to Section 72 of *Republic Act No. 7653*. Under this law, the Monetary Board of the BSP, with the approval of the President of the Philippines, in the imminence of or during a foreign exchange crisis or in times of national emergency, may temporarily suspend or restrict sales of foreign exchange by the BSP, subject all transactions in gold and foreign exchange to licensing by the BSP, and require any person residing in or operating in the Philippines to deliver any foreign exchange obtained by such person to the BSP or to any bank or agent designated by the BSP, at the then effective exchange rate or rates.

IV. Taxes, Tariffs and Duties

Please do not provide any in-depth comments on tax structuring. However, please provide your general comments on the typical amount of withholding tax that would apply and whether a "gross-up" provision contained in a franchise agreement would be enforceable in your country.

Payments of royalties for the use of intellectual property rights or franchise fees arising from Philippine sources are generally subject to a 20% final withholding tax ("FWT"), except for payments made to non-resident alien individuals who are not engaged in trade or business in the Philippines and to non-resident corporations, which are subject to 25% FWT and 30% FWT respectively.[162] Tax treaties entered into by the Philippines may also entitle residents of foreign contracting states receiving

---

[161] *Id.*

[162] *Rep. Act No. 8424 (1997). This is the National Internal Revenue Code of the Philippines, as amended.*

royalty income from Philippine sources to claim preferential tax rates. The Philippines is a party to agreements/treaties for the avoidance of double taxation with a number of countries.[163]

It is mandatory for all TTAs to include a provision requiring the franchisor to bear the Philippine taxes on all payments relating to the TTA.[164] Thus, a tax gross-up provision, which passes on the burden to pay income taxes on the royalties or franchise fees to the franchisee, may render the entire agreement unenforceable for being violative of this mandatory provision. However, value added tax ("VAT") payable on the royalties or fees, may be passed on to the franchisee (subject to obtaining an exemption from compliance with Section 88.4 of the IP Code from the DITTB), considering that the same may be used as an input tax creditable against the output VAT of the franchisee.

V. Trademarks

Please advise us as to whether there are any special requirements for granting a valid trademark license, including the use of a registered user agreement or a short trademark license agreement and any required filing of such an agreement with the trademark authorities.

Apart from complying with the provisions of Sections 87 and 88 of the IP Code as discussed above, any license contract concerning the registration of a mark, or an application therefor, shall provide for effective control by the franchisor of the quality of the goods or services of the franchisee in connection with which the mark is used. If the license contract does not provide

[163] Australia, Austria, Bahrain, Bangladesh, Belgium, Brazil, Canada, Chile, China, Czech Republic, Denmark, Finland, France, Germany, Hungary, India, Indonesia, Israel, Italy, Japan, Korea, Malaysia, Netherlands, New Zealand, Norway, Pakistan, Poland, Romania, Russian Federation, Singapore, Spain, Sweden, Switzerland, Thailand, Turkey, United Arab Emirates, United Kingdom, United States of America, Vietnam, and Yugoslavia.

[164] Rep. Act No. 8293, sec.88.4.

for such quality control, or if such quality control is not effectively carried out, the license contract shall not be valid.[165]

The law also requires the submission of a trademark license agreement to the IPO. The IPO shall record the agreement and publish a reference to it but its contents shall be kept confidential. A license agreement shall have no effect against third parties until it is recorded by the IPO.[166]

The procedure for the recordal of a trademark license agreement is as follows:

- □ Prior to its recordal, the trademark license agreement shall be filed with the DITTB for clearance. The proof of payment of the filing fee shall be filed with the agreement.
- □ Within a period of ten days, the DITTB shall determine whether the agreement violates any of the provisions of Sections 87 or 88 of the IP Code.
- □ If the agreement does not violate Sections 87 and 88 of the IP Code, the DITTB shall issue a certificate of clearance and the agreement shall be recorded by the appropriate officer in the IPO.
- □ Should any provision of the agreement violate Sections 87 and 88 of the IP Code, the DITTB shall issue a notice to the parties to the agreement informing them of the violation and requiring them to comply with the pertinent provision of the IP Code prior to recordal.[167]

VI. Restrictions on Transfer

Please advise as to whether there are any restrictions (1) on a franchisor to restrict transfers by a master franchisee, any

---

[165] *Id.* sec. 150.1.

[166] *Id.* sec. 150.2.

[167] IPO Rules, Rules 17 to 20.

interest in a master franchisee, or the assets of the master franchisee or (2) the ability of a master franchisee to control and/or restrict transfers of a subfranchisee's rights under a master franchise agreement, interest in the subfranchisee, or the assets of the subfranchisee.

There are no specific restrictions under Philippine law on (i) the ability of the franchisor to restrict transfers by a master franchisee of any of its interest or assets, or (ii) the ability of a master franchisee to control and/or restrict transfers of a subfranchisee's rights under a master franchise agreement, interest in the subfranchisee, or assets of the subfranchisee. The parties may freely provide for such restrictions in their agreement, provided that such provisions are not contrary to law, morals, good customs, public order, or public policy.[168] In this regard, as mentioned above, Section 87.5 of the IP Code prohibits a provision in a TTA (such as a franchise agreement) that establishes a full or partial purchase option in favor of the licensor (such as a franchisor).

In general, however, an assignment of incorporeal rights should appear in a public instrument in order to be binding against third persons.[169]

VII. Termination

Please advise us as to any laws relating to termination in your country, such as agency laws, required indemnity provisions, notice or "good cause" requirements, or other laws affecting termination of a franchise agreement. Please describe.

There are no specific provisions governing the termination of a franchise agreement under Philippine law. The parties are free to stipulate on the grounds, required indemnities and procedures for termination. In any case, a party should not exercise its right to

---

[168] New Civil Code of the Philippines, art.1306.

[169] *Id,* art. 1625.

terminate the agreement in an arbitrary or abusive manner. Otherwise, it may be held liable for damages.

In general, the following are the grounds for extinguishment of obligations:[170]

- payment or performance,
- loss of the thing due,
- condonation or remission,
- confusion or merger of the rights of the creditor and debtor,
- compensation,
- novation,
- annulment,
- rescission,
- fulfillment of a resolutory condition,
- prescription, and
- expiration of the term or period.

VIII. Governing Law, Jurisdiction and Dispute Resolution

A. Choice of Law of Foreign Jurisdiction

Please confirm whether the choice of law of a foreign jurisdiction would likely to be upheld under the law of the country, except for certain matters such as trademarks, bankruptcy, and competition matters, which we assume would be governed by the law in your country.

As a general rule, the parties to a contract may freely stipulate a choice of law, provided that (i) such choice does not contravene Philippine law, morals, good customs, public order, or public policy[171] and (ii) the law stipulated bears a relationship to the parties or their transaction (as when one of the parties is a

[170] *Id,* art. 1231 and art. 1193

[171] *Id,* art. 1306.

resident of, or the elements of a transaction have taken place in, the jurisdiction of the place of the chosen law). However, notwithstanding the choice of a foreign law as the governing law, a Philippine court may, in disregard of any provision of the foreign law, apply the laws of the Philippines (i) with respect to matter bearing upon the authority and capacity of any Philippine national to enter into or perform the obligations under the agreement, and (ii) in determining compliance with all requirements of governmental approvals in the Philippines.

The IP Code specifically requires that the interpretation of TTAs or voluntary license contracts shall be governed by Philippine law.[172] Thus, the parties cannot provide for any law of a foreign jurisdiction as the governing law of the agreement.

B. International Arbitration Dispute Resolution

Please confirm that a court in your country would honor an election of international arbitration dispute resolution, and therefore refuse to hear any disputes arising under a franchise agreement.

The parties to a TTA may provide for international arbitration as the mechanism for dispute resolution, and such election will be respected by Philippine courts. The IP Code provides that in the event that the TTA provides for arbitration as a mode of dispute resolution, the procedure of arbitration of (i) the Arbitration Law of the Philippines or (ii) the Arbitration Rules of the United Nations Commission on International Trade Law or (iii) the Rules of Conciliation and Arbitration of the International Chamber of Commerce shall apply. Moreover, the venue of arbitration shall be the Philippines or any neutral country.[173]

---

[172] Rep. Act No. 8293, sec. 88.1.

[173] Section 88.3, IP Code.

Philippines

The Philippines is a signatory to the *1958 Convention on the Recognition and Enforcement of Foreign Arbitral Awards* ("New York Convention").

IX. Non-Competition Provisions

If the franchise agreement prohibits the master franchisee from engaging in certain competitive activities during the term of the agreement, and for a 12-month period after the termination or expiration of the agreement, please comment on the enforceability of non-competition covenants in your country.

The parties to a franchise agreement may freely and validly provide for non-competition covenants, as long as these covenants are not contrary to law, morals, good customs, public order, or public policy.[174] The Supreme Court has ruled that a contract in restraint of trade, including a non-involvement clause, is valid provided there is a limitation upon either time or place and the restraint upon one party is not greater than the protection the other party requires.[175]

However, the IP Code prohibits certain anti-competitive provisions in a TTA or franchise agreement, for examples:

1. clauses that prohibit the franchisee from exporting the licensed product, unless justified for the protection of the legitimate interest of the franchisor (such as exports to countries where exclusive licenses to manufacture and/or

---

[174] New Civil Code of the Philippines, art. 1306.

[175] *Daisy B. Tiu v. Platinum Plans Phil., Inc.*, G.R. No. 163512, February 28, 2007.

distribute the licensed product(s) have already been granted);[176] and

2. contractual provisions that restrict the use of technology supplied after the expiration of the TTA, except in cases of early termination of the TTA due to reasons attributable to the franchisee.[177]

X. Language Requirements

Does the law in your country require that a franchise agreement be translated into the local language in order to be enforceable between the parties?

There is no requirement under Philippine law for documents to be written in the local language in order to be enforceable between the parties. The parties may use English which is one of the official languages of the Philippines.

XI. Other Significant Matters

A. Binding Letter of Intent and Taking Deposit

The parties to a proposed franchise contract may sign a binding letter of intent or take a fee or deposit. However, under Philippine law governing option agreements, when the offeror has allowed the offeree a certain period to accept, the offer may be withdrawn at any time before acceptance by communicating such withdrawal, except when the option is founded upon a consideration, as something paid or promised.[178]

---

[176] Rep. Act No. 8293, sec.87.8.

[177] *Id.* sec. 87.9.

[178] New Civil Code of the Philippines, art. 1324.

B. Franchise Association

The Philippine Franchise Association ("PFA") is the pioneer and largest franchise association in the Philippines. The PFA is a self-regulating organization and membership therein is voluntary. Its members range from micro to large enterprises engaged in the food, retail, services, and other industries. The PFA is committed to the promotion of franchising as a tool for economic development and nation building through enterprise development and employment generation.[179] A list of the PFA's current officers and directors and its contact details are available on its website: http://www.pfa.org.ph/.

There are other franchise associations such as the Filipino International Franchise Association ("FIFA") and the Association of Filipino Franchisers Inc. ("AFFI"). The FIFA is also a non-stock, non-profit organization whose officers are experienced executives in the franchise business. It seeks to bring together franchisors, franchisees, and those with interest in the franchise sector to facilitate the process of learning and sharing information and to encourage high standards of conduct.[180] The AFFI, on the other hand, is committed to promote responsible micro, small, and medium enterprise businesses through franchising and consists of Filipino corporate presidents, CEOs, and prominent businessmen who recognize the competitive potential of the local franchising industry in the global market.[181]

C. Franchised Brands

Examples of international franchised brands operating in the Philippines are McDonald's, 7-Eleven, KFC, Krispy Kreme, Subway, Wendy's, T.G.I. Friday's, The Body Shop, GNC,

---

179 http://www.pfa.org.ph/last accessed on June 7, 2015.

180 http://www.fifa.ph/ last accessed on June 7, 2015.

181 http://affi.com.ph/ last accessed on June 7, 2015.

Philippines

Starbucks, Outback, Yellow Cab, Papa John, Dominos, Pizza Hut, Shakey's and Marithe Francois Girbaud.

Franchising in South Korea

Brendon Carr

YULCHON LLC

Seoul, South Korea

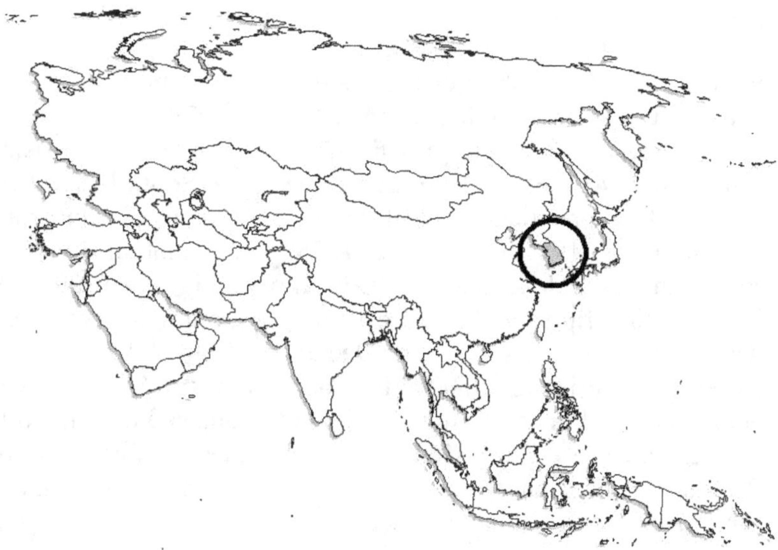

South Korea

I. Introduction

A. Historical Background of the Country

After World War II, a democratic-based government (Republic of Korea, ROK) was set up in the southern half of the Korean Peninsula while a communist-style government was installed in the north (Democratic People's Republic of Korea, DPRK). During the Korean War (1950–53), U.S. troops and UN forces fought alongside ROK soldiers to defend South Korea from a DPRK invasion supported by China and the Soviet Union. A 1953 armistice split the peninsula along a demilitarized zone at about the 38th parallel.

Park Chung-Hee took over leadership of the country in a 1961 coup. During his regime, from 1961 to 1979, South Korea achieved rapid economic growth, with per capita income rising to roughly 17 times the level of North Korea. South Korea held its first free presidential election under a revised democratic constitution in 1987, with former ROK Army General Rog Tae-Woo winning a close race. In 1993, Kim Young-Sam (1993–98) became the first civilian president of South Korea's new democratic era. President Kim Dae-Jung (1998–2003) won the Nobel Peace Prize in 2000 for his contributions to South Korean democracy and his "Sunshine" policy of engagement with North Korea. President Park Geun-Hye, daughter of former ROK President Park Chung-Hee, took office in February 2013 and is South Korea's first female leader.

South Korea holds a non-permanent seat (2013–14) on the UN Security Council and will host the 2018 Winter Olympic Games. Serious tensions with North Korea have punctuated inter-Korean relations in recent years, including the North's attacks on a South Korean ship and island in 2010, nuclear and missile tests, and its temporary closure of the inter-Korean Kaesong Industrial Complex in 2013.

South Korea

B. Economy of the Country

South Korea over the past four decades has demonstrated incredible growth and global integration to become a high-tech industrialized economy. In the 1960s, GDP per capita was comparable with levels in the poorer countries of Africa and Asia. In 2004, South Korea joined the trillion-dollar club of world economies, and is currently the world's 12th largest economy. Initially, a system of close government and business ties, including directed credit and import restrictions, made this success possible. The government promoted the import of raw materials and technology at the expense of consumer goods, and encouraged savings and investment over consumption.

The Asian financial crisis of 1997–98 exposed longstanding weaknesses in South Korea's development model including high debt/equity ratios and massive short-term foreign borrowing. GDP plunged by 6.9% in 1998, and then recovered by 9% in 1999–2000. South Korea adopted numerous economic reforms following the crisis, including greater openness to foreign investment and imports. Growth moderated to about 4% annually between 2003 and 2007. South Korea's export focused economy was hit hard by the 2008 global economic downturn, but quickly rebounded in subsequent years, reaching 6.3% growth in 2010.

The U.S.-Korea Free Trade Agreement was ratified by both governments in 2011 and went into effect in March 2012. Throughout 2012 and 2013 the economy experienced sluggish growth because of market slowdowns in the United States, China, and the Eurozone. The administration in 2014 is likely to face the challenge of balancing heavy reliance on exports with developing domestic-oriented sectors, such as services. The South Korean economy's long-term challenges include a rapidly aging population, inflexible labor market, dominance of large conglomerates ("*chaebols*"), and heavy reliance on exports, which comprise about half of GDP.

South Korea

C. Franchise Legal Overview

The *Fair Transactions in Franchise Business Act* (the "Act") was enacted on November 1, 2002 and was amended in 2008, 2010 and 2013. In February 2014, certain key amendments to the Act became effective (the "Amendment"). The new legislation addresses franchise relationship issues and heightens disclosure requirements.

A *Presidential Enforcement Decree, last amended January 6, 2015*, ("Presidential Decree") clarifies and further details certain provisions of the Act, including the Amendment.

II. Regulatory Requirements

A. Pre-Sale Disclosure

Please describe any pre-sale franchise disclosure or similar requirements that may apply to franchise transactions.

In South Korea, franchise transactions are regulated specifically by Article 2 of the Act. The Korean franchise law is generally quite friendly to franchisors. However, in practice the Korea Fair Trade Commission (the "KFTC") exhibits a strong bias in favor of the smaller party, typically the franchisee, in any disputes over interpretation of the law or franchise agreement.

The principal notable features of the Act are the requirements to deliver a registered disclosure document prior to taking any monies from a prospective franchisee, the requirement to escrow franchise fees for a certain period after delivery, and the mild limitations on the ability of the franchisor to quickly terminate the agreement (e.g., requires six (6) month notice before expiration, two written notices of default, 60-day cure period for default). Under the Act, acceptance of a franchise fee or execution of a franchise agreement is prohibited unless the franchisor provides a registered disclosure document within the 14-day time period. The 14-day time period may be amended to seven (7) days if the franchisee has consulted either an attorney or a licensed franchise dealer. The Act is silent as to whether disclosures need to be furnished to a prospective franchisee or master franchisee prior to their signing a letter of intent for franchise rights.

B. Government Approvals, Registrations, Filing Requirements

Please describe any necessary government approvals, registrations, or filing requirements that may apply to franchise transactions.

Article 3 of the Act provides for an exemption where the Act will not be applicable (e.g., in those case where the delivery of a disclosure document to a prospective franchisee is not required), if the total franchise fee paid by the franchisee to the franchisor for a six (6) month period beginning from the date of initial payment of the franchise fee does not exceed an amount of KRW 1 million (approximately US$ 985) or if the annual sales of the franchisor is less than KRW 50 million (approximately US$ 49,000) (amounts of KRW are specifically prescribed by the Presidential Decree of the Act).

To register a disclosure document, the franchisor must prepare the disclosure and all required appendixes in the Korean language and in a prescribed format ready to be used in the KFTC's on-line disclosure-document database. Review of the disclosure document in principle shall be completed within 30 days of submission; however, in practice, it is not uncommon for KFTC to deem a submission "incomplete" until the examining officer is ready to approve the document, and the review period may be extended up to approximately 60 days as the officer's curiosity is sated.

KFTC review of submitted registrations may be substantive as well as procedural. Examining officers may direct changes to the disclosure document or the proposed franchise agreement.

C. Limits on Fees and Typical Term of Franchise Agreement

Please describe any limits upon the nature and extent of fees and the term of a typical franchise agreement.

Royalties and service fees are common fees found in franchise agreements in Korea. It is also common for a franchisor to set development quotas. There are no threshold limits on fees.

III. Currency

If all payments under a franchise agreement must be made in immediately available U.S. Dollars, please advise as to any restrictions, reporting requirements, or regulations concerning the exchange, repatriation or remittance of U.S. Dollars.

Outbound foreign currency payments must be reported to a licensed foreign exchange bank and documented by a copy of the transaction agreements. Payments may be subject to withholding taxes subject to the relevant tax treaty, if any.

At the time of remittance of fees, a report must be filed with the remitting bank, which in turn reports to the Bank of Korea. Sometimes the bank may require a copy of the underlying agreement giving rise to the entitlement to the payment, which in the case of a franchise relationship would include the franchise agreement. Reports required for outbound foreign currency payments are not public records, and would not be expected to be disclosed to any other party by the bank.

IV. Taxes, Tariffs, and Duties

Please do not provide any in-depth comments on tax structuring. However, please provide your general comments on the typical amount of withholding tax that would apply and whether a "gross-up" provision contained in a franchise agreement would be enforceable in your country.

Franchisees are required to withhold tax on certain payments such as royalties and service fees.

Korea has a double taxation treaty with the United States.

V. Trademarks

Please advise us as to whether there are any special requirements for granting a valid trademark license, including the use of a registered user agreement or a short trademark license agreement and any required filing of such an agreement with the trademark authorities.

In general, there is no requirement under the Act for a franchisor to report or file with any government agency its trademark license to the franchisee pursuant to a franchise agreement. However, under the Trademark Act an exclusive license must be recorded with the Korea Intellectual Property Office to be effective. In this regard, the entire franchise agreement can be filed. However, it is customary to file a separate short form license that only reveals the essential trademark license information, so that all of the contents of the franchise agreement are not disclosed to the public.

VI. Restrictions on Transfer

Please advise as to whether there are any restrictions (1) on a franchisor to restrict transfers by a master franchisee, any interest in a master franchisee, or the assets of the master franchisee or (2) the ability of a master franchisee to control and/or restrict transfers of a subfranchisee's rights under a master franchise agreement, an interest in the subfranchisee, or the assets of the subfranchisee.

Under Korean franchise law, there are no requirements, restrictions or special provisions regarding transfers.

South Korea

VII. Termination

Please advise us as to any laws relating to termination in your country, such as agency laws, required indemnity provisions, notice or "good cause" requirements, or other laws affecting termination of a franchise agreement. Please describe.

The Act requires the franchisor to notify the franchisee of a decision not to renew a franchise agreement at least six (6) months prior to scheduled expiration; otherwise the franchisee may demand renewal.

Termination for default requires at least two written notices over a period of 60 days. If the franchisee shall cure the default during the 60-day period, termination shall not be permitted.

As with other countries, it is important to make clear that the franchise agreement does not create an agency relationship with the franchisee because there are specific issues regarding the agency relationship, including termination, which may require the principal or franchisor to pay its agent or franchisee compensation of up to one year's earnings.

VIII. Governing Law, Jurisdiction, and Dispute Resolution

A. Choice of Law of Foreign Jurisdiction

Please confirm whether the choice of law of a foreign jurisdiction would likely to be upheld under the law of the country, except for certain matters such as trademarks, bankruptcy and competition matters, which we assume would be governed by the law in your country.

Contracting parties are free to determine the governing law for their agreement, and their selection will be respected. However, in respect of mandatory provisions of the Act or other applicable statutes of Korea, Korean law will apply to the relationship regardless of the choice of law language in any agreement between the parties.

B. International Arbitration Dispute Resolution

Please confirm that a court in your country would honor an election of international arbitration dispute resolution, and therefore refuse to hear any disputes arising under a franchise agreement.

Korea is a signatory to the *Convention on the Recognition and Enforcement of Foreign Arbitral Awards* (the "New York Convention"). Although it is common for franchisors to require the parties engage in mediation or arbitration to resolve disputes, in practice most franchisor-franchisee disputes end up being resolved by the administrative investigation of the KFTC, the country's fair trade enforcement agency. KFTC is loath to decline jurisdiction over disputes on the basis of an agreement to arbitrate.

IX. Non-Competition Provisions

If the franchise agreement prohibits the franchisee from engaging in certain competitive activities during the term of the agreement, and for a 12-month period after the termination or expiration of the agreement, please comment on the enforceability of non-competition covenants in your country.

There are no legal restrictions on non-competition provisions provided that the non-compete obligation is not objectively unfair based on the circumstances.

X. Language Requirements

Does the law in your country require that a franchise agreement be translated into the local language in order to be enforceable between the parties?

The Act itself does not prescribe an official language for either the required franchise disclosure documents, or for franchise agreements. However, under Korea's law concerning adhesion contracts, the *Standardized Agreements Control Act,* where a weaker party is presented an adhesion contract which cannot be negotiated in practice, the Korean language is mandatory. Additionally, the KFTC generally requires franchisors to submit all documents to KFTC in the Korean language for purposes of registered disclosure documents. The registered disclosure document will include a sample standard franchise agreement, in addition to the other mandatory disclosure elements. Therefore, it is a practical requirement that if English is used, that all documents are also provided with Korean translations.

XI. Other Significant Matters

Please advise as to whether there are any significant matters not addressed above of which a franchisor should be aware in connection with its entering into a franchise agreement in your country.

The Korea Franchise Association represents the country's franchise sector. Membership is optional for both franchisors and franchisees.

In addition, franchisors with operations in Korea should pay close attention to changes made to the Act under the Amendment, most of which commenced on 14 February 2014.

The key changes are summarized below:

1. Requirement to provide sales revenue

    □ The Act requires franchisors to provide prospective franchisees with anticipated sales revenue and the basis for the calculation. The Presidential Decree stipulates that the franchisor must provide a range of projected sales revenue that reflects the minimum and maximum projected sales revenue of the prospective franchise unit at the location being considered. Moreover, the Presidential Decree requires a rather precise estimate: the maximum projection cannot be greater than 70% more than the minimum projection.

2. Requirement to share remodeling costs

   □ The legislation prohibits a franchisor from forcing a franchisee to remodel without just cause. In the case that a franchisor demands renovation or remodeling of a franchise unit, but does not require relocation of the unit, the franchisor shall be liable to bear 20% of the franchisee's costs. In the case that a move is required by the franchisor, the franchisor shall be liable to bear 40% of such costs. Currently, this percentage does not differ among industries.

3. Requirement for a territory and no competition in it from the franchisor group

   □ From 14 August 2014, franchisors are required to specify a franchise territory in a franchise agreement. Once specified in the agreement, no change can be made to the territory, except for a reason prescribed by the Presidential Decree. Importantly, franchisors and their affiliates are prohibited from opening their own or a franchise unit engaging in the same industry as that of the franchisee within that territory, without just cause.

4. Limits on ability to determine opening hours

   □ Franchisors will be prohibited from unfairly restricting franchisees' business hours or requiring franchisees to engage in late-night trading if the revenue from the late-night business is significantly lower than the cost of trading in the extended hours.

Franchising in Taiwan

Patricia Ginsberg
PAMIR LAW GROUP

Taipei, Taiwan

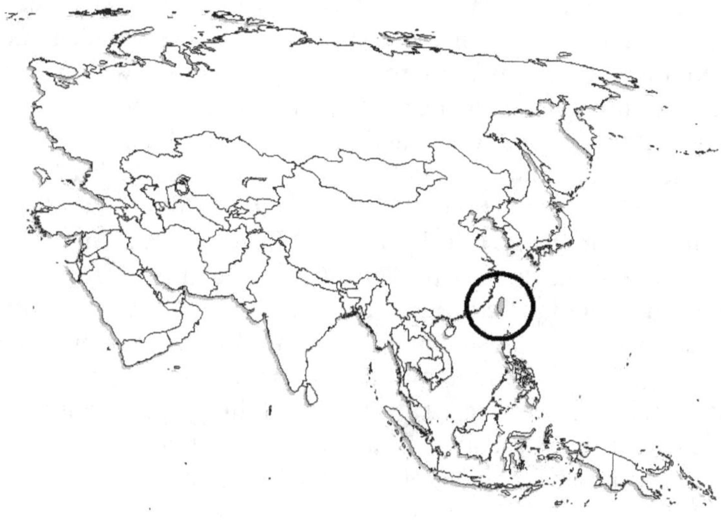

Taiwan

I. Introduction

A. Historical Background of the Country

Taiwan, which was a Japanese colony from 1895 to 1945, came under Chinese Nationalist control after World War II. Following Mao Tse-tung's communist victory on mainland China in 1949, two million Nationalists fled to the island of Taiwan and established a government using the 1947 constitution originally intended for all of China. The Nationalist ("KMT") government ruled Taiwan under strict martial law until the late 1980s when Taiwan gradually began the process of democratization, incorporating more and more local population within the governing structure and permitting economic liberalization. Throughout this period, the island prospered and became one of East Asia's economic "Tigers." In 1996, Taiwan had its first direct presidential election. After more than 50 years of an authoritarian one-party rule by the KMT government, in 2000, Taiwan underwent its first peaceful transfer of power from the KMT to the Democratic Progressive Party ("DPP") when a DPP candidate won the presidential election. At the moment, the dominant political issues continue to be the management of sensitive relations between Taiwan and China—specifically the question of Taiwan's status as a recognized state—as well as domestic priorities for economic reforms and growth.

B. Economy of the Country

Taiwan has a dynamic capitalist economy. Exports, led by high-tech products, electronics, machinery, and petrochemicals, have provided the primary impetus for economic development. This heavy dependence on exports, however, does expose the economy to impact from fluctuations in world demand. Geographically, it is strategically located in Asia, with major cities within one to five hours flight away making it an excellent hub as a business center for Asia. The Taiwanese population tends to be highly educated providing a sophisticated work force and consumer group. The populace has substantial spending power, thus attracting major international consumer brands to enter the Taiwanese market. It has proven to be a successful market for international franchise brands such as Subway, McDonald's, Chili's, Texas Roadhouse, Swenson's, Shane English School, Montesori, Domino's, Gymboree, TGI Friday's and so forth. Taiwan has also home-grown a number of successful brands which are branching overseas (e.g., 85 café in U.S., China, Australia, and Hong Kong; Coco Bubble Tea in New York; and Dante Coffee in Indonesia and Kuwait).

Free trade agreements have proliferated in East Asia over the past several years. Following the landmark Economic Cooperation Framework Agreement (ECFA) signed with China in June 2010, Taiwan executed a free trade deal with New Zealand in July 2013. This is Taiwan's first ever trade agreement with a country with which it does not maintain official diplomatic relations. In November of the same year, Taiwan inked a trade pact with Singapore. In addition to these nations, Taiwan has bilateral free trade agreements with Panama, El Salvador, Guatemala, Honduras, and Nicaragua.

The island runs a large overall trade surplus mainly because of its surplus with China, and its foreign reserves are the world's sixth largest, behind China, Japan, Saudi Arabia, Russia, and Switzerland. Japan, China, and U.S. are Taiwan's largest sources of importers for the past 14 years. China and nations in Southeast Asia (Philippines, Indonesia, Malaysia, Thailand, Cambodia, Singapore, and Vietnam) are presently the island's top destinations for its direct investment overseas with several Southeast Asian nations rapidly attracting labor-intensive industries due to changes in China's business environment, labor, and investment related laws and other economic factors.

C. Franchise Legal Overview

In Taiwan, franchise activities are not regulated by any franchise specific legislation. However, the *Taiwan Fair Trade Act* ("Act") addresses matters concerning fair trade and competition and thus the Act applies to franchise transactions. The Taiwan Fair Trade Commission ("TFTC") has promulgated guidelines concerning franchising. In 1999, the TFTC issued the "*Guidelines on the Disclosure of Information by franchisors*" (renamed as the "*Fair Trade Commission Disposal Directions (Policy Statements) on the Business Practices of franchisors")*[182] ("Guidelines"). The Guidelines are designed to promote fair dealing and prevent franchisors from concealing important information during solicitation of potential franchisees.

II. Regulatory Requirements

A. Pre-Sale Disclosure

Please describe any pre-sale franchise disclosure or similar requirements that may apply to franchise transactions.

Under the Guidelines, a franchisor must disclose material information in writing to a prospective franchisee at least ten days before entering into a franchise agreement (or within a reasonable period of time, depending on the specifics of a case). The Guidelines stipulate that material information includes, but is not limited to, the following items:

1. expenses before operation such as any applicable franchise fee[s], training charges, expenses for product purchases and capital equipment, etc. (each such item, its corresponding amount, and total estimate must be clearly listed);

2. expenses during operation such as license fee calculation and payment, management instruction fees, products, and raw material costs (each such item, its corresponding amount and total estimate must be clearly listed);

182 The Guidelines were amended on November 20, 2003, December 24, 2008, May 18, 2011 and February 8, 2012.

3. the trademark right, patent and copyright involved, and their contents, validity periods, extent of authorization, and restrictive conditions;

4. management assistance, training, and instruction;

5. plans for setting up other franchisees under the same franchise system in the franchisee's operating area;

6. the total number and location of franchisees under the same franchise system in the same county or city, and the statistics (ratio) of contract cancellation and termination in the previous year;

7. restrictions regarding the franchise relationship during the contract period, including:

   a. terms concerning supply of products, raw materials, capital equipment, etc. (specifications and names of suppliers or contractors);

   b. items and quantities of products or raw materials to be purchased; and

   c. any other restrictions with regard to the franchise relationship; and

8. conditions on amendment and termination.

In addition to the advance disclosure of material information, the franchise agreement itself must be provided to a prospective franchisee at least five days prior to signing to enable the prospective franchisee an opportunity to review the agreement. The parties should execute the agreement in duplicate, with one original held by the franchisee.

B. Government Approvals, Registrations, Filing Requirements.

Please describe any necessary government approvals, registrations, or filing requirements that may apply to franchise transactions.

With the exception of the requirements stipulated in the Guidelines described above, it is not necessary to have governmental approvals or registrations before parties enter into a franchise arrangement. Furthermore, there is no registration or filing requirements that apply once the parties have signed the franchise agreement and entered into the franchise relationship. Please note, however, where it is necessary to convert Taiwanese currency to the relevant foreign currency, franchise fee payments made overseas may be subject to additional reporting requirements (See Section III).

C. Limits on Fees and Typical Term of Franchise Agreement

Please describe any limits upon the nature and extent of fees and the term of a typical franchise agreement.

In general, franchisors and franchisees are free to agree on the relevant fees and the conditions of their transaction. There are no upper or lower limits on the amount of fees that a franchisor charges its franchisee. Although parties are free to agree on the terms and conditions, a franchisor should not abuse its position and the dependence of its franchisees. The Guidelines identify several prohibited activities that violate fair trade and dealings under the Act:

1. Differentiated Treatment

A franchisor would be deemed to violate Article 19(2) of the Act if the franchisor engages in differentiated treatment regarding price, trading terms or transactions with various franchisees or other businesses at the same competition level without justifiable reasons and such conduct leads to competition restriction or impediment of fair competition.

2. Improper Restrictions on franchisees

In order to protect their intellectual property rights, brand image and interests, or the overall business reputation of the franchise system, franchisors may impose necessary but reasonable restrictions. Improper and unreasonable restrictions leading to competition restriction or impediment of fair competition violate Article 19(6) of the Act. Examples of such illegal conduct include, but are not limited to, the following:

a. Tie-In Sales

Without justifiable reasons, a franchisor demands its franchisee to buy additional different product(s) when the franchisee is purchasing certain products.

b. Trading Counterpart Restriction

Without justifiable reasons, a franchisor imposes restrictions on its franchisee with regard to product sales, capital equipment, raw materials, and furnishing of work, such as the mandatory engagement of suppliers or contractors designated by the franchisor. Such conduct will most likely be regarded as leading to competition restriction or to the impediment of fair competition. The franchisor, however, may make recommendations so long as the selection of suppliers or contractors is not mandatory.

c. Compulsory Purchase Amounts

Without justifiable reasons, a franchisor demands its franchisee to purchase specific quantities of products or raw materials and prohibits their return and such quantities exceed what the franchisee is able to sell within a reasonable number of business days or surpass the stock quantities a franchisee requires. Such conduct will most likely be regarded as leading to competition restriction or to the impediment of fair competition.

III. Currency

If all payments under a franchise agreement must be made in immediately available U.S. Dollars, please advise as to any restrictions, reporting requirements, or regulations concerning the exchange, repatriation or remittance of U.S. Dollars.

Payments under a franchise agreement do not need to be denominated in U.S. Dollars. Under the "*Regulations Governing the Declaration of Foreign Exchange Receipts and Disbursements or Transaction,*"[183] if an amount wired overseas is greater than Five Hundred Thousand New Taiwan Dollars (NT$500,000, roughly US$ 16,666 at an exchange rate of US$ 1:NT$30), then the local bank must report to the Central Bank of the Republic of China (Taiwan) ("Central Bank") regarding the purpose of the remittance. If a single remittance by a company is at or over One Million United States Dollars (US$ 1,000,000), then besides reporting to the Central Bank, one would need to submit the "transaction documents" such as the franchise agreement. For an entity (as opposed to a natural

[183] Promulgated on August 30, 1995, and amended on December 27, 1995, June 11, 1997, December 31, 2001, March 30, 2002, April 30, 2003, and June 01, 2010.

person), the annual remittance for an entire year should not be greater than Fifty Million United States Dollars (US$ 50,000,000) in the aggregate. If the remittance will exceed such maximum figure, prior approval of the Central Bank is required.

IV. Taxes, Tariffs and Duties

Please do not provide any in-depth comments on tax structuring. However, please provide your general comments on the typical amount of withholding tax that would apply and whether a "gross-up" provision contained in a franchise agreement would be enforceable in your country.

Absent tax treaties, the withholding tax levied on a franchisee's payment made to a foreign franchisor with no permanent existence in Taiwan is twenty percent (20%). "Gross up" provisions are enforceable in Taiwan.

Taiwan is a signatory of double taxation treaties with the following countries: Australia, Belgium, Denmark, Gambia, Indonesia, Macedonia, Malaysia, New Zealand, Senegal, Singapore, South Africa, Swaziland, Sweden, the Netherlands, United Kingdom, Vietnam, India, Israel, Thailand, France, Germany, Hungary, Slovakia, and Paraguay. Additionally, Taiwan has double taxation agreements for the shipping or air transport industry with: Canada, the European Union, Germany, Israel, Japan, Korea, Luxembourg, Macau, the Netherlands, Norway, Sweden, Thailand, and the United States.

V. Trademarks

Please advise us as to whether there are any special requirements for granting a valid trademark license, including the use of a registered user agreement or a short trademark license agreement and any required filing of such an agreement with the trademark authorities.

Taiwan

The agency in charge of intellectual property in Taiwan is the Intellectual Property Office of the Ministry of Economic Affairs ("Taiwan Intellectual Property Office"). There are no special requirements for granting a valid trademark license. The Taiwan Intellectual Property Office does not require users to register or file their license agreement. Mutual consent alone will suffice. A franchisor can still register the trademark license with the Taiwan Intellectual Property Office. By doing this, the trademark license registration can act as a defense against certain types of third-party claims. For this reason, it is recommended that franchisors and franchisees apply to the Registrar Office at the Taiwan Intellectual Property Office to record the license.

A franchisor who has not registered its trademark in Taiwan is recommended to do so since Taiwan Trademark Law applies the "first to file" principle and affords protection to a trademark upon registration. It is, therefore, important to file trademark application(s) on the earliest possible date. A foreign individual or entity must appoint an agent in Taiwan to apply for the registration of a mark on its behalf to the Taiwan Intellectual Property Office.

Priority can be claimed for a trademark application if it is filed within six months from the date of the first registration application of the same trademark in a country that has a treaty or agreement with Taiwan concerning reciprocal trademark protection. Taiwan became a member of the World Trade Organization ("WTO") on January 1, 2002; thus, priority can be claimed by any applicant of any other WTO member state.

In Taiwan, registered marks are designated as "trademarks," regardless of whether they cover goods or services. One application can cover one mark for goods or services in one or more class(es). However, a multi-class application will not be permitted if the priority date for one class is from one country and the priority date for another class is from a different country. In that case, separate applications must be made.

In terms of timing, the Taiwan Intellectual Property Office normally takes about eight to ten months to process a trademark application once all required supporting documents have been properly submitted. After the application is approved, an approval letter will be sent to the applicant. Registration fees must be paid within two months from the date the approval letter is received. After the payment of registration fees, the Taiwan Intellectual Property Office will publish the mark as a registered trademark in the *Government Gazette*. The applicant will obtain the trademark rights and certificate as of the publication date. Anyone may file an opposition to the registration within three months from the publication date. Therefore, although the certificate is given, the trademark rights are not fully valid until three months after the publication and as long as no objections by third parties are made.

VI. Restrictions on Transfer

Please advise as to whether there are any restrictions (1) on a franchisor to restrict transfers by a master franchisee, any interest in a master franchisee, or the assets of the master franchisee or (2) the ability of a master franchisee to control and/or restrict transfers of a subfranchisee's rights under a master franchise agreement, an interest in the subfranchisee, or the assets of the subfranchisee.

Under Taiwanese laws, there is no specific law regulating franchise businesses. The franchisor-franchisee relationship is subject to the franchise agreement itself under general contract rules and principles, which are covered by the *Civil Code of Taiwan* ("Civil Code"). There are no restrictions (1) on a franchisor to restrict transfers by a master franchisee, any interest in a master franchisee, or the assets of the master franchisee or (2) the ability of a master franchisee to control and/or restrict transfers of a subfranchisee's rights under a master franchise agreement, an interest in the subfranchisee, or the assets of the subfranchisee. Terms and conditions should be clearly stated in the franchise agreement, should be conscionable and should not violate public order or morale and cannot violate fair and reasonable trading order.

VII. Termination

Please advise us as to any laws relating to termination in your country, such as agency laws, required indemnity provisions, notice or "good cause" requirements, or other laws affecting termination of a franchise agreement. Please describe.

As mentioned above, Taiwan does not have specific laws regulating franchise businesses. The franchisor-franchisee relationship is subject to the franchise agreement itself under general contract rules and principles, which are covered by the Civil Code. There are no restrictions or requirements concerning indemnity provisions or termination for good cause. The parties are free to agree on terms and conditions of their franchise relationship; provided however, that the terms should be conscionable and should not violate public order or morale. Terms and conditions regarding termination should be clearly stated in the franchise agreement and cannot violate fair and reasonable trading order.

VIII. Governing Law, Jurisdiction and Dispute Resolution

A. Choice of Law of Foreign Jurisdiction

Please confirm whether the choice of law of a foreign jurisdiction would likely to be upheld under the law of the country, except for certain matters such as trademarks, bankruptcy and competition matters, which we assume would be governed by the law in your country.

Under Taiwan's conflict of laws principles, contracting parties are free to determine the governing law for their agreement, and their selection will be respected. If the parties do not agree on the governing law, courts in Taiwan will apply the law with the greatest connection to the case in accordance with the type of dispute. For instance, if the dispute concerns a debt relation (e.g., the franchisee owes the franchisor royalties), then the location where the debtor's actions took place is assumed to be the greatest connection to such type of cases.

B. International Arbitration Dispute Resolution

Please confirm that a court in your country would honor an election of international arbitration dispute resolution, and therefore refuse to hear any disputes arising under a franchise agreement.

Under Taiwanese law, contracting parties are free to determine their dispute resolution method, including their selection to pursue arbitration instead of court litigation. The parties may also agree to select foreign arbitration instead of domestic arbitration. According to the *Arbitration Act of Taiwan*, if a party to an arbitration agreement files a lawsuit contrary to the arbitration agreement, the adverse party has the right to petition the court to suspend the lawsuit. The court would then order the parties to submit to arbitration. In such cases, if the party fails to submit to arbitration, the court will dismiss the legal action.

Taiwan is not a party to the *Convention on the Recognition and Enforcement of Foreign Arbitral Awards* (the "New York Convention") because it is not a member of the United Nations. Despite not being a signatory to the New York Convention, foreign arbitral awards can nevertheless be recognized and enforced in Taiwan. The *Arbitration Act in Taiwan* is based on the *UNCITRAL Model Law of 1985* ("UNCITRAL Law"), and it applies to both domestic and international arbitrations. Except on narrow grounds relating to the lack of jurisdiction, the improper constitution of the tribunal, serious procedural irregularity, or an award countering public policy, countries such as Taiwan that have adopted UNCITRAL Law will usually recognize and enforce foreign arbitral awards.

In the case of Taiwan, the courts do, however, have the additional discretion to refuse recognition if the country where the award was made or under whose law the award was issued, refuses to recognize Taiwanese arbitral awards. The party wishing to enforce a foreign award in Taiwan should first apply to a Taiwanese court for recognition. The application should include the original arbitration agreement together with the original arbitral award document (if any of the originals are not available, then an authenticated copy is required).

These documents submitted to the court must be translated into Chinese if they are in a foreign language and must be legalized by the Taiwanese embassy or its functional equivalent located at the applicable jurisdiction. The petitioner must comply with these formalities to prevent the application from being dismissed. An award would be recognized and enforced unless the court determines that the award contravenes public order or good morals of Taiwan or if the dispute could not be arbitrated under the laws of Taiwan or pursuant to any of the narrow grounds stated above.

Even if such narrow grounds do not exist, the court may still, at its discretion, dismiss an application for the award recognition if the country where the arbitral award is made or whose laws govern the arbitral award does not recognize arbitral awards from Taiwan. After recognition by the court, the petitioner should then apply to the Civil Execution Department of the relevant District Court for enforcement of the award. An execution fee for enforcement would be determined and must then be paid.

IX. Non-Competition Provisions

If the franchise agreement prohibits the franchisee from engaging in certain competitive activities during the term of the agreement, and for a 12-month period after the termination or expiration of the agreement, please comment on the enforceability of non-competition covenants in your country.

To protect the intellectual property and business interests of the franchisor, a non-competition clause with a reasonable non-compete period is allowed under Taiwanese law. There is no black letter law stipulating the exact period a non-compete would be considered reasonable or permissible; however, in practice, a period of up to two years after the termination or expiration of the agreement will usually be enforceable.

X. Language Requirements

Does the law in your country require that a franchise agreement be translated into the local language in order to be enforceable between the parties?

Taiwan does not require that a franchise agreement be in the Chinese language to be valid and enforceable between the parties. However, in the event of a dispute presented to Taiwanese courts, all evidence and documents, including the franchise agreement, would need to be translated into Chinese. Should the case be arbitrated, the parties are free to decide the language in which the arbitration is to be conducted as well as the language of the evidentiary documents.

XI. Other Significant Matters

Please advise as to whether there are any significant matters not addressed above of which a franchisor should be aware in connection with its entering into a franchise agreement in your country.

Taiwan has a few franchise associations, which are not affiliated with the government. Their names and contact details are provided below:

Taiwan Chain Stores and Franchise Association
4F, No. 180, Nanking E. Road,
Section 4, Taipei 105, Taiwan
TEL: 886-2-2579-6262 FAX: 886-2-2579-1176
http://www.tcfa.org.tw/

Taiwan

Association of Chain and Franchise Promotion, Taiwan
7F., No.82, Sec. 1, Zhongshan N. Rd.,
Zhongshan Dist., Taipei City 104, Taiwan
TEL: 886-2-2523-5118 FAX: 886-2-2523-0229
http://www.franchise.org.tw/about_e.php

Franchising in Tajikistan

Rustam M. Nazrisho and Sherzod S. Sodatkadamov

Nazrisho & Mirzoev, LLC

Dushanbe, Tajikistan

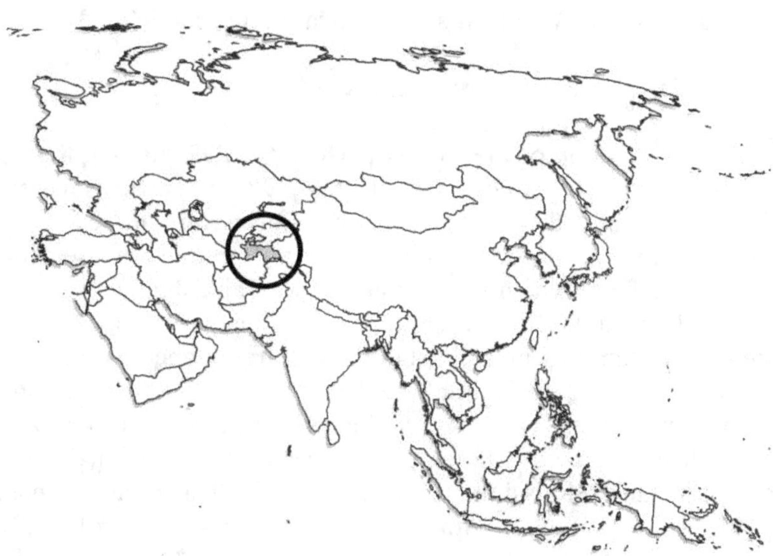

Tajikistan

I. Introduction

A. Historical Background of the Country

Historically, Tajikistan was home to kingdoms ruled by people of different faiths and cultures as well as by numerous empires and dynasties. What now constitutes Tajikistan became an independent state in 1991 as a result of the breakup of the Soviet Union. The country experienced a civil war from 1992 to 1997. Although the country remains the poorest in the former Soviet sphere, the newly established political stability and foreign aid have allowed the country's economy to grow. Tajikistan became a member of the World Trade Organization in March 2013.

B. Economy of the Country

Tajikistan has one of the lowest per capita GDPs among the 15 former Soviet republics. The 1992–1997 civil war severely damaged an already weak economic infrastructure and caused a sharp decline in industrial and agricultural production. Because of limited employment opportunities in Tajikistan, more than one million Tajik citizens work abroad, roughly 90% in Russia–supporting families in Tajikistan through remittances. Less than 7% of the land area is arable and cotton is the most important crop. Until 2008, cotton production was closely monitored and controlled by the government. In the wake of the National Bank of Tajikistan's admission in December 2007 that it had directed the AgroInvestBank to improperly lend money to politically connected investors in the cotton sector, the IMF canceled its stand-by assistance program in Tajikistan. As part of the Tajik government's subsequent reforms, over a half billion dollars in farmer debt has been forgiven. In 2008 Tajikistan passed new law authorizing farmers to decide for themselves what crops to grow, and this has resulted in a gradual decrease in cotton output.

Tajikistan imports approximately 60% of its food, most of which comes by rail. Uzbekistan closed one of the rail lines into Tajikistan in late 2011, hampering the transit of goods to and from the southern part of the country. As a result, food and fuel prices increased to the highest levels since 2002. Mineral resources include silver, gold, uranium, and tungsten.

Industry consists mainly of small obsolete factories in food processing and light industry, substantial hydropower facilities, and a large aluminum plant–currently operating below 25% of capacity. Electricity output expanded with the completion of the Sangtuda-1 hydropower dam–finished in 2009 with Russian investment. The smaller Sangtuda-2 hydropower dam, built with Iranian investment, began operating in 2012 at a limited capacity. The Tajik government is tens of millions of dollars in arrears for both Sangtuda dams, and Sangtuda-2 has been closed for "maintenance" since January 2014. The government has pinned its drive for energy independence on completion of the Roghun dam.

In 2010, the government began a coerced sale of shares in the Roghun enterprise to its population, ultimately raising over US $ 180 million before stopping under intense criticism from international donors, but the dam is likely to cost billions of dollars. The World Bank funded two feasibility studies (technical-economic, and social-environmental) for the dam. If built according to plan, Roghun will be the tallest dam in the world, will operate year-round, and will significantly expand Tajikistan's electricity output. In 2013, the Tajik government finalized an agreement to import one million tons of fuel and oil products from Russia each year, at reduced prices. Tajikistan's economic situation remains fragile due to uneven implementation of structural reforms, corruption, weak governance, seasonal power shortages, and its large external debt burden.

C. Franchise Legal Overview

The legal system of the Republic of Tajikistan (Tajikistan) is similar to those of other Central Asian countries. It is based on statutory law rather than case law. The main legal act that regulates private relations, such as contractual relations, intellectual property matters, ownership rights and other issues is the *Civil Code of Tajikistan (Kodeksi Grazhdani)* which is composed of three parts. Chapter forty-nine of the *Civil Code of Tajikistan* dated December 11, 1999 (Civil Code) titled Commercial Concession Contract[184] is the main piece of legislation governing franchise contracts. The Civil Code describes this type of contract as an agreement where one party (the right holder-franchisor) provides to the other party (the user-franchisee) for value, and for a term or without a term, the right to use a set of exclusive rights belonging to the right holder, including the right to the firm name and/or commercial name of the right holder, protected commercial information, as well as other exclusive rights stipulated in the agreement— trademarks, service marks, etc.

According to Tajik Law, a franchise agreement is enforceable, if the franchisor provides to the franchisee at least the following exclusive rights, generally referred to as "mandatory objects of franchise agreement,"——the right to (1) firm name and (or) commercial name and (2) protected commercial information. Thus, any franchise agreement, should have a provision on the transfer to a franchisee the mandatory objects of franchise agreement.[185]

---

184 It is worth noting that the *Civil Code* does not use the term "franchise contract," instead it employs the term "Commercial Concession Contract". For the purposes of this chapter the term "franchise agreement" is used instead of "Commercial Concession Contract".

185 In theory, though there are different views on this issue, as some experts consider that not all mandatory objects should be provided to the franchisee, but at least one of them. Taking into account that these kind of contracts are rare and the lack of relevant judicial precedents, the aforesaid issue remains disputable.

Tajikistan

II. Regulatory Requirements

A. Pre-Sale Disclosure

Please describe any pre-sale franchise disclosure or similar requirements that may apply to franchise transactions.

Under Tajik Law there are no pre-sale franchise disclosures or similar requirements applicable to franchise transactions.

B. Governmental Approvals, Registrations, Filing Requirements

Please describe any necessary government approvals, registrations or filing requirements that may apply to franchise transactions.

To be a fully effective and enforceable franchise transaction, it should be registered according to Tajik Law. The registration process consists of two stages:

1) The franchise contract should be registered with the local department on state registration of legal entities and individual entrepreneurs of the Tax Committee under the Government of Tajikistan (*Kumitai andozi nazdi hukumati Jumhurii Tojikiston*) where the franchisee is registered, if the franchisor is a foreign national.

2) Where the franchise agreement provides for the transfer of objects protected by intellectual property legislation (such as trademarks and service marks), such agreement should be registered with the Patent Office (*Markazi millii patentu ittiloot*) of Tajikistan as well, otherwise the franchise agreement will be deemed void. This procedure follows the abovementioned registration with the local department on state registration of legal entities and individual entrepreneurs of the Tax Committee.

Under default rules, the franchisor is responsible for registration of the franchise agreement with the state authorities described above. Notwithstanding the above, there is no legal normative act that specifically regulates the registration procedures of franchise transactions.

C. Limits on Fees and Typical Term of Franchise Agreement

Please describe any limits upon the nature and extent of fees and the term of a typical franchise agreement.

Tajik contract law is based on the principle of freedom of contract. As a general rule, the parties to a contract are free to incorporate any terms or conditions to such contract to the extent permitted by law. In the case of franchise agreements, Tajik Law does not stipulate any limits with regards to fees and terms of the franchise transaction. The law does provide that the parties to the contract, the franchisor and the franchisee, should be individual entrepreneurs and/or commercial legal entities.

III. Currency

If all payments under a franchise agreement must be made in immediately available U.S. Dollars, please advise as to any restrictions, reporting requirements, or regulations concerning the exchange, repatriation or remittance of U.S. Dollars.

According to the *Law On Currency Regulation and Currency Control (Qonun "Dar borai tanzimi as'or va nazorati as'or")* dated June 13, 2013, payments in U.S. Dollars are treated as currency operations that are not subject to any restrictions, reporting requirements, or regulations concerning the exchange, repatriation, or remittance of U.S. Dollars.

IV. Taxes, Tariffs and Duties

Please do not provide any in-depth comments on tax structuring. However, please provide your general comments on the typical amount of withholding tax that would apply and whether a "gross up" provision contained in a franchise agreement would be enforceable in your country.

Pursuant to *Tax Code (Kodeksi Andoz)* dated September 17, 2012 (effective on January 1, 2013), any income, in the form of royalty, derived from sources within Tajikistan by a foreign company without a permanent establishment in Tajikistan is subject to a 15% withholding tax.

Tajikistan is signatory to double taxation treaties with the following countries: Azerbaijan, Armenia, Belgium, Belorussia, China, Czech Republic, Germany, India, Iran Indonesia, Japan, Kazakhstan, Kyrgyzstan, Latvia, Moldova, Poland, Pakistan, Russia, Romania, Switzerland, Turkey, Turkmenistan, Ukraine, and United Arab Emirates.

Pursuant to most of the tax treaties mentioned above, the rate of withholding tax with respect to royalties is reduced to 10%. In some treaties however, the tax is set at the rate of 8% (China), 5% (Switzerland) and 15% (Belorussia).

The enforceability of "gross-up" provisions contained in a franchise agreement is a disputable issue, but in practice is widely used in other commercial transactions.

V. Trademarks

Please advise us as to whether there are any special requirements for granting a valid trademark license, including the use of a registered user agreement or a short trademark license agreement and any required filing of such an agreement with the trademark authorities.

The *Law on Trademarks and Service Marks (Qonun "Dar borai tamghahoi moli va tamghai khizmatrasoni")* dated March 5, 2007, is the main piece of legislation relating to trademarks. The only provision specific to license agreements is reflected in Article 31 of the *Law on Trademarks and Service Marks*. In accordance with this Article, the owner (licensor) of the registered trademark is allowed to grant, on a contractual basis, the registered trademark to another individual or entity (the licensee). The license agreement should include a provision that the quality of the licensee's goods should not be lower than the quality of the licensor's goods and that the licensor must monitor the implementation of this provision. The law also provides that the license contract should be registered with the Patent Office in order to be effective and enforceable.

Article 962 of the Civil Code obligates the franchisor to transfer licenses to the franchisee if provided by the franchise agreement and must follow the established procedures. Notwithstanding the above, there is no need for the parties to a franchise agreement to enter into a separate license agreement, as the license agreement itself could be a part of the franchise agreement. In this case, the franchise agreement should be registered with the Patent Office following the registration with tax authorities as mentioned in Section II(B) above.

VI. Restrictions on Transfer

Please advise as to whether there are any restrictions (1) on a franchisor to restrict transfers by a master franchisee, any interest in a master franchisee, or the assets of the master franchisee or (2) the ability of a master franchisee to control and/or restrict transfers of a subfranchisee's rights under a master franchise agreement, interest in the subfranchisee, or the assets of the subfranchisee.

There are no specific restrictions under Tajik Law on a franchisor's ability to restrict transfers by a master franchisee of the rights provided under franchise agreement. Pursuant to the Civil Code, the franchisor may allow or restrict the master franchisee to transfer the exclusive rights. As to the transfer of interest in a master franchisee, or the assets of the master franchisee, the franchisor could not restrict the transfers directly, as similar restrictions are subject only to the corporate documents of the master franchisee.

There are also no specific restrictions under Tajik Law on the ability of a master franchisee to control and/or restrict transfers of a subfranchisee's rights. As to the transfer of interest in a master franchisee, or the assets of the master franchisee, the master franchisee could not restrict the transfers directly, as similar restrictions are subject only to the corporate documents of the subfranchisee.

VII. Termination

Please advise us as to any laws relating to termination in your country, such as agency laws, required indemnity provisions, notice or "good cause" requirements, or other laws affecting termination of a franchise agreement. Please describe.

There are commonly accepted rules of termination that may be used in the franchise agreement, such as (i) mutual agreement of the parties; (ii) unilateral termination by one party of a termless franchise agreement with six months prior notice, unless another period is provided by the contract; (iii) by a court decision upon the application of one of the parties (a) in the case of a material violation of the contract by the other party and (b) in the case of a material change of circumstances, unless otherwise stipulated by the contract; and (iv) the occurrence of any of the events as may be agreed between the parties. Furthermore, the *Civil Code* provides that the early termination of the franchise agreement requires the registration of the termination agreement with the agencies set forth in Section II(B) above.

VIII. Governing Law, Jurisdiction and Dispute Resolution

A. Choice of Law of Foreign Jurisdiction

Please confirm whether the choice of law of a foreign jurisdiction would likely to be upheld under the law of the country, except for certain matters such as trademarks, bankruptcy and competition matters, which we assume would be governed by the law in your country.

The Civil Code sets out the general principle that the parties may freely choose the law governing their cross-border transactions, unless otherwise provided by Tajik Law. The parties are allowed to choose the law applicable to the entire contract or to separate parts thereof. Thus, as a general rule the choice of law of a foreign jurisdiction in a cross-border transaction most likely would be upheld under Tajik Law, unless otherwise provided by specific rules.

B. International Arbitration Dispute Resolution

Please confirm that a court in your country would honor an election of international arbitration dispute resolution, and therefore refuse to hear any disputes arising under a franchise agreement.

The settlement of disputes by means of arbitration is not widespread among Tajik businesses, and there is no reputable arbitration institution, despite the existence of the *Law On Arbitration Tribunals* (*Qonun "Dar borai sudhoi hakami"*) dated January 5, 2008 and a newly passed *Law On International Commercial Arbitration dated March 18, 2015*. The only available option for foreign investors is the use of arbitration clauses in contracts (or arbitration agreements) that refers all disputes or claims to foreign arbitration institutions. In 2012, Tajikistan acceded to the *1958 New York Convention on Recognition and Enforcement of Foreign Arbitral Awards.* Consequently, it is now possible to enforce foreign arbitral awards in Tajikistan, although with some limitations such as inapplicability of the convention to disputes related to real estate (immovable property).

IX. Non-Competition Provisions

If the franchise agreement prohibits the master franchisee from engaging in certain competitive activities during the term of the agreement, and for a 12-month period after the termination or expiration of the agreement, please comment on the enforceability of non-competition covenants in your country.

According to the *Civil Code*, the franchise agreement may provide for restrictions of the parties' rights, such as (i) the master franchisee's obligation not to compete with the franchisor in the territory and with respect to the business covered by the contract and (ii) the master franchisee's renunciation of the right to obtain similar rights under other franchise agreements from the franchisor's competitors or potential competitors. The law does not restrain the parties from agreeing to apply the abovementioned non-competition covenants for a 12-month period after the termination or expiration of the agreement, and such covenants would likely be effective and enforceable. However, it should be noted that non-competition covenants may be invalidated upon request of antimonopoly agencies or other concerned parties, if such covenants are in contradiction with the antimonopoly laws.

X. Language Requirements

Does the law in your country require that a franchise agreement be translated into the local language in order to be enforceable between the parties?

Pursuant to *Law On Official Language of the Republic of Tajikistan (Qonun "Dar borai zaboni davlatii Jumhurii Tojikiston")* dated October 5, 2009, all paperwork of organizations operating in Tajikistan must be in the Tajik language. Moreover, since franchise agreements are registered with the state authorities mentioned in Section 1(B) above, for registration purposes the authorities require a certified translated copy of the franchise agreement. In practice, despite the requirements of Tajik laws, most of the contracts in the country are drafted in the Russian language.

XI. Other Significant Matters

Please advise as to whether there are any significant matters not addressed above of which a franchisor should be aware in connection with its entering into a franchise agreement in your country.

In general, it is clear that the laws of franchising in Tajikistan are incomplete. This is attributed to the fact that franchising transactions in Tajikistan are virtually non-existent. Nevertheless, based on the present structure of the relevant law in the country, it is safe to assume that the laws are lax and somewhat welcoming for franchising. In practice, however, franchisors must keep in mind that the laws will evolve as there is more investment in Tajikistan through franchise agreements.

Franchising in Thailand

Sriwan Puapondh and Alan Adcock

TILLEKE & GIBBINS

Bangkok, Thailand

Thailand

I. Introduction

A. Historical Background of the Country

A unified Thai kingdom was established in the mid-14th century. Thailand is the only Southeast Asian country never to have been taken over by a European power. A bloodless revolution in 1932 led to a constitutional monarchy. In alliance with Japan during World War II, Thailand became a U.S. treaty ally in 1954 after sending troops to Korea and later fighting alongside the United States in Vietnam. Thailand since 2005 has experienced several rounds of political turmoil including a military coup in 2006 that ousted then Prime Minister Thaksin Chinnawat, followed by large-scale street protests by competing political factions in 2008, 2009, and 2010. Thaksin's youngest sister, Yinglak Chinnawat, in 2011 led the Puea Thai Party to an electoral win and assumed control of the government. A blanket amnesty bill for individuals involved in street protests, altered at the last minute to include all political crimes–including all convictions against Thaksin–triggered months of large-scale anti-government protests in Bangkok beginning in November 2013. In early May 2014 Yinglak was removed from office and in late May 2014 the Royal Thai Army staged a coup against the caretaker government.

B. Economy of the Country

With a well-developed infrastructure, a free-enterprise economy, generally pro-investment policies, and strong export industries, Thailand achieved steady growth due largely to industrial and agriculture exports——mostly electronics, agricultural commodities, automobiles and parts, and processed foods.

Unemployment, at less than 1% of the labor force, stands as one of the lowest levels in the world, which puts upward pressure on wages in some industries. Thailand also attracts nearly 2.5 million migrant workers from neighboring countries. The Thai government in 2013 implemented a nation-wide 300 baht (US$ 10) per day minimum wage policy and deployed new tax reforms designed to lower rates on middle-income earners. The Thai economy has weathered internal and external economic shocks in recent years. The global economic recession severely cut Thailand's exports, with most sectors experiencing double-digit drops. In late 2011 Thailand's recovery was interrupted by historic flooding in the industrial areas in Bangkok and its five surrounding provinces, crippling the manufacturing sector. The government approved flood mitigation projects worth US$ 11.7 billion, which were started in 2012, to prevent similar economic damage, and an additional US$ 75 billion for infrastructure over the following seven years. This was expected to lead to an economic upsurge but growth has remained slow, in part due to ongoing political unrest and resulting uncertainties. Spending on infrastructure will require re-approval once a new government is seated.

C. Franchise Legal Overview

Thailand has no specific legislation or set of regulations that deal with franchising. Accordingly, the ordinary principles of contract and the common law will apply to franchises in Thailand. As such, there is no need for pre-sale franchise disclosure, government approvals nor are there any restrictions to the nature and extent of fees that may be charged. These matters are solely matters for the franchisor and franchisee.

II. Regulatory Requirements

A. Pre-Sale Disclosure

Please describe any pre-sale franchise disclosure or similar requirements that may apply to franchise transactions.

In Thailand, there are no franchise disclosure requirements. Note, however, the draft Franchising Business Act, outlined in Section XI.

B. Governmental Approvals, Registrations, Filing Requirements.

Please describe any necessary government approvals, registrations, or filing requirements that may apply to franchise transactions.

There are no required governmental approvals, registrations, or other filing requirements.

C. Thai Legislation

Currently, there are no specific laws in Thailand regarding franchise regulation (although, as discussed in Section XI, the enactment of the draft *Franchising Business Act* would change this). Nonetheless, franchise relations are not completely without restrictions. While no specific franchise law currently exists, the courts utilize various other laws broadly covering contracts and business operations in governing franchise agreements.

The following local laws are relevant:

- *The Civil and Commercial Code;*
- *The Thailand Trademark Act B.E. 2534 (1991), as amended by the Trademark Act (Number 2) B.E. 2543 (2000);*
- *The Thailand Patent Act B.E. 2522 (1979), as amended by the Patent Act (Number 2) B.E. 2535 (1992) and Patent Act (Number 3) B.E. 2542 (1999);*
- *The Thailand Copyright Act B.E. 2537 (1994);*
- *The Trade Secrets Act B.E. 2545 (2002);*
- *The Unfair Contract Terms Act B.E. 2540 (1997);*
- *The Trade Competition Act B.E. 2542 (1999);*
- *The Act Relating to Price of Merchandise and Service B.E. 2542 (1999);*
- *The Revenue Code B.E. 2481 (1938);*
- *The Direct Sales and Direct Marketing Act B.E. 2545 (2002); and*
- *The Product Liability Act B.E. 2551 (2008).*

Many ministerial regulations executing and further articulating these acts are also helpful to the courts in handling franchising disputes. Note, however, that after the franchisor and the franchisee finalize terms in a franchise agreement and commence executing those terms, Thai courts will generally defer to the contract's terms unless doing so would violate law or public policy.

D. Limits on Fees and Typical Term of Franchise Agreement

Please describe any limits upon the nature and extent of fees and the term of a typical franchise agreement.

While Thai courts generally work to enforce contractual terms, certain terms are not allowed by law.

For example, parties cannot contract in advance to absolve a debtor for their own fraud or gross negligence. Such an agreement would be void as a matter of law.[186] Other terms that might violate the Thai *Unfair Contract Terms Act* include those that:

- □ Permit one party to unreasonably delay or not comply with its contractual obligations;
- □ Permit unreasonable or capricious contract termination;
- □ Except or limit liability resulting from breach of contract;
- □ Permit one party to impose further obligations upon the other party than those originally agreed upon;
- □ Permit confiscation of a deposit (or liquidated damages), when the amount is disproportionately high in light of the actual damages resulting from breach of the contract under which the deposit was placed; and

186 Civil and Commercial Code, Section 373

- Comprise language seeking to preemptively except or limit liability for infringement or breach of contract resulting in the bodily injury or death of a third person, when such contract violation constituted a deliberate or negligent act committed by the party seeking to avoid liability, or by others to whom that party must be further liable.

Beyond this kind of exculpatory language, a party's consent to terms excepting or limiting liability for contract infringement or breach constituting illegal behavior that violates public order or morality is further invalid.

While the *Unfair Contract Terms Act* confers upon the courts significant discretion in reviewing the legitimacy of contract terms, it does instruct the courts to consider the following general guidelines in doing so:

- the time and place of contract's drafting or execution;
- whether one party's obligations significantly outweighed the other's;
- typical industry-specific protocol and processes; and
- the parties' respective trustworthiness, bargaining power, and financial positions, and expertise.

So that they might satisfy the above guidelines, the Act permits the courts to hear expert testimony during hearings. This framework means that franchisors must be careful in ensuring that their contracts' terms are reasonable, lest a court later strike those terms down as unfairly limiting competition, and thus unenforceable.

For example, in drafting a franchising arrangement involving the use of patented technology, the franchisor might naturally wish to include a "tying arrangement," whereby the franchisee would be obligated to purchase materials or services for use in the production of a particular item exclusively from the franchisor or its agent. While such an arrangement would make good sense for the franchisor, it would likely be prohibited as unfairly limiting competition.

III. Currency

If all payments under a franchise agreement must be made in immediately available U.S. Dollars, please advise as to any restrictions, reporting requirements, or regulations concerning the exchange, repatriation or remittance of U.S. Dollars.

Thai law restricts local franchisees ability to convert Thai Baht into U.S. Dollars. The rules regulating exchange control in Thailand are prescribed by the *Exchange Control Act* (B.E. 2485) and *Ministerial Regulation No. 13* (B.E. 2497) issued under said Act. These laws set out the principles of controls under which Notifications of the Ministry of Finance and Notices of the Competent Officer were issued to regulate the conversion of Baht into foreign currencies. Commercial banks are authorized by the Bank of Thailand (BOT) to approve the remittance of certain foreign exchange transactions. Remittance of foreign currencies for purposes other than those approvable by commercial banks shall require approval of the BOT.

Approval requirements for the remittance of foreign currencies are as described below:

A. Import of Goods

Commercial banks are authorized to approve the remittance of unlimited amounts for payments of imported goods. Remittance of the equivalent of US$ 20,000 or higher requires the submission of a Foreign Exchange Transaction (FET) Form to the commercial banks together with the following related documents:

- □ purchase and sale agreement,
- □ price list, and

- □ invoice from the supplier.

B. Royalty Fees and Consulting Services Fees

Commercial banks are authorized to approve the remittance of unlimited amounts for payments of royalty fees, consulting services fees global marketing funds, development deposits, and remedies for non-performance. Remittance of the equivalent of US$ 20,000 or higher shall require the submission of a FET Form to the commercial banks together with documents indicating an obligation to make payments to persons abroad, such as agreements, invoices, etc.

For the purchase or exchange of foreign currencies under (1) and (2) above, the applicant must be an obligor whose name is stated in the related documents. For the purchase or exchange by persons with no obligation on behalf of such obligator, the commercial banks shall request a power of attorney.

In case of payment to recipients whose names are not stated in the evidence, the commercial banks shall request an order from a beneficiary abroad authorizing such persons to receive such payment, or any related documents, on the beneficiary's behalf.

For the purchase or exchange of foreign currencies under (1) and (2) above, but where the documents submitted are not completed as prescribed therein, commercial banks shall submit the applications to the BOT for prior approval together with the following documents:

- □ application explaining the relevant details;
- □ relevant evidence for each case; and
- □ evidence showing the applicant's identification, such as a copy of an identification card (in cases of natural persons), or Memorandum of Association, Certificate of Registered Capital, or list of shareholders or partners,

certified by the Ministry of Commerce (MOC), in cases of juristic (legal) persons.

C. Global Marketing Funds, Development Deposits and Remedies for Non-performance

Commercial banks may not approve such purchases or exchanges and shall submit the applications to the BOT for prior approval together with the following documents:

- □ application explaining the relevant details;
- □ relevant evidence for each case; and
- □ evidence showing the applicant's identification, such as a copy of an identification card (in cases of natural persons), or Memorandum of Association, Certificate of Registered Capital, or list of shareholders or partners, certified by the MOC, in cases of juristic (legal) persons.

IV. Taxes, Tariffs and Duties

Please do not provide any in-depth comments on tax structuring. However, please provide your general comments on the typical amount of withholding tax that would apply and whether a "gross-up" provision contained in a franchise agreement would be enforceable in your country.

Franchise fees and royalties paid by Thai franchisees or licensees to foreign franchisors or licensors not carrying on business in Thailand are subject to Thai income tax in the form of withholding tax at a rate of 15%. The franchisee or licensee, as the payer of franchise fees and royalties, shall be obligated to deduct the 15% withholding tax and remit the same to the Thai Revenue Department within the seventh day of the month following the month in which the franchise fees and royalties were paid.

Thailand

Foreign franchisors sometimes require that Thai franchisees spend a certain amount of money on advertising, marketing, and/or promotional initiatives in order to promote the franchisor's products or trademarks (e.g., trade names, trademarks, and logos). These expenses may be deemed as part of the franchise fees, in which case they will be subject to the 15% withholding tax, although they were not paid directly to the foreign franchisor.[187]

Thailand has entered into Double Taxation Avoidance Agreements ("DTAs"), which are now effective with 59 countries to date. Under some of these DTAs, the 15% withholding tax may be reduced where a lower rate is specified therein.

In eliminating double taxation, some DTAs provide for the credit method to be used, whilst in other DTAs, the exemption method is to be applied.

In principle, under the credit method, the 15% withholding tax paid to the Thai Revenue Department may be used as credit against the licensor's income tax, payable on such franchise fees/royalties in the resident country. On the other hand, under the exemption method, franchise fees/royalties subject to tax in Thailand would, in principle, be exempt from income tax in the resident country. A franchisor/licensor would also need to check domestic law in its country of residence.

There is no duty to inform the Revenue Department of the payment of franchise fees or royalties. The franchisee or licensee must file a withholding tax return and remit the tax to the Revenue Department within the seventh day of the month following the month in which the payment was made. Nonetheless, since a foreign franchisor/licensor may need to present a withholding tax certificate issued by the Thai Revenue Department as evidence for tax credit in the resident country, it

187 Supreme Court Judgment 4440/2552 (2009)

is typical for a franchisor to name the Thai franchisee or licensee as its appointee on an application for a withholding certificate.

The required documents for an application for a withholding certificate include the franchise or license agreement, a copy of the withholding tax return, the receipts issued by the Revenue Department, and a power of attorney.

V. Trademarks

Please advise us as to whether there are any special requirements for granting a valid trademark license, including the use of a registered user agreement or a short trademark license agreement and any required filing of such an agreement with the trademark authorities.

According to Section 68 of the *Trademark Act*, it is compulsory to register the license agreement of a registered trademark with the Thai Trademark Office to make it valid and enforceable. The consequence of a non-registered license agreement is that it is non-enforceable under Thai law, and the use by a licensee is not legitimate to defend non-use cancellation action.

Work Description	Official Fee	Counsel Fee
Registration of a license agreement for one mark	THB 500 (per mark) (approx. US$ 15)	THB 9,300 (approx. US$ 286)
For each additional mark (if any)	THB 500 (per mark) (approx. US$ 15)	THB 3,800 (approx. US$ 117)
Issuing of license certificate	THB 1,000 (per agreement) (approx. US$ 31)	THB 2,400 (approx. US$ 74)
Translation fee from English into Thai		THB 60 per line (approx. US$ 2)

These costs do not include actual expenses and Value Added Tax of 7%.

According to the same section, application for registration of a trademark license agreement shall at least provide the following particulars:

- conditions and terms of the agreement between the trademark proprietor and the person applying to be an authorized licensee, which must actually enable the former to control the quality of the goods manufactured by the latter;

- the goods on which the licensed trademark is to be used. In practice, the Trademark Office will register the license agreements only for goods covered by those registered trademarks. The wording of the licensed goods must be identical to the wording of the goods covered in the licensed trademarks.

To record a license agreement, the following documents are required:

License Agreement

An original license agreement executed by the authorized directors of the licensor and licensee duly notarized before a Notary Public. If the licensee is a Thai company, it is simply required to have authorized representative(s) sign in the presence of two witnesses and affix the company seal; or

A certified copy of the license agreement. However, such a copy is acceptable only with a Notary Public's certification that the document is a true copy of the original agreement, when the licensor and licensee companies still exist under its incorporated laws, and when true signatures and proper power of the signors are established.

Thailand

Foreign Licensor/Licensee

Powers of Attorney from licensor and licensee must be duly notarized before a Notary Public. They must be signed by the same authorized directors of the licensor and licensee who executed the license agreement to avoid possible rejection by the Registrar.

Thai Licensee

A Power of Attorney duly signed by the authorized director(s) of the company and affixed with the company seal;

A signed copy of the passport or identity card of the authorized director(s);

An original Certificate of Incorporation issued no later than six months prior.

After an application to register a license agreement is filed, the Registrar will take about 8-12 months from the application date to examine and issue a decision. If the license agreement does not comply with requirements or the required documents are not in order, the Registrar will issue a Notification requesting the party to rectify any errors. There is no specific deadline to comply with the Registrar's Notification. However, if the license agreement and the required documents are in order, the Registrar will issue a Notification requesting the payment of the Registration Fee. The party is required to make the payment within 30 days of the receiving date of the Notification. The certificate evidencing the license agreement registration will be issued within 30 days of the payment date. For a straightforward case, it normally takes about 12-18 months from the filing date to obtain a certificate evidencing the license agreement registration.

An unregistered license is void and hence unenforceable under Thai law. However, a practical problem arises when the Trademark Registrar at the Department of Intellectual Property

(DIP) sometimes refuses to record a franchise agreement based on the reasoning that a franchise agreement is not equivalent to a trademark licensing agreement. From this perspective, the franchise agreement is not required to be registered under the law. However, Thai courts have varying views on this issue. Some judges see that trademark licensing is inseparable from franchising relationships. If the franchising agreement is not registered, the whole agreement is void. Other judges, however, see that the license of trademark use rights only forms part of a broader commercial agreement between the parties. If the trademark license has not been registered properly, the terms regarding trademark licensing are void, but other commercial terms will survive.

For legal compliance, some clients enter into a separate trademark licensing agreement in Thai with the franchisee, and register the agreement with the DIP. The DIP allows the parties to conceal parts of the agreement that are irrelevant to trademark licensing and conditions required under the trademark law (short form recordal).

VI. Restrictions on Transfer

Please advise as to whether there are any restrictions on (1) a franchisor to restrict transfers by a master franchisee, any interest in a master franchisee, or the assets of the master franchisee or (2) the ability of a master franchisee to control and/or restrict transfers of a subfranchisee's rights under a master franchise agreement, interest in the subfrranchisee, or the assets of the subfranchisee.

Thai law does not restrict a foreign franchisor from prohibiting its local franchisee from transferring equity interests in the subsidiary franchise business without the foreign franchisor's prior written consent.

A provision to prohibit the transfer of equity interests without obtaining prior written consent from other shareholders may be validly incorporated as a condition in the Articles of Association

(AOA). Therefore, if the franchisor is a shareholder in the new subsidiary, the franchisor may effectively prohibit the transfer of equity interests without its consent by incorporating such provision in the company's AOA, which shall also bind third parties, as the AOA is a public document registered with the Department of Business Development.

With respect to practical restrictions on foreign franchisors, disregarding a limited provision on the registration of liens on machinery, there are currently no laws in Thailand providing means by which a franchisor can secure liens against the franchisee's personal property (e.g., equipment, inventory, and accounts receivables).

Accordingly, that property, as well as the franchise-unique knowledge it represents, is vulnerable. For example, when a franchisee defaults on a loan and becomes subject to a creditor's claims, the franchisor has few real options toward protecting the franchisee's franchise-unique equipment and inventory from being taken by third-party creditors totally unanticipated by the franchise agreement.

While Thai law better provides for the protection of real property, foreign franchisors must be wary of multiple issues. First, in order for a lease of real property to be assignable, the contract must contain express language providing for assignment. Without this express language, if the franchisee defaults, the franchisor will be unable to retake possession of the franchise location. Accordingly, franchisors should be diligent in confirming that any lease of retail space to a franchisee expressly contain the landlord's guarantee that the leasehold will be assigned back to the franchisor (or the franchisor's replacement appointee) and, ultimately, to a new franchisee.

Nonetheless, a properly drafted lease may not be enough to fully protect the franchisor. Even assuming the franchise location is transferred back to the franchisor, if that franchisor is a foreigner, Thai law may prohibit him from resuming operation of the franchise.

The *Alien Business Act* prohibits foreigners from operating certain businesses. Specifically, foreigners are strictly prohibited from engaging in any retail and many service businesses. This situation makes foreign franchisors even more vulnerable in cases of defaulting franchisees.

VII. Termination

Please advise us as to any laws relating to termination in your country, such as agency laws, required indemnity provisions, notice or "good cause" requirements, or other laws affecting termination of a franchise agreement. Please describe.

A. Practical Barriers to Termination

Foreign franchisors often appoint their local franchisees to ensure that the franchise business remains compliant with relevant regulations of the Food and Drug Administration or the Ministry of Agriculture. For example, the franchise agreement generally obligates the franchisee, as the appointed local entity, to apply for and maintain product registration and import licenses.

This arrangement typically serves the interests of both the franchisor and the franchisee. Nonetheless, it may also lead to a situation in which the local entity, after growing local business for the franchised products or services, is tempted (and well-positioned) to unfairly compete and/or otherwise infringe upon the original franchise relationship.

This scenario can result in a rogue ex-franchisee problem (or a hijacked certificate), whereby the foreign franchisor may have significant difficulties in terminating a franchise agreement with a franchisee who is the exclusive distributor in the local market.

B. Material Breach and Termination

Many different factors (from economic downturns to livestock epidemics) may impact a local franchisee's business, leading to necessary adjustments to the franchisee's market position. This may mean, for example, that the franchisee needs to change the operation's minimum sales targets or advertising spending. Such situations will not constitute breach of contract sufficient to warrant termination of the franchising relationship.

Nonetheless, it is important for foreign franchisors to carefully monitor their local franchisees' behavior and to regularly report unacceptable performance in order to proactively avoid situations in which full-scale impropriety results in contract termination. For example, it is easy for a foreign franchisor to search whether his franchisee has applied for a trademark similar to the franchisor's own, or filed his own trademark for goods similar to the franchisor's products.

A foreign franchisor can also easily investigate whether the local franchisee is selling the same or similar products, and if so, in what type of packaging. For example, the franchisor can first determine whether the local franchisee has recently re-registered the franchisor's business as a manufacturing operation, and also whether the franchisee has obtained a manufacturing license. If this turns out to be the case, the franchisor can then determine whether the relevant manufacturing approvals are for products the same as, or similar to, its own. These enquiries can be made at the relevant Ministry of Commerce tax office. Furthermore, foreign franchisors should (and often do) maintain the right, via express provision within the franchise agreement, to make unannounced inspections of the franchise operation.

C. Preparing for Termination

If the above searches confirm unacceptable behavior on the part of the franchisee, the franchisor, together with the franchisee, should consult the franchise agreement to determine whether such behavior constitutes material breach, and if so, to confirm proper consequences. Common breach situations include:

- Registration of a similar trademark for an identical product;

- ☐ Unauthorized manufacture and/or sale of a competitive product;
- ☐ Unreasonable and/or unjustified non-observance of agreed-upon targets; and
- ☐ Marked decrease in sales of certain products against normal sales of others.

The parties should also be sure to follow the dispute resolution and termination processes set forth in the agreement. If the agreement calls for arbitration, the parties should determine whether an exceptional provision for court-granted injunctive relief exists for cases of intellectual property infringement or breach of confidentiality.

If such a provision exists, the franchisor need not wait for the arbitration panel's decision, but can instead head straight to court to seek an injunction. The parties should also confirm whether termination is effective immediately or after a designated period of days.

In case of breach by the franchisee, the franchisor should carefully follow the termination process, and be prepared to produce a paper trail of earlier warnings, so as to neutralize any potential impact of the franchisee's counterclaims of good faith. The termination notice should refer to any and all breaches in order to mitigate the likelihood of the franchisee's challenging the allegations, and of the franchisee's counsel attempting to prolong the litigation process via an unnecessarily drawn-out exchange of clarification letters.

It is important that the notification of termination be carefully and precisely worded, lest it later be presented in litigation as evidence of defamation or unlawful termination.

Furthermore, in order to ensure that the relationship is fully terminated, the notification should list all documents to be returned by the franchisee. This list should include the certificate of free sale and a cancellation of the import license (or the transfer back of the license to the franchisor or a newly appointed franchisee) in order to discourage the ex-franchisee from engaging in unauthorized sales of the franchisor's products.

D. Post-termination Considerations

When a foreign franchisor determines that the time has come to terminate, it is crucial to consult the agreement to determine under whose name the products were registered. This will generally be that of the local franchisee because, as aforementioned, foreign franchisors often appoint their local franchisees to serve as applicants in registering the franchised products with relevant local ministries.

In Thailand, a foreign franchisor seeking to change the registrant's name on a product registration certificate (i.e., from the ex-franchisee to either the franchisor or the newly appointed franchisee), cannot simply amend the product registration application. Instead, the franchisor must reapply for a new product registration certificate. This arrangement is both advantageous and burdensome for the franchisor: while the local partner may not be aware of the new applications, the franchisor will sustain both delay and costs in waiting for the new product registration certificate (while the process generally takes a few months, it may take longer if the examiner determines that retesting is required).

VIII. Governing Law, Jurisdiction and Dispute Resolution

A. Choice of Law of Foreign Jurisdiction

Please confirm whether the choice of law of a foreign jurisdiction would likely to be upheld under the law of the country, except for certain matters such as trademarks, bankruptcy and competition matters, which we assume would be governed by the law in your country.

A foreign franchisor's choice of law of a foreign jurisdiction would likely be upheld by the Thai courts in governing a master franchise agreement.

B. International Arbitration Dispute Resolution

Please confirm that a court in your country would honor an election of international arbitration dispute resolution, and therefore refuse to hear any disputes arising under a franchise agreement.

Unlike foreign judgments, foreign arbitral awards may be enforced in Thailand, so long as an award rendered in a foreign country is governed by a treaty, convention, or international agreement to which Thailand is a party. Foreign arbitral awards rendered in member countries of the *New York Convention on Recognition and Enforcement of Foreign Arbitral Awards* and the *Geneva Protocol* are recognized and enforced in Thailand, which is a member of both conventions.

Note, however, that in order to enforce a foreign arbitral award, a Thai court judgment will need to be obtained. Accordingly a petition for enforcement of an award must be filed with the Thai Court within three years of the date when the award can be enforced. The process for the enforcement of the award usually takes approximately 12 to 18 months from the date the petition is submitted to the Thai courts.

Note also that the Thai Court may refuse enforcement of the award on limited grounds only, such as lack of capacity of one of the parties, lack of notice given to one of the parties, the arbitral award having been beyond the scope of the arbitration agreement, or the arbitral tribunal or arbitration procedure having been inconsistent with the arbitration agreement.

Thailand

IX. Non-Competition Provisions

If the franchise agreement prohibits the franchisee from engaging in certain competitive activities during the term of the agreement, and for a 12-month period after the termination or expiration of the agreement, please comment on the enforceability of non-competition covenants in your country.

Foreign franchisors should always be aware of the risk that an ex-franchisee will take the knowledge and experience gained from running the franchise operation and open a competitive business or franchise.

Intellectual property rights infringement is an area of particular risk, and thus, while Thai law independently protects foreign franchisors' IP rights, those franchisors should further protect themselves by using clear and robust language in the franchising agreement.

Beyond this, franchisors should also include language in their franchise agreements prohibiting franchisees from opening competing businesses. This prohibition should not be limited to the lifetime of the franchise agreement, but rather run beyond its expiration or termination.

Thai courts generally uphold such non-competition provisions, assuming those provisions are reasonable and do not practically deny an individual from working in his profession or industry of choice. For an extreme example of an exception to the general rule, the courts would probably strike down a clause that barred a photographer from working in any competing photography studio in Thailand. On the other hand, the courts would be more likely to uphold non-competition provisions specifying the following limitations:

- □ a particular kind of photograph (e.g., period costume photographs);

- □ a particular geographic zone (e.g., within a one-kilometer radius of the franchisor's present or future photography studio locations); and
- □ a fixed term (e.g., for six years).

The above examples represent the three general limitation categories that the courts will consider in determining whether a non-competition provision is enforceable:

- □ the definition of competing operation,
- □ the geographic effect, and
- □ the chronological term.

Accordingly, foreign franchisors should ensure that these limitations are clearly established in the non-competition provisions in their franchising agreements, and more generally that the provisions fairly reflect not only the franchisor's protection interests, but also the franchisee's interest in pursuing work in his profession or industry of choice.

X. Language Requirements

Does the law in your country require that a franchise agreement be translated into the local language in order to be enforceable between the parties?

Under Thai law, there are no requirements that franchising agreements be translated into Thai in order to be enforceable between the parties. However, if both Thai and English versions of the agreement are executed, and there are discrepancies between the two versions, the document executed in Thai shall govern, unless there is clear indication that the English version is to prevail. Accordingly, it is advisable that foreign franchisors draft only one version of the master franchising agreement.

XI. Other Significant Matters

Please advise as to whether there are any significant matters not addressed above of which a franchisor should be aware in

connection with its entering into a franchise agreement in your country.

The draft *Franchising Business Act* defines "franchise," mandating, for example, that a franchise business incorporate some form of intellectual property, and focuses on franchise registration and restrictions.

The draft *Franchising Business Act* has four main objectives:

- to stipulate criteria and reasons for regulating franchising;
- to appoint a committee to be in charge of providing franchise business support, to submit promotion and development plans to the Minister of Commerce, and to consider complaints;
- to stipulate protective measures with a view toward protecting both franchisors and franchisees, e.g,. to prevent exaggerated advertisements and to ensure the fairness of contracts, the availability of clear business operating manuals, and the disclosure of sufficient data to facilitate decision-making regarding the purchase of franchises; and
- to stipulate criminal and administrative penalties to be imposed for breaches of the law.

Restrictions

Compliance with specified restrictions on business operations will be required of both franchisors and franchisees. For example, franchise agreements will necessarily be written, and franchisors will be required to disclose all necessary operational data, including clear working manuals for franchisees' instruction and reference. To protect franchisors, franchisees will be prohibited from disclosing such operational data. Nonetheless, if foreign franchisors are serious about protecting their most important assets, it will remain crucial that they ensure that their franchising agreements incorporate clear and robust confidentiality and intellectual property provisions.

Registration

Any franchisor seeking to establish a franchise business with a Thai franchisee will be required to meet specified qualifications and to register with the Ministry of Commerce. The draft *Franchising Business Act* follows the Chinese model (outlined in the People's Republic of China's Ministry of Commerce's *Administrative Measures on Commercial Franchising 2005* and the *Franchise Regulations 2007*) by further mandating that before filing his registration application, a franchisor must have profitably operated two franchise business outlets for at least two years.

If the parties to a franchising agreement do not comply with the above, the Committee for the Consideration of Administrative Punishment may revoke the franchise, and such revocation will prevent the business operator not only from engaging in further relevant solicitations or advertising, but also from operating a new franchise business in the future.

Scope of Enforcement

The draft *Franchising Business Act* does not apply to franchise operations in which the foreign franchisor maintains residency abroad. Accordingly, agreements between a foreign franchisor and a Thai franchisee will not be required by law to follow the above rules and regulations. Nonetheless, if the relevant agreement allows the Thai franchisee to grant subfranchising agreements to other Thais, those subfranchising agreements will be subject to the full force of the law.

Franchised brands currently operating in Thailand include Zara and Gap (clothing and accessories), Krispy Kreme (food), Engel & Volkers (real estate) and Ikea (home accessories).

Franchising in Vietnam

Mai Thi Minh Hang and Ngo Viet Hoa

RUSSIN & VECCHI

Hanoi, Vietnam

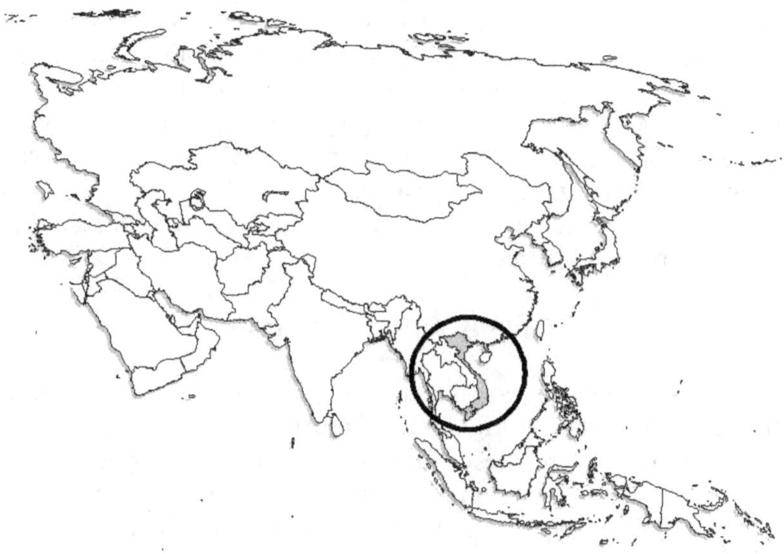

Vietnam

I. Introduction

A. Historical Background of the Country

Vietnam declared independence from France after World War II, but France continued to rule until its 1954 defeat by communist forces under Ho Chi Minh. Under the Geneva Accords of 1954, Vietnam was divided into the communist North and anti-communist South. U.S. economic and military aid to South Vietnam grew through the 1960s in an attempt to bolster the government, but U.S. armed forces were withdrawn following a cease-fire agreement in 1973. Two years later, North Vietnamese forces overran the South reuniting the country under communist rule. Despite the return of peace, for over a decade the country experienced little economic growth because of conservative leadership policies, the persecution and mass exodus of individuals - many of them successful South Vietnamese merchants - and growing international isolation. However, since the enactment of Vietnam's "*doi moi*" (renovation) policy in 1986, Vietnamese authorities have committed to increased economic liberalization and enacted structural reforms needed to modernize the economy and to produce more competitive, export-driven industries.

B. Economy of the Country

Vietnam is a densely-populated developing country that has been transitioning from the rigidities of a centrally-planned economy since 1986. Vietnamese authorities have reaffirmed their commitment to economic modernization in recent years. Vietnam joined the World Trade Organization in January 2007, which has promoted more competitive, export-driven industries. Vietnam became an official negotiating partner in the Trans-Pacific Partnership Trade Agreement in 2010. Agriculture's share of economic output has continued to shrink from about 25% in 2000 to less than 20% in 2013, while industry's share increased from 36% to more than 42% in the same period. State-owned enterprises account for about 40% of GDP. Poverty has declined significantly, and Vietnam is working to create jobs to meet the challenge of a labor force that is growing by more than one million people every year. The global recession hurt Vietnam's export-oriented economy, with GDP in 2013 growing at 5%, the slowest rate of growth since 1999. In 2013, however, exports increased by more than 12%, year-on-year; several administrative actions brought the trade deficit back into balance. Between 2008 and 2011, Vietnam's managed currency, the dong, was devalued in excess of 20%, but its value remained relatively stable in 2013. Hanoi has oscillated between promoting growth and emphasizing macroeconomic stability in recent years. In February 2011, the government shifted from policies aimed at achieving a high rate of economic growth, which had stoked inflation, to those aimed at stabilizing the economy, through tighter monetary and fiscal control. Although Vietnam unveiled a broad, "three pillar" economic reform program in early 2012, proposing the restructuring of public investment, state-owned enterprises, and the banking sector, little perceptible progress has been made. Vietnam's economy continues to face challenges from an undercapitalized banking sector. Non-performing loans weigh heavily on banks and businesses.

C. Franchise Legal Overview

The basic regulations on franchising are provided in the *Commercial Law*, adopted by the National Assembly on June 14, 2005 ("Commercial Law"). These regulations are elaborated on in *Decree No. 35/2006/ND-CP* of the Government (March 31, 2006) ("Decree 35") as amended by *Decree No. 120/2011/ND-CP* of the Government (December 16, 2011) ("Decree 120"), and *Circular No. 09/2006/TT-BTM* of the Ministry of Trade[188] (May 25, 2006) ("Circular 09"). Regulations related to franchising can also be found in the *Law on Intellectual Property*, adopted by the National Assembly on November 29,

188 The Ministry of Trade is currently known as the Ministry of Industry and Trade.

2005, and the *Law on Technology Transfer*, adopted on November 29, 2006.

II. Regulatory Requirements

Vietnamese franchise laws apply to franchising activities between Vietnamese parties, to a foreign franchisor who grants a franchise to a franchisee in Vietnam, and to a Vietnamese franchisor who grants a franchise to a franchisee in a foreign country.

A. Pre-Sale Disclosure

Please describe any pre-sale franchise disclosure or similar requirements that may apply to franchise transactions.

1. Initial Disclosure

Under *Decree 35*, an information disclosure document titled "Franchise Description Document" (the "FDD") must be submitted to the Ministry of Industry and Trade (the "MOIT") as part of its registration dossier (discussed below). The FDD must be prepared according to a standard form provided by the MOIT under *Circular 09*.

The contents of the FDD must include:

- □ information about the franchisor, including: the franchisor's name, address of head office, incorporation date, scope of business, type of business to be franchised, and a description of the organizational structure of the franchisor, including the department that is in charge of the franchising activities of the franchisor;
- □ whether the franchisor is the master franchisor or a subfranchisor (master franchisee);
- □ litigation history related to franchising activities;
- □ initial costs payable by the franchisee;
- □ other financial obligations of the franchisee;
- □ initial investment by the franchisee;

- information on trademarks and service marks that will be used in association with the franchised business;
- obligations of the franchisee to buy or lease equipment as designated by the franchisor;
- obligations of the franchisor, including: obligations prior to the execution of the franchise agreement; obligations during the course of operation of the franchise system; obligations to consider the franchisee's proposed premises for the franchised business; and obligations to provide training, including initial training, and other training programs;
- description of the market of the goods/services to be franchised;
- a summary of the franchise agreement;
- information on the franchise system, including: number of outlets, both currently in operation and those that have ceased to operate; number of franchise agreements the franchisor has signed with franchisees; the number of franchise agreements that have been transferred by franchisees to third parties; the number of franchise agreements that have been terminated or renewed;
- financial statements of the franchisor; and
- information on awards or recognition that the franchisor may have received;

Decree 35 also requires the franchisor to provide the franchisee or master franchisee (a franchisee with the right to act as a subfranchisor by granting a franchise to a subfranchisee) with the above FDD and a copy of the franchise agreement at least 15 working days prior to the execution of the franchise agreement.

If a master franchisee wishes to grant a franchise to a subfranchisee, the master franchisee must comply with the disclosure requirements as if it were the franchisor. The master franchisee must also provide a subfranchisee with the contents of the Master Franchise Agreement (the "MFA") and information about the franchisor. It must also inform a subfranchisee of legal remedies in the case the MFA is terminated.

If a foreign franchisor grants a master franchise to a local master franchisee, the foreign franchisor is not required to provide disclosure to local subfranchisees. This is the responsibility of the local master franchisee.

2. Ongoing disclosure

Besides the initial disclosure requirement mandated in the FDD, a franchisor is required to keep its franchisees updated concerning all significant changes related to its franchise system. A "significant change" is defined to be any change that may have an impact on the business activities of a franchisee.

Circular 09 requires the franchisor to report to the MOIT any change in: (a) the name of the franchisor; (b) address of the head office; (c) telephone and fax number; (d) scope of business; or (e) type of business to be franchised. The report must be made within 30 days from the date on which the change occurs.

B. Government Approvals, Registrations, and Filing Requirements

Please describe any necessary government approvals or similar requirements that may apply to franchise transactions.

1. Offshore franchisors

An offshore franchisor must register its franchising activity and file it with the MOIT. The registration dossier must include: (1) a registration form of the franchising activity, made on a standard form provided in *Circular 09*; (2) the FDD; (3) a certified copy of the franchisor's business registration; and (4) a certified copy of patents and certificates of intellectual property rights of the prospective franchisor, if any. If any of these documents are in a foreign language, a certified translation into Vietnamese into Vietnamese is required. The fee to register a franchise is VND 16,500,000 (equivalent to about US$ 810.00)

If the applicant is a master franchisee, the above dossier must include a document issued by the franchisor that shows permission to subfranchise the business.

The franchising agreement itself need not be included in the dossier unless it is necessary to register the licensing of intellectual property rights that are associated with a franchised business and that fall within the regulations on intellectual property. See Section V (Trademarks) on licensing regulations under the *Law on Intellectual Property*.

The MOIT has discretion to determine whether the documentation filed to register the franchising activity meets disclosure requirements. If the MOIT finds the documentation to be incomplete or invalid, it must provide written notice to the applicant that it needs to supplement the necessary documents in order to complete the registration. The applicant has the right to request that the MOIT clarify what additional materials the applicant must provide.

If the registration dossier is approved, *Circular 09* stipulates that the MOIT will register the franchising activity within 05 working days. In practice, however, the time frame can be as long as a month.

2. Vietnamese franchisors

A Vietnamese franchisor, whether it grants a franchise to a foreign or domestic franchisee, is not required to register its franchising activity with the MOIT. Instead, it must report its franchising activity to the provincial Services of Industry and Trade (the "SOITs"). There is no specific provision under *Decree 120* that specifies the content of the report, nor the procedure by which the report is filed. Thus, the report requirement currently appears not to be fully operational.

C. Limits of Fees and Typical Term of Franchise Agreement

Please describe any limits upon the nature and extent of fees and the term of a typical franchise agreement.

The law imposes no limits relating to the nature and extent of fees in a franchisee agreement. Similarly, there are no limits in regards to the duration of a franchise agreement. As such, a franchisor and franchisee may freely negotiate the terms and conditions of a franchise agreement. Decree 35 gives some suggested terms and conditions which can be used for reference, but it is not compulsory to include them in the franchisee agreement.

III. Currency

If all payments under a franchise agreement must be made in immediately available U.S. Dollars, please advise as to any restrictions, reporting requirements, or regulations concerning the exchange, repatriation or remittance of U.S. Dollars.

Generally, there is no exchange control issue in a franchise arrangement. In particular, *Article 6* of the *Ordinance on Foreign Exchange* provides that all payments and money remittances in relation to "current transactions" (including payment for imported goods/services) between a resident and a non-resident may be freely conducted. The remittance of franchise fees by a Vietnamese franchisee to a foreign franchisor is treated as a current transaction, which is freely conducted. Of course, a commercial bank will examine relevant papers and documents in accordance with regulations of the State Bank of Vietnam before it wires money.

IV. Taxes, Tariffs and Duties

Please do not provide any in-depth comments on tax structuring. However, please provide your general comments on the typical amount of withholding tax that would apply and whether a "gross-up" provision contained in a franchise agreement would be enforceable in your country.

Under *Circular No. 103/2014/TT-BTC* of the Ministry of Finance dated August 6, 2014 ("Circular 103"), an offshore franchisor is subject to withholding taxes which include value added tax ("VAT") and corporate income tax ("CIT"). Because the offshore franchisor usually is a nonresident and does not have a permanent establishment in Vietnam, the Vietnamese franchisee is generally responsible for the payment of VAT and CIT incurred by the offshore franchisor.

1. CIT

CIT applies to the offshore franchisor's income generated from royalty fees at a rate of 10%. As a matter of practice, income from services, including development and initial franchise fees may be subject to a CIT rate of 5%.

2. VAT

VAT applies to services provided by the offshore franchisor to the Vietnamese franchisee. The amount of VAT that applies to such services is equal to 50% [189] of the revenue that is received by that offshore franchisor before netting of any taxes, multiplied by the VAT rate of 10%.

Under the VAT law, VAT does not apply to royalties the offshore franchisor receives from the Vietnamese franchisee.

3. Double Taxation Relief

An offshore franchisor may find taxation relief under an applicable double taxation agreement ("DTA"), if any. Currently, Vietnam has double taxation treaties in effect or signed with numerous countries (69 as at July 15, 2014). Of note,

---

[189] 50% is the percentage of added value assigned for services.

however, is that Vietnam currently does not have a DTA signed with the United States.

4. "Gross-up" Provisions

There is currently no law precluding the enforceability of a gross-up provision within a franchise agreement. However, because the Vietnamese franchisee is generally responsible to register, declare, and make payment of CIT and VAT incurred by the offshore franchisor, such a provision would pose an enormous financial burden on the franchisee and likely render the franchise agreement impracticable.

V. Trademarks

Please advise us as to whether there are any special requirements for granting a valid trademark license, including the use of a registered user agreement or a short trademark license agreement and any required filing of such an agreement with the trademark authorities.

A non-resident franchisor must register its trademark in Vietnam for its trademark to be recognized by law. However, an agreement to license the right to use a legally recognized trademark (a trademark licensing agreement) need not be registered with any authority for it to be effective. Nevertheless, the parties to such a licensing agreement may wish to register such an agreement with the National Office of Intellectual Property ("NOIP"), as registration will protect the trademark from a third party's claim.

VI. Restrictions on Transfer

Please advise as to whether there are any restrictions (1) on a franchisor to restrict transfers by a master franchisee, or the assets of the master franchisee, or (2) the ability of a master franchisee to control and/or restrict transfers of a subfranchisee's rights under a master franchise agreement, an interest in the subfranchisee, or the assets of the subfranchisee.

Decree 35 contains no restrictions on the franchisor's ability to restrict transfers by a master franchisee. Similarly, *Decree 35* contains no restrictions on the ability of a master franchisee to control or restrict transfers of a subfranchisee's rights under a master franchise agreement, an interest in the subfranchisee, or the assets of the subfranchisee.

VII. Termination

Please advise us as to any laws relating to the termination in your country, such as agency laws, required indemnity provision, notice or "good cause" requirements, or other laws affecting termination of a franchise agreement. Please describe.

As a matter of background, a franchise agreement is listed as a commercial contract under the *Commercial Law*. The right to unilaterally terminate a commercial contract is generally set out in the *Commercial Law*. In particular, a party to a contract can unilaterally terminate a contract if:

(i) the other party commits a breach of the contract of a type that the parties agreed to be grounds for the non-default party to terminate the contract; or

(ii) there was a material breach of contract by the other party. A material breach is defined as a breach that causes damages to the non-defaulting party such that the non-defaulting party is unable to achieve the purposes of the contract. Due to this qualitative approach, it is therefore up to the courts or arbitrators to decide whether there was a material breach by a party on a case-by-case basis.

In addition, *Decree 35* specially provides for the right of either a franchisee or franchisor to unilaterally terminate a franchise agreement in certain circumstances, as follows:

A franchisee may unilaterally terminate a franchise agreement if the franchisor fails to:

- □ provide to the franchisee guiding documents on the franchise system;
- □ provide initial training and regular technical assistance;
- □ design the operating premises of the franchisee;
- □ ensure the intellectual property rights of subject matters of the franchise agreement; or
- □ treat franchisees in its franchising system fairly and equally.

A franchisor may unilaterally terminate a franchise agreement if the franchisee:

- □ fails to maintain the Business Registration Certificate ("BRC") or other equivalent certificate that is required by law to operate the franchised business;
- □ is insolvent or dissolved;
- □ commits a material violation of the law that may cause significant damage to the prestige of the franchising system; or
- □ fails to remedy, in a reasonable time, a minor breach of a franchise agreement upon the receipt of the franchisor's written notification of such breach.

VIII. Governing Law, Jurisdiction and Dispute Resolution

A. Choice of Law of Foreign Jurisdiction

Please confirm whether the choice of law of a foreign jurisdiction would likely to be upheld under the laws of the country, except for the certain matters such as trademarks, bankruptcy and competition matters, which will assume would be governed in your country.

The choice that a foreign law is to govern a transaction in which one of the parties is a foreign party, is generally permissible, pursuant to the Civil Code and the *Commercial Law*, but subject to certain general conditions. One such condition holds that the application, or the consequence of such application of foreign law, must not be contrary to the basic principles of Vietnamese law. There would, however, only be narrow grounds for challenging a choice of foreign law on the basis that such condition has not been satisfied.

The choice of which law should govern the franchise agreement depends on which venue is chosen to settle a dispute under the franchisee agreement. If the franchise agreement refers a dispute to a venue in Vietnam, either to Vietnamese courts or Vietnamese arbitrators, then a foreign law cannot be the governing law of the franchise agreement. This is simply because, as a matter of practice, the Vietnamese courts and Vietnamese arbitrators may not have sufficient expertise or knowledge on such foreign law to interpret the franchise agreement properly.

B. International Arbitration Dispute Resolution

Please confirm a court in your country would honor an election of international arbitration dispute resolution, and therefore refuse to hear any dispute arising under the franchise agreement.

Vietnam is a signatory to the 1958 New York *Convention on the Recognition and Enforcement of Foreign Arbitral Awards* (the "New York Convention").

Under Vietnamese law, arbitration is acceptable as the exclusive remedy for resolving disputes, except for those disputes that are specified in the Civil Procedure Code to be subject to the exclusive jurisdictions of the courts. The disputes that would arise from a franchise agreement do not fall within the exclusive jurisdiction of the courts and can thus be referred to arbitrators. If the parties agree under the franchise agreement to refer disputes to arbitration, neither party may initiate a court claim.

Vietnam

IX. Non-Competition Provisions

If the franchise agreement prohibits the franchisee from engaging in certain competitive activities during the term of the agreement, and for a 12 month period after the termination or expiration of the agreement, please comment on the enforceability of non-competition covenants in your country.

A non-competition clause in a franchise agreement is permissible under Vietnamese law as a matter of freedom of contract.

However, in practice it would be difficult to enforce such a clause. In particular, the only action that a franchisor can take to prevent the franchisee from engaging in competitive activities is to seek a court's injunctive relief. However, it is not always convenient to do so. This is because the franchisor must have evidence that the franchisee is going to engage in such activities. Such evidence is not easily obtained.

Furthermore, when the competitive activities have already been completed, the franchisor can only rely on remedies for breach of the franchise agreement.

Injunctive relief is available under the Civil Procedure Code to:

- address an urgent request of the claimant;
- protect evidence; or
- prevent the occurrence of a serious consequence.

An injunctive relief can be sought only after the applicant has initiated a petition to the court, a petition to the arbitrator, or together with filing of a petition to the court in respect of a breach of the party against whom the injunctive relief is sought.

The applicant must file a request for an injunctive relief with the court with which the petition is filed, or, if the petition is made to the arbitrator, the court of the province in which the arbitrator sits. An application must address the following matters:

(i) name, address of the applicant, and the party against whom the injunctive relief is sought;

(ii) summary of the dispute or breach of the party against whom the injunctive relief is sought;

(iii) the grounds for the request; and

(iv) the specific measures needed to be taken.

A court must decide whether to grant injunctive relief within 48 hours in cases of extreme urgency, and generally, within three days of receiving the request. An injunctive relief, if granted, must be sent to a competent Department of Civil Judgment Execution for enforcement.

X. Language Requirements:

Does the law in your country require that a franchise agreement be translated into the local language in order to be enforceable between the parties?

The law of Vietnam requires that all franchise agreements to be made in the Vietnamese language. The regulator has explained that this requirement has been included because many local franchisees are small- and medium-size entrepreneurs who are not familiar with foreign languages. A franchising agreement made in Vietnamese is intended to ensure that a local franchisee thoroughly understands and properly performs the agreement, and to avoid disputes due to misinterpretation. This language restriction, however, does not apply to a franchise agreement under which a Vietnamese franchisor grants a franchise in a foreign country.

XI. Other Significant Matters:

Please advise as to whether there are any significant matters not addressed above of which a franchisor should be aware in

connection with its entering into a franchise agreement in your country.

There are no other significant matters to be addressed.

Appendices

Appendix A
Form of Questionnaire

Regulatory Requirements

A. Pre-Sale Disclosure

Please describe any pre-sale franchise disclosure or similar requirements that may apply to franchise transactions.

B. Government Approvals, Registrations, Filing Requirements

Please describe any necessary government approvals, registrations, or filing requirements that may apply to franchise transactions.

C. Limits on Fees and Typical Term of Franchise Agreement

Please describe any limits upon the nature and extent of fees and the term of a typical franchise agreement.

Currency

If all payments under a franchise agreement must be made in immediately available U.S. Dollars, please advise as to any restrictions, reporting requirements, or regulations concerning the exchange, repatriation or remittance of U.S. Dollars.

Taxes, Tariffs, and Duties

Please do not provide any in-depth comments on tax structuring. However, please provide your general comments on the typical amount of withholding tax that would apply and whether a "gross-up" provision contained in a franchise agreement would be enforceable in your country.

Trademarks

Please advise us as to whether there are any special requirements for granting a valid trademark license, including the use of a registered user agreement or a short trademark license agreement and any required filing of such an agreement with the trademark authorities.

Restrictions on Transfer

Please advise as to whether there are any restrictions on (1) a franchisor to restrict transfers by a master franchisee, any interest in a master franchisee, or the assets of the master franchisee or (2) the ability of a master franchisee to control and/or restrict transfers of a subfranchisee's rights under a master franchise agreement, interest in the subfranchisee, or the assets of the subfranchisee.

Termination

Please advise us as to any laws relating to termination in your country, such as agency laws, required indemnity provisions, notice or "good cause" requirements, or other laws affecting termination of a franchise agreement. Please describe.

Governing Law, Jurisdiction, and Dispute Resolution

A. Choice of Law of Foreign Jurisdiction

Please confirm whether the choice of law of a foreign jurisdiction would likely to be upheld under the law of the country, except for certain matters such as trademarks, bankruptcy and competition matters, which we assume would be governed by the law in your country.

B. International Arbitration Dispute Resolution

Please confirm that a court in your country would honor an election of international arbitration dispute resolution, and therefore refuse to hear any disputes arising under a franchise agreement.

<u>Non-Competition Provisions</u>

If the franchise agreement prohibits the franchisee from engaging in certain competitive activities during the term of the agreement, and for a 12-month period after the termination or expiration of the agreement, please comment on the enforceability of non-competition covenants in your country.

<u>Language Requirements</u>

Does the law in your country require that a franchise agreement be translated into the local language in order to be enforceable between the parties?

<u>Other Significant Matters</u>

Please advise as to whether there are any significant matters not addressed above of which a franchisor should be aware in connection with its entering into a franchise agreement in your country.

Appendix B
Bibliography of International Franchise Resources For Asia

Keri A. McWilliams
NIXON PEABODY LLP

Washington, D.C.

General

Mark Abell, Gary R. Duvall, and Andrea Oricchio Kirsh, *International Franchise Legislation* B1, ABA FORUM ON FRANCHISING (1996)

Kathleen C. Anderson and Anthony M. Stiegler, *Put Muscle in Your Marks: Enforcing Intellectual Property Rights* W14, ABA FORUM ON FRANCHISING (1995)

Richard M. Asbill and Jane W. LaFranchi, *International Franchise Sales Laws—A Survey* W7, ABA FORUM ON FRANCHISING (2005)

Jeffery A. Brimer, Alison C. McElroy, and John Pratt, *Going International: What Additional Restraints Will You Face?* W4, ABA FORUM ON FRANCHISING (2011)

Michael G. Brennan, Alexander Konigsberg, and Philip F. Zeidman, *Globetrotting: A Workshop on International Franchising* 10/W8, ABA FORUM ON FRANCHISING (1994)

Michael G. Brennan, Alexander Konigsberg, and Philip F. Zeidman, *Globetrotting: Strategies for Launching U.S. Franchisors Abroad* 2/P2, ABA FORUM ON FRANCHISING (1994)

Christopher P. Bussert and Jennifer Dolman, *Regaining Your Trademark After Abandonment or Misappropriation* W7, ABA FORUM ON FRANCHISING (2011)

Ronald T. Coleman and Linda K. Stevens, *Trade Secrets and Confidential Information: Rights and Remedies* W2, ABA FORUM ON FRANCHISING (2000)

Finola Cunningham, *Commerce Department Helps Franchisors Go Global*, in FRANCHISING WORLD 63 (Dec. 2005)

Michael R. Daigle and Alex S. Konigsberg, *Meeting Off-Shore Disclosure and Contract Requirements* F/W13, ABA FORUM ON FRANCHISING (1992)

Jennifer Dolman, Robert A. Lauer, and Lawrence M. Weinberg, *Structuring International Master Franchise Relationships for Success and Responding When Things Go Awry* W22, ABA FORUM ON FRANCHISING (2007)

Gary R. Duvall, Paul Jones, and Jane LaFranchi, *Planning for the International Enforcement of Franchise Agreements* W6, ABA FORUM ON FRANCHISING (1999)

William Edwards, *International Expansion: Do Opportunities Outweigh Challenges?* in FRANCHISING WORLD (February 2008)

George J. Eydt and Stuart Hershman, *Bringing a Foreign Franchise System to the United States* W9, ABA FORUM ON FRANCHISING (2009)

William A. Finkelstein and Louis T. Pirkey, *International Trademarks* W15, ABA FORUM ON FRANCHISING (1991)

William A. Finkelstein, *Protecting Trademarks Internationally: Current Strategies and Developments* B3, ABA FORUM ON FRANCHISING (1996)

Stephen Giles, Lou H. Jones, and Lawrence Weinberg, *Negotiating and Documenting Complex International Franchise Agreements* W21, ABA FORUM ON FRANCHISING (2006)

Steven M. Goldman, Stephen Giles, Marc Israel, and Stanley Wong, *Competition Round Up from Around the World* LB2, ABA FORUM ON FRANCHISING (2004)

David C. Gryce and E. Lynn Perry, *Trademarks and Copyrights in the International Arena* 6/W4, ABA FORUM ON FRANCHISING (1993)

Kenneth S. Kaplan, Andrew P. Loewinger, and Penelope J. Ward, *System Standards in International Franchising* W14, ABA FORUM ON FRANCHISING (2005)

Edward Levitt and Jorge Mondragon, *A Survey of International Legal Traps and How to Avoid Them—Beyond the Franchise Laws* W20, ABA FORUM ON FRANCHISING (2007)

Ned Levitt, Kendal H. Tyre, and Penny Ward, *The Impossible Dream: Controlling Your International Franchise System* W4, ABA FORUM ON FRANCHISING (2010)

Michael K. Lindsey and Andrew P. Loewinger, *International (Non-U.S.) Franchise Disclosure Requirements* W9, ABA FORUM ON FRANCHISING (2002)

Andrew P. Loewinger and John Pratt, *Recent Changes and Trends in International Franchise Laws* W4, ABA FORUM ON FRANCHISING (2008)

Andrew P. Loewinger and Thomas M. Pitegoff, *Avoiding the Long Arm of the Law in International Franchising: Issues and Approaches* W8, ABA FORUM ON FRANCHISING (1995)

Craig J. Madson and Katherine C. Spelman, *Similarity and Confusion in the Intellectual Property Arena* W11, ABA FORUM ON FRANCHISING (1997)

Christopher A. Nowak, John Pratt, and Carl E. Zwisler, *Franchising Internationally with Countries with Opaque Legal Systems* W20, ABA FORUM ON FRANCHISING (2006)

Kerry Olson, Frank Robinson, and Kendal H. Tyre, *From LOI to Closing: Getting an International Franchise Deal Done* W23, ABA FORUM ON FRANCHISING (2014)

E. Lynn Perry and John L. Sullivan Jr., *Trademark Compliance and Enforcement Techniques* E/W12, ABA FORUM ON FRANCHISING (1992)

Leonard Polsky, Mark Abell, Ruby Asturias, and Sun Chang, *Post Expiration and Termination Issues in Master Franchising – The Fate of Unit Franchises and Other Issues*, INT'L J. FRANCHISING L., Issue 6, at 3 (2014)

Marcel Portmann, *Franchising Sector Proves Global Reach*, in FRANCHISING WORLD (January 2007)

John Pratt and Luiz Henrique O. do Amaral, *Civil Law for Common Law Practitioners (or How to Draft an Agreement for Use Overseas)* W4, ABA FORUM ON FRANCHISING (2002)

Kirk W. Reilly, Robert F. Salkowski and Geoffrey B. Shaw, *Determining the Rules of Engagement in Litigation Here and Abroad* W5, ABA FORUM ON FRANCHISING (2008)

Catherine Riesterer and Frank Zaid, *Basics of International Franchising* L/B2, ABA FORUM ON FRANCHISING (1997)

W. Andrew Scott and Christopher N. Wormald, *Stranger in a Strange Land: Contrasting Franchising in International Expansion* W2, ABA FORUM ON FRANCHISING (2003)

Donald Smith and Erik Wulff, *International Franchising: The Unraveling of an International Franchise Relationship* 15/W13, ABA FORUM ON FRANCHISING (1993)

Francesca R. Turitto, Luciana Bassani, Dominic Hui, David W. Koch, and Sajai Singh, *A Marriage Made in Heaven? Private Equity and International Franchising*, INT'L J. FRANCHISING L., Issue 1, at 1 (2015)

Kendal H. Tyre and Phil Wilkins, *Who is Making an Impact on Diversifying Their Brands*, in FRANCHISING WORLD (June 2008)

Frank Zaid, Pamela Mills, and Michael Santa Maria, *Essential Issues in International Franchising* LB/1, ABA FORUM ON FRANCHISING (2001)

Mark Abell, *What is Franchising?,* in THE FRANCHISE LAW REVIEW 1 (Mark Abell ed. 2014)

Mark Abell, *Franchising as Part of an International Multichannel Strategy,* in THE FRANCHISE LAW REVIEW 3 (Mark Abell ed. 2014)

Mark Abell, *The Regulation of Franchising Around the World,* in THE FRANCHISE LAW REVIEW 8 (Mark Abell ed. 2014)

Sarah Charles, *Commercial Planning*, in THE FRANCHISE LAW REVIEW 29 (Mark Abell ed. 2014)

Steven Frost & Mark Abell, *Sustaining Relationships,* in THE FRANCHISE LAW REVIEW 36 (Mark Abell ed. 2014)

Allan Poulter & Robert Williams, *Intellectual Property,* in THE FRANCHISE LAW REVIEW 43 (Mark Abell ed. 2014)

Matthew Oliver, *Tax Considerations,* in THE FRANCHISE LAW REVIEW 50 (Mark Abell ed. 2014)

Ruth Boardman, Francis Aldhouse & Elizabeth Upton, *Data Protection,* in THE FRANCHISE LAW REVIEW 98 (Mark Abell ed. 2014)

Victoria Hobbs, *Resolving International Franchise Disputes,* in THE FRANCHISE LAW REVIEW 106 (Mark Abell ed. 2014)

Mark Abell, *The Competition Law of the European Union,* in THE FRANCHISE LAW REVIEW 119 (Mark Abell ed. 2014)

Mark Abell, *Editor's Global Overview,* in THE FRANCHISE LAW REVIEW 121 (Mark Abell ed. 2014)

Duke Johnston, *Case Study – The Dwyer Group,* in THE FRANCHISE LAW REVIEW 589 (Mark Abell ed. 2014)

Fidel Porcuna, *Dispute Resolution Appendix,* in THE FRANCHISE LAW REVIEW 593 (Mark Abell ed. 2014)

ASIA

Stephen Giles, Andrew P. Loewinger, and Sherin Sakr, *Go East Young Franchisor: Franchising in Asia-Pacific Other Than China and India* W21, ABA FORUM ON FRANCHISING (2011)

Stephen Giles, *Franchising in Asia-Pacific Region, Who's Who Legal*: FRANCHISE 2012 (2012)

China

Mark Abell, Daniela C. Brito, and Paul D. Jones, *Franchising in the BRIC Markets (Brazil, Russia, India, and China)* W18, ABA FORUM ON FRANCHISING (2008)

Vivien Chan, *Franchising in China: (Un)Fair Competition,* INT'L J. FRANCHISING L., Issue 1, at 32 (2010)

Grace Chen & Marcus Vass, *China,* in THE FRANCHISE LAW REVIEW 225 (Mark Abell ed. 2014)

Ella S.K. Cheong, *China*, in INT'L FRANCHISING CHN/1 (Dennis Campbell gen. ed. 2011)

Babette Märzheuser-Wood and Vicky Reinhardt, *China – Initiative to Update and Modernise Franchise Regulation*, INT'L J. FRANCHISING L., Issue 5, at 10 (2011)

Dr. Martin Mendelsohn, *China: New Franchising Law*, INT'L J. FRANCHISING L. , Issue 2, at 23 (2005)

Yu Qin and Richard L. Wageman, *China*, in INT'L FRANCHISE SALES LAWS China-1 (Andrew P. Loewinger and Michael K. Lindsey eds. 2010)

Tao Xu, *Developments in Chinese Franchising Regulation*, INT'L J. FRANCHISING L. , Issue 3, at 38 (2014)

Ren Yanling, *Changes to Chinese Franchise Law: An improved Balance Between the Interests of Franchisors and Franchisees*, INT'L JOURNAL OF FRANCHISING LAW, Issue 3, at 27 (2012)

Jie Zhou, *The Legal Regime for Franchising in China: Civil or Administrative?*, INT'L JOURNAL OF FRANCHISING LAW, Issue 1, at 29 (2013)

Hong Kong

Vivien Chan, *Franchising and the New Competition Law in Hong Kong*, INT'L J. FRANCHISING L., Issue 6, at 5 (2010)

Andrea S.Y. Fong, *Hong Kong*, in INT'L FRANCHISING HK/1 (Dennis Campbell gen. ed. 2011)

Marcus Vass & Alex Wong, *Hong Kong*, in THE FRANCHISE LAW REVIEW 283 (Mark Abell ed. 2014)

India

Mark Abell, Daniela C. Brito and Paul D. Jones, *Franchising in the BRIC Markets (Brazil, Russia, India, and China)* W18, ABA FORUM ON FRANCHISING (2008)

Nipun Gupta & Divya Sharma, *India,* in THE FRANCHISE LAW REVIEW 305 (Mark Abell ed. 2014)

Preeti Mehta, *India—Termination of Master Franchise Agreements and the Consequences*, INT'L J. FRANCHISING L., Issue 3, at 5 (2007)

Preeti Mehta, *Liberalisation of Indian Government's Policy on Payments for Technical Collaboration & Franchises,* INT'L J. FRANCHISING L., Issue 6, at 25 (2010)

Divya Sharma, *Franchising Disputes in India—Choices Dictate the Consequences*, INT'L J. FRANCHISING L., Issue 4, at 41 (2014)

Sajai Singh, *Franchising — A Viable Option in the Indian Retail Sector*, INT'L J. FRANCHISING L., Issue 5, at 23 (2013)

Yoginder Pal, *Franchising in India*, FRANCHISING WORLD (October 2006)

Indonesia

Sigit Ardianto and Rivan F. Ramadhan, *Indonesia*, in INT'L FRANCHISING INA/1 (Dennis Campbell gen. ed. 2011)

Rick Beckman and Ferry P. Madian, *Indonesia*, in INT'L FRANCHISE SALES LAWS Indonesia-1 (Andrew P. Loewinger and Michael K. Lindsey eds. 2010)

Richard Cornwallis and Norma Mutalib, *Indonesia's Franchise Regulations*, INT'L J. FRANCHISING L. Issue 3, at 17 (2010)

Graeme Payne and Gordon Drakes, *New Franchise Regulations in Indonesia: A Fine Line Between Stimulating the Local Market and Protectionism*, INT'L J. FRANCHISING L. Issue 1, at 27 (2013)

Kendal H. Tyre, Jr. & Pierce Haesung Han, *The Ministry of Trade of Indonesia Limits Growth of Food and Beverage Franchises*, NIXON PEABODY LLP: FRANCHISE ALERT (February 2013)

Japan

Takenari Shimizu, *Japan*, in INT'L FRANCHISING JAP/1 (Dennis Campbell gen. ed. 2011)

Souichirou Kozuka and Takashi Kanai, *Japan*, in INT'L FRANCHISE SALES LAWS Japan-1 (Andrew P. Loewinger and Michael K. Lindsey eds. 2010)

Kazakhstan

Aigoul Kenjebayeva et al., *Kazakhstan*, in THE FRANCHISE LAW REVIEW 348 (Mark Abell ed. 2014)

Nick Green, *Modernization of Kazakhstan's Intellectual Property Legislation*, INT'L J. FRANCHISING L., Issue 2, at 41 (2015)

Malaysia

Leela Baskaran, *Malaysia*, in INT'L FRANCHISING MAY/1 (Dennis Campbell gen. ed. 2011)

Mohd Bustaman Hj Abdullah and Wong Sai Fong, *Malaysia*, in INT'L FRANCHISE SALES LAWS Malaysia-1 (Andrew P. Loewinger and Michael K. Lindsey eds. 2010)

Lin Li Lee, *Franchising Cases in Malaysia*, INT'L J. FRANCHISING L., Issue 1, at 37 (2015)

Su Siew Ling, *Malaysia – Changes to Franchise Law*, INT'L J. FRANCHISING L., Issue 3, at 34 (2013)

Kendal H. Tyre, Jr. & Pierce Haesung Han, *Malaysian Government Actively Promotes Growth in Franchise Sector*, NIXON PEABODY LLP: FRANCHISE ALERT (October 2013)

Kendal H. Tyre, Jr. & Pierce Haesung Han, *Tapping Into Malaysia's Aggressive Franchising Goals*, PORTFOLIO MEDIA, INC.: LAW360 (November 2013)

Gurmeet Kaur Sidhu & Siew Ling Su, *Malaysia,* in THE FRANCHISE LAW REVIEW 373 (Mark Abell ed. 2014)

Nancy Weingartner, *Doing Business: Malaysia Has One of the Fastest-Growing Franchise Markets,* in FRANCHISE TIMES 83 & 86 (October 2014)

Philippines

Claro F Certeza, *Philippines,* in THE FRANCHISE LAW REVIEW 428 (Mark Abell ed. 2014)

Singapore

Daniel Lim, Bernard Lui, Michele The, and Vanessa Chew, *Singapore*, in INT'L FRANCHISING SIN/1 (Dennis Campbell gen. ed. 2011)

Sheena Jacob & Angelique Chan, *Singapore*, in THE FRANCHISE LAW REVIEW 485 (Mark Abell ed. 2014)

South Korea

Brendon Carr and Jae-Hoon Kim, *South Korea*, in INT'L FRANCHISE SALES LAWS South Korea-1 (Andrew P. Loewinger and Michael K. Lindsey eds. 2010)

Soowon Hong, *Recent Trends in Enforcement of Laws in Korea*, INT'L J. FRANCHISING L., Issue 1, at 33 (2015)

Jae-Hoon Kim, *Changes to Korean Franchise Regulation*, INT'L J. FRANCHISING L., Issue 3, at 47 (2014)

Kendal H. Tyre, Jr. & Pierce Haesung Han, *South Korea's Fair Trade Commission Imposes Largest Possible Fine on Franchise for Unfair Practices*, NIXON PEABODY LLP: FRANCHISE LAW ALERT (October 2014)

Kendal H. Tyre, Jr. & Pierce Haesung Han, *South Korea Adopts Major Amendments to the Fair Transactions in Franchise Business Act*, NIXON PEABODY LLP: FRANCHISE LAW ALERT (January 2014)

Taiwan

Wellington Liu and David Lu, *Taiwan*, in INT'L FRANCHISE SALES LAWS Taiwan-1 (Andrew P. Loewinger and Michael K. Lindsey eds. 2010)

Thailand

Alan Adcock and Sriwan Puapondh, *Thailand*, in INT'L FRANCHISING THA/1 (Dennis Campbell gen. ed. 2011)

Vietnam

Mai Minh Hang and Nguyen Anh Tran, *Vietnam*, in INT'L FRANCHISE SALES LAWS Vietnam-1 (Andrew P. Loewinger and Michael K. Lindsey eds. 2010)

Appendix C
Quick Reference Guide

	Bangladesh	China	Hong Kong	India	Indonesia	Japan	Kazakhstan	Malaysia	Nepal	Philippines	South Korea	Taiwan	Tajikistan	Thailand	Vietnam
Pre-Sale Disclosure Requirement		X			X	X	X	X			X	X			X
Double Taxation Treaty with United States	X	X		X	X	X	X			X	X		X	X	
Trademark License Registration	X*	X	X*	X*		X*	X	X	X*	X	X*	X*	X*	X	X*
Central Bank Filing	X	X^		X^	X	X^	X^	X^	X	X^	X^	X^		X^	
Signatory to New York Convention	X	X	X	X	X	X	X	X	X	X	X		X	X	X

* recommended or best practice
^ certain payment thresholds

4818-6761-0403.5

www.ingramcontent.com/pod-product-compliance
Lightning Source LLC
LaVergne TN
LVHW052241200926
848481LV00002B/236